HAWKS, DOVES,

AND OWLS

HAWKS, DOVES, AND OWLS

AN AGENDA FOR AVOIDING NUCLEAR WAR

Graham T. Allison
Albert Carnesale
Joseph S. Nye, Jr.

Editors

W. W. NORTON & COMPANY
New York · London

Published simultaneously in Canada by Penguin Books Canada Ltd., 2801 John Street, Markham, Ontario L3R 1B4,
Printed in the United States of America.

The text of this book is composed in Times Roman, with display type set in Palatino. Composition and manufacturing by The Haddon Craftsmen, Inc.

First Edition

Library of Congress Cataloging in Publication Data
Main entry under title:

Hawks, doves, and owls.

   Bibliography: p.
   Includes index.
   1. Nuclear warfare. 2. Nuclear disarmament.
I. Allison, Graham T. II. Carnesale, Albert.
III. Nye, Joseph S.
U263.H39 1985   327.1'74   84–29485

ISBN 0-393-01995-0

W. W. Norton & Company, Inc., 500 Fifth Avenue, New York, N. Y. 10110
W. W. Norton & Company Ltd., 37 Great Russell Street, London WC1B 3NU

1 2 3 4 5 6 7 8 9 0

CONTENTS

III. *Conclusions*

THE AUTHORS

Graham T. Allison is Dean of the John F. Kennedy School of Government, Harvard University. He is author of *Essence of Decision: Explaining the Cuban Missile Crisis, Remaking Foreign Policy* (co-authored with Peter Szanton), and numerous other articles and books on American foreign policy and security issues.

Albert Carnesale is Academic Dean of the John F. Kennedy School of Government. He is a nuclear engineer and was a member of the SALT I delegation. He currently consults for the Departments of State and Defense. He is co-author of *Living with Nuclear Weapons* and co-editor of *International Security.*

Joseph S. Nye, Jr. is Dillon Professor of International Affairs at Harvard University. He was Deputy to the Undersecretary of State for Security Assistance, Science and Technology and chaired the National Security Council Group on Nonproliferation of Nuclear Weapons. He is co-author of *Living with Nuclear Weapons.* His most recent book is *The Making of America's Soviet Policy.*

Paul Bracken teaches in the political science department and in the School of Organization and Management at Yale University. He was formerly associated with the Hudson Institute and is most recently author of *The Command and Control of Nuclear Forces.*

Richard K. Betts is a senior fellow at the Brookings Institution in Washington, D.C. He has been a staff member to the Senate Select Committee on Intelligence and a consultant to the National Security

Council. He is author of *Soldiers, Statesmen, and Cold War Crises* and *Surprise Attack,* as well as co-author of *The Irony of Vietnam* and *Nonproliferation and U.S. Foreign Policy.*

Fen Osler Hampson is a postdoctoral fellow at the John F. Kennedy School of Government and coordinator of the Project on Avoiding Nuclear War. He was a member of Harvard's Energy and Security Project and a contributer to *Energy and Security.* He has written on international security and defense issues.

Francis Fukuyama is senior analyst on Soviet and Middle Eastern Affairs with the RAND Corporation in Santa Monica, California. He was formerly with the policy planning staff in the Department of State. He is author of numerous articles and monographs on Middle Eastern security issues.

Henry S. Rowen is a professor at the Graduate School of Business and a member of the Hoover Institution at Stanford University. He served in the Defense Department during the Kennedy and Johnson administrations and as Chairman of the National Intelligence Council of the CIA from 1981 to 1983.

Stephen M. Meyer is a member of the political science department at the Massachusetts Institute of Technology and Director of the Soviet Security Studies Working Group at MIT's Center for International Studies. He is a consultant to the Department of Defense and the Central Intelligence Agency. His publications include *The Dynamics of Nuclear Proliferation.*

PREFACE

THE DEBATE over national security and arms control has focused primarily on weapons: more or fewer weapons, different kinds of weapons. During the 1984 presidential campaign, for example, President Ronald Reagan defended his administration's military buildup, the biggest in peacetime. Former Vice President Walter Mondale advocated a freeze on deploying new weapons. Numbers and types of arms have preoccupied governments and specialists on both the right and the left.

This definition of the problem is far too narrow. Suppose the United States completed the current strategic buildup, or that superpower arsenals were cut in half. In both cases the United States and the Soviet Union would retain thousands of strategic nuclear warheads. Each would still be able to attack or retaliate and destroy the other society. For the foreseeable future, then, we must focus on the fundamental question: What practical steps can the United States take to *avoid* a major nuclear war with the Soviet Union?

This book begins with a simple—some will say simplistic—proposition: the primary objective of the United States in either building up or building down nuclear arms should be to protect and defend U.S. values and institutions by *avoiding nuclear war* with the Soviet Union. The first question to be asked about a proposed increase or reduction in nuclear arms is how it would affect the probability of such a nuclear war. An even more important responsibility is to look beyond numbers and types of nuclear armaments and ask what else affects the probability of a nuclear war between the United States and the Soviet Union. Recent discussion has paid too little attention to this critical question.

This book emerges from a multiyear project at Harvard's John F. Kennedy School of Government, funded by the Carnegie Corporation. It builds on an earlier book written by the Harvard Nuclear Study Group. But whereas *Living with Nuclear Weapons* sought to summarize current thinking about nuclear issues for the general public, this work stretches beyond recent discussions by reexamining various issues of nuclear weapons acquisition, policies for use and non-use, diplomatic initiatives, and arms control in the light of a single fundamental criterion: *net effects on the likelihood of a major nuclear war between the United States and the Soviet Union.* More specifically, the aims of this book are first, to develop a conceptual framework for examining risks of nuclear war and second, to identify actions that could be taken to reduce the likelihood of nuclear war.

We have written this book for many different readers: first, for members of the policymaking community; second, for the interested public of citizens concerned about the threat of war; and third, for experts on nuclear weapons and international security. Finally, we are also writing for students. All these readers will, we hope, find this volume a provocative entry in the debate about the most important issue of our time.

ACKNOWLEDGMENTS

THIS BOOK results from a collaboration among the three co-authors that goes back many years. For forcing what would otherwise have remained interesting discussions to become a project with a product, we are most thankful to David Hamburg and the Carnegie Corporation. By establishing the Avoiding Nuclear War Project at Harvard's John F. Kennedy School of Government, the Carnegie Corporation has focused the minds of many individuals—faculty, postdoctoral students, doctoral students—on the question of how to avoid nuclear war.

The ideas in this book, as well as their presentation, have benefited from this attention. The book reflects hours of discussion among members of the project's Working Group, including Bruce Allyn, Robert Beschel, James Blight, John Borawski, Morton Halperin, Ronald Heifetz, Christann Gibson, Charles Glaser, Sean Lynn-Jones, Ernest May, Howard Raiffa, Scott Sagan, Thomas Schelling, Kiron Skinner, William Ury, Stephen Walt, Anne Wortham, and Paul Zigman.

Authors of the particular chapters are, of course, primarily responsible for their own work. But these chapters, as well as our own, are informed by a week-long seminar at Big Sky, Montana, in July 1984. In addition to members of the Working Group, participants in that seminar included: Robert Blackwill, Leslie Gelb, Alexander George, Arnold Horelick, Robert McNamara, Michael May, Fritz Mosher, Helmut Sonnenfeldt, James Thompson, and Edward Warner.

Many others provided comments and ideas, including Francis Bator, McGeorge Bundy, George Bunn, Antonia Chayes, Ashton

Carter, John Deutch, Paul Doty, Randall Forsberg, Jim Goldgeier, Stanley Hoffmann, Robert Jervis, Robert Keohane, John Mack, Fritz Mosher, Richard Pipes, Ralph Potter, Mark Ramee, George Rathjens, David Robinson, Larry Smith, and Dorothy Zinberg.

For the help of these, and many others, we express our grateful thanks. For the errors that remain, we are responsible.

I. The Shape of the Problem

1 INTRODUCTION

by Graham T. Allison, Albert Carnesale,
and Joseph S. Nye, Jr.

PHILOSOPHERS have observed that the most common form of human stupidity is forgetting what one is trying to do. Nations are as prone to stupidity as individuals. In the realm of national security, defense, and arms control we should continually ask ourselves, What is the United States trying to do?

In recent congressional debate about the defense budget, the nuclear freeze, and the MX missile, many objectives have been offered. For example:

- to rebuild U.S. strength after decades of neglect;
- to stop the arms race—three decades of piling up arms seemingly without limit;
- to reduce expenditures on arms, especially as budget deficits persist;
- to achieve deep cuts in strategic nuclear arsenals; and
- to insist that "enough is enough."

Each of these proposals addresses part of the problem. None focuses directly on the key objective. What are we trying to do?

Our one-line answer is: To protect U.S. values and institutions, which requires avoiding nuclear war between the United States and the Soviet Union. The United States must manage the political competition with the Soviet Union so as to avoid a major nuclear war. American policymakers will pursue other objectives as well, but this is the necessary condition that must be satisfied if we are to have the opportunity to pursue any other goal. It is the first criterion by which to evaluate proposed actions to enhance U.S. security. In this book, avoiding nuclear war becomes the prism through which we examine a complex array of issues, including weapons, arms control, and indeed international relations.

Some believe that avoiding a *major* nuclear war is too narrow an objective. Should we not avoid *any* war between the superpowers, even one fought solely with conventional (that is, non-nuclear) weapons or with a small number of nuclear weapons? The answer is "yes." Large-scale conventional wars and "limited" nuclear wars would be tragic occurrences in and of themselves and could also lead to all-out nuclear war. Nonetheless, in the hierarchy of objectives, avoiding major nuclear war deserves preeminence.

A situation in which one or several nuclear weapons were used— accidentally or intentionally, by a nation, a madman, or a terrorist organization—would be a disaster. But it would pale beside a conflict in which hundreds, or thousands, or tens of thousands of nuclear weapons were employed. No matter how much damage had already been done, it would make sense to try to prevent more. Our goal must be to avoid all wars. But if, despite our efforts, some nuclear weapons were used, we should try to prevent the use of still more. Conventional wars or "limited" nuclear wars are not therefore acceptable. But among all potential human catastrophes, a major nuclear war would be the worst. We must thus consider how to prevent an initial use of nuclear weapons from leading to still greater disaster.

Avoiding a major nuclear war is clearly not the only objective of American foreign policy, but it is one that must be achieved if we are to reach any other goals. Secretary of State George Shultz has put the matter clearly. Testifying before the Senate Foreign Relations Committee on U.S.-Soviet relations, he said,

We must defend our interests and values against a powerful Soviet adversary that threatens both. And we must do so in a nuclear age, in which a global war would *even more* thoroughly threaten those interests and values [emphasis added].[1]

A key question, then, is one of tradeoffs: how large a risk of nuclear war should we be willing to accept in pursuit of other objectives?

Unfortunately, neither we nor others have found a way to escape the traditional, painful tradeoffs in national security policy. The goal of avoiding nuclear war may conflict with other foreign policy objectives and with avoiding conventional war. Efforts to reduce the probability of global war may make its potential consequences more grave. Enhancing deterrence may raise the risk of accidents and may entail significant political and monetary costs at home and abroad. When these tradeoffs are clarified in a specific choice, individuals will differ. For example, some people oppose any action that reduces the risks of a nuclear war at the price of increasing the risks of a major conventional war. Many initiatives involve hard tradeoffs that must be weighed case by case; nevertheless, we begin with a presumption in favor of actions that reduce the risks of a major nuclear war.

We must also recognize that some actions intended to reduce the risks of a major nuclear war could be counterproductive. Consider Europe. A major U.S.-Soviet nuclear war in Europe would be most likely to come about through escalation from a conventional war. The probability of such an outcome depends on both (1) the probability of a conventional war in Europe and (2) the probability of escalation from such a war to a major nuclear war. If reducing one element in this combination increases the other disproportionately, the net effect will be unfavorable. Some steps that might be taken to reduce the likelihood of escalation to a nuclear war (for example, a pledge of "no first use" of nuclear weapons) might increase the likelihood of conventional aggression enough that the overall effect would be to make nuclear war more, not less, likely. Similarly, attempts to reduce the likelihood of conventional conflict by increasing the potential for escalation to nuclear war (for example, by deploying relatively vulnerable intermediate-range nuclear weapons delivery systems in Western Europe) could also be counterproductive. The debate about "no first use" dances around this paradox.

Our approach begins with three key questions:

1. *The Shape of the Problem:* What are the major features of the problem of nuclear weapons and nuclear war?
2. *The Implications of the Problem:* Reflecting on this problem, how does it affect our lives and prospects?
3. *A Strategy for Attacking the Problem:* How should we think about *what is to be done?* What actions should (and should not) be taken?

The Shape of the Problem

Everyone can agree that a major nuclear war would be a global catastrophe. Then why do the superpowers maintain such enormous nuclear arsenals? What do they want from their nuclear weapons?

The question is simple; the answer is not. Nuclear weapons are supposed to serve many purposes, perhaps too many. They are expected to deter attacks—both nuclear and conventional—on the homeland, on allies, and on other areas of vital interest; to be used in fighting a war if deterrence should fail; to support foreign policies; to provide leverage in arms control negotiations; and to serve as symbols of status and strength at home and abroad.

The problem of nuclear weapons and war has been well described by strategic analysts over the past four decades. Our list of major features is a familiar one, presented primarily to remind us and our readers of the hard facts. These central features include:

- At any moment the Soviet leadership chooses, the Soviet Union can execute a nuclear attack that will kill most Americans and destroy the United States as a functioning society.
- The Soviet Union faces an identical threat from the United States.
- No defense against this threat is currently possible. Today, and in the foreseeable future, the U.S. population stands *hostage* to Soviet military forces—and vice versa.
- A revolution in weaponry—nuclear weapons and missile delivery systems—has transformed the age-old problem of war.[2] In history, armies primarily defended citizens and countries. Usually, it was necessary to defeat an enemy's forces before destroying or dominating the population. After military victory, human beings managed to kill their fellows in large numbers: Genghis Khan's invasion of Persia in the early thirteenth century destroyed a majority of the population; in the Thirty Years' War of the seventeenth century, over 30 percent of the German population died; World War II claimed fifty million victims. Now, however, the United States and the Soviet Union have the power to destroy the opponent's population or society before engaging its military forces.
- Given the consequences of a nuclear war, common sense might

suggest that neither the United States nor the Soviet Union would ever intentionally engage in such a suicidal undertaking. Yet, over the last three decades, each nation has repeatedly taken actions that, in the view of the decision-makers, increased the risks of nuclear war. Some of these actions, such as the Soviet emplacement of missiles in Cuba, have led to crises in which the risks of nuclear war were substantial (in the Cuban missile crisis, President Kennedy estimated the risk to be one in three). Moreover, leaders of both superpowers have relied on the threat of nuclear war to achieve other objectives (for example, when the United States declared a nuclear alert in the 1973 Mideast War, or in 1980 when President Carter declared a vital American interest in the Persian Gulf and committed the United States to defend the region against a Soviet invasion "by any means necessary"). Indeed, today the United States and its European allies rely on nuclear weapons and the threat of nuclear war to keep the conventional peace in Europe.

Each point could be elaborated; additional points could be added. But this sketch will serve as a chilling reminder of the nuclear landscape.

The Implications of the Problem

Warfare has been a constant condition of mankind. Human nature and human societies have evolved over thousands of years in an environment that has required and rewarded some degree of aggressiveness. Yet since 1945 we have avoided world war. By grace, and good fortune, and good work, we have already exceeded by two decades the period of relative peace enjoyed after World War I. The limitation of warfare over the past forty years is especially remarkable in view of geopolitical conditions.

An evolutionary perspective sheds some light on our problem.[3] Mammals have been on the earth for more than seventy million years. Primates were among the first mammals. A manlike creature appeared several million years ago, our own species 50,000 to a million years ago. Agriculture has been practiced for 10,000 years; the industrial revolution occurred some 250 years ago. Nuclear weapons have been on this earth for forty years. Two countries have had the capacity to destroy each other for less than twenty years. Thus, in a moment of evolutionary time, the human environment has been transformed.

What does this evolutionary perspective suggest about the species? Human biology and behavioral tendencies have been environmentally shaped over millions of years. Specifically, the tendency of individuals, groups, tribes, and nations to fight among themselves has functioned adaptively during the course of this evolution to provide access to food, water, and shelter, and to resolve disputes among groups.

Today human beings face a radically different environment, one in which the species might destroy itself and the ecosystem. Other species confronted with such drastic change have not fared well. Today they are mostly to be found in museums.

At the same time, human beings can think and, through thought, take initiative to shape their social institutions. We may be less a prisoner of biological determinism than other species have been. But given the dramatic change in our environment, and the deep roots of key social institutions such as the nation-state, it is not clear that we will adapt in time. That nuclear war might kill us all does not make rapid or radical adaptation inevitable—as any review of other species facing similar challenges shows. A critical question will be whether we can reduce risks, buy enough time, and muster the intelligence and courage to adapt our institutions. The United States and the Soviet Union must discover ways to overcome history-as-usual.

Should we be encouraged by the record of the past forty years? World War II ended with the defeat of Germany and Japan—but left in place an array of antagonisms and instabilities that under conditions of history-as-usual might well have led to another world war. The conditions of the mid-twentieth century were at least as bad as those of its first decade, which led to World War I. One starts with a fundamental geopolitical competition between the United States and the Soviet Union. The ingredients of that contest were recognized 150 years ago by de Tocqueville, who noted: "There are now two great nations in the world which, starting from different points, seem to be advancing towards the same goal. Their point of departure is different and their paths diverse; nevertheless each seems called by some secret design of Providence one day to hold in its hands the destiny of half the world."[4] The two nations de Tocqueville identified were the Soviet

Union (Russia at the time) and the United States (or the Anglo-Americans, as he called them).

Add to this tension Soviet defensive paranoia and ideological aggressiveness and American tendencies to define security broadly in terms of the status quo in various regions, and the result has been a series of political conflicts loosely characterized as "cold war." Moreover, since the end of the colonial era the number of poor and fragile states has increased rapidly, engaging real and imagined U.S. and Soviet interests and providing many additional fuses for war.

Yet we have so far avoided another world war. There have been wars—wars that claimed some ten million victims—but U.S.-Soviet relations have been most extraordinarily cautious.

Why? Part of the answer lies in the "sublime irony" described by Churchill in 1955, that "safety will be made the sturdy child of terror, and survival the twin brother of annihilation."[5] Survival and annihilation have become twin brothers—Siamese twins.

Nuclear weapons have forced on the United States and the Soviet Union a vital common bond: survival. The nuclear threat creates a solidarity of interest between the two superpowers—against a total war in which they would be the greatest victims. Nuclear weapons have a crystal ball effect, enabling the leaders of each country to see that by attacking the other they could be committing suicide for themselves and their societies.[6] Tragically, crystal balls can be shattered by accident, mishandling, or willful risk-taking. Again comes the key question—can we reduce such risks and buy the time needed for longer-term adaptation of our institutions?

A Strategy for Attacking the Problem

The late Herman Kahn enjoyed provoking colleagues by offering a prize of $1,000 to anyone who could devise a *plausible* scenario for nuclear war between the United States and the Soviet Union. The prize was never awarded, since Kahn reserved to himself the judgment about "plausibility" and never found a scenario that he believed qualified.

Most analysts would agree that it is hard (though perhaps not impossible) to develop a plausible scenario. Indeed, this difficulty represents an important obstacle to thinking constructively about nuclear war. The costs of a major nuclear war would be so catastrophic, so far exceeding any conceivable benefits, that the mind boggles at the prospect of any government's choosing such a course of action. But unlikely and implausible are not the same as impossible.

To structure our analysis of risks of nuclear war, we begin with a simple framework of three elements:

- *general paths* to a major nuclear war;
- *factors* that affect the likelihood of war along each path; and
- *actions* that could be taken to diminish that likelihood.

Table 1 fleshes out this framework.

The five general paths to nuclear war will be familiar to students of this subject:

1. *Accidental or unauthorized use,* resulting from malfunctions of machines or of minds;

2. *Surprise attack:* a bolt-from-the-blue attack on the nuclear forces of one of the superpowers;

3. *Preemption in crisis:* an attack launched in desperation in time of crisis because one side believes (rightly or wrongly) the other intends soon to strike first;

4. *Escalation of conventional war,* in which battlefield, or tactical, nuclear weapons are used after a clash of conventional forces (for example, between NATO and Warsaw Pact troops in Europe, or between Soviet and American forces in the Middle East or the Persian Gulf); and

5. *Catalytic war,* triggered deliberately or inadvertently by actions of third parties, including in particular the use of nuclear weapons by a nation or terrorist group.

For each of these general paths, more specific scenarios of events can be constructed. By analyzing these scenarios, we can identify *factors* that affect the likelihood of war occurring along each path and discover *actions* to reduce that likelihood.

Consider, for example, the path of escalation in Europe. How might the war begin? Imagine a spontaneous labor uprising in East Germany like that of Solidarity in Poland. To suppress the uprising and restore order, Soviet troops are sent in—much as they were in 1956 in Hungary, in 1968 in Czechoslovakia, and in 1979 in Afghanistan. The East Germans resist, and large-scale fighting ensues. Some West German citizens and volunteer military personnel cross into East Germany to assist their fellow Germans. After several days of fighting, large numbers of East Germans begin seeking sanctuary in West Berlin. The Soviets blockade all roads and air routes leading to that city. That act engages NATO's commitment to the security and freedom of West Berlin. After several days of warning, threat, and negotiations fail to open transit routes to West Berlin, the United States and its NATO allies conclude that the Soviet Union intends to absorb West Berlin as part of the resolution of the crisis. To prevent this, NATO aircraft begin to resupply West Berlin. Soviet and Warsaw Pact aircraft resist, and several aircraft crash, in both accidents and engagements. As the airlift fails, and again after warning, NATO sends military units along the major land route to West Berlin. These forces confront Warsaw Pact forces, and fighting begins.

The conflict expands along much of Europe's central front as Soviet reinforcements arrive and NATO defenses begin to crumble. Despite warnings to the Soviets to halt the conflict or suffer the consequences, Soviet forces accelerate their movement westward. World War III begins.

Suddenly, four key bridges across the Elbe River being used by the Soviets to supply their advance are destroyed by low-yield nuclear explosions. The Soviet leadership, assuming (perhaps correctly) that this crossing of the nuclear threshold has been authorized by the highest authorities in the West, is convinced that the United States is likely soon to follow up with a massive attack on Soviet nuclear forces in Europe. Moreover, the Soviet command is especially worried about the independent French nuclear strike force and the possibility of the destruction of Moscow. Thus, in a manner consistent with Soviet doctrine and exercises—but to the surprise of NATO—the Soviet Union strikes massively at all nuclear forces in Europe, causing widespread destruction in Germany, France, England, and most of the rest of Central Europe. At the same time, the Soviet leader sends a Hot Line message to the President of the United States stating that no nuclear weapons have yet been used against the U.S. (or Soviet) homeland and proposing that if the president has not lost his control he should agree to stop the fighting now.

The American president then faces the hardest choice any presi-

TABLE 1

GENERAL PATHS to Nuclear War	FACTORS Affecting Likelihood Along Path	ACTIONS to Reduce Likelihood Along Path
· Accidental or Unauthorized Use	○ Numbers, location, protective devices, and processes for use of nuclear weapons ○ Communications systems	○ Reduce numbers and locations; improve protective devices and processes for their use ○ Improve C^3I (Command, Control, Communications, and Intelligence) ○ Systematize crisis prevention and management
· Surprise Attack	○ Extreme U.S.-Soviet hostility ○ Objective nuclear balance of U.S.-Soviet forces that allows leaders to expect net positive advantage from first strike ○ Objective C^3I that allows leaders to expect net positive advantage from attack ○ Misperceptions-misunderstandings of objective facts about forces or C^3I	○ Strengthen incentives for peace and cooperation ○ Maintain objective conditions—robust, invulnerable, and redundant strategic nuclear forces—that make any first strike obviously crazy ○ Maintain objective C^3I that is obviously robust, invulnerable, and redundant ○ Pursue arms control agreements that maintain confidence in retaliatory second-strike capabilities while reducing confidence in successful first strikes ○ Develop processes to limit misperceptions-misunderstandings of objective conditions

TABLE 1 (Continued)

GENERAL PATHS to Nuclear War	FACTORS Affecting Likelihood Along Path	ACTIONS to Reduce Likelihood Along Path
· Preemption in Crisis	○ Perception that war is imminent and unavoidable ○ Objective nuclear balance of U.S.-Soviet forces . . . (see above) ○ Objective C^3I . . . (see above) ○ Misperceptions-misunderstandings . . . (see above)	○ Systematize crisis prevention and management ○ Maintain objective conditions . . . (see above) ○ Maintain objective C^3I . . . (see above) ○ Pursue arms control agreements . . . (see above) ○ Develop processes to limit misperceptions-misunderstandings . . . (see above)
· Escalation of Conventional War	○ Involvement of United States or USSR or both in conventional war ○ Objective or perceived balance of conventional forces that tempts escalation ○ Involvement of United States or USSR client state in local war ○ Misperceptions-misunderstandings of objective factors ○ Vulnerability, doctrine, and location of theater nuclear weapons ○ Misperceptions-misunderstandings in "fog of war"	○ Systematize crisis prevention and management ○ Maintain objective balance of conventional forces that deters or provides adequate defense ○ Have in place processes to limit misperceptions-misunderstandings ○ Reduce vulnerability of and reliance upon theater nuclear forces ○ Improve theater C^3I
· Catalytic War	○ Numbers of third parties with weapons and delivery systems ○ Sophistication of weapons and delivery systems	○ Restrain nuclear proliferation ○ Systematize crisis prevention and management ○ Improve intelligence capabilities

dent has ever had to make. Millions of Europeans, and hundreds of thousands of Americans in Europe, have been killed. America's NATO allies have instantly suffered a catastrophe many times worse than World War II. By policy and commitment, as well as all considerations of justice, the United States must retaliate against the Soviet perpetrators of this near-ultimate crime. But a president who takes this step risks the destruction of the United States as well.

Soviet military units continue marching west. Both U.S. and Soviet forces have been on the highest level of alert for almost ten days. American intelligence agencies believe that it is now nearly certain that some Soviet strategic nuclear forces will be fired against the United States, if only by accident. Soviet intelligence learns of this discussion in the United States. As the confusion spirals, the Soviet leadership becomes convinced that the only question is which side will strike the first blow. Because Soviet strategic forces are overwhelmingly land-based, a U.S. preemptive strike could leave the Soviet Union in a decisively inferior military position. The Soviet leadership could still retaliate against U.S. cities—at the price of a further American response to destroy Soviet cities. But at the end of the exchange, the U.S. would retain a substantial nuclear reserve while Soviet nuclear forces would have been spent. By striking first, the Russian generals do not claim to be able to "disarm" the United States or even to approach that goal. They do maintain that a Soviet preemptive attack could be sufficiently disruptive to attenuate greatly, and perhaps even to prevent, the expected retaliatory blow. By every measure, they argue, the Soviet Union is better off striking first than being struck first. Persuaded by their military advisers, the Kremlin leaders order an all-out attack against the nuclear forces and command and control centers of the United States. This hypothetical World War III has now become a major nuclear war.

Is this sequence of events likely? No. Is it possible? Yes. Likelihoods of such scenarios are, of course, matters of judgment. The more specific the details, the less likely that events will develop in precisely that form. But we believe that such a sequence of actions and reactions (and similar scenarios presented in chapters 2 through 6) provides not-implausible paths to a major nuclear war between the United States and the Soviet Union.

Thinking about scenarios allows us to ask questions about the two other elements of our framework: factors and actions. In the European scenario, the likelihood of nuclear war between the superpowers is influenced by several factors, including the defensibility or vulnerability of American and Soviet commitments to allies (West Berlin or East Germany); the balance of U.S.-Soviet conventional forces and those of their allies; the presence, vulnerability, doctrine, and plans for use of tactical and theater nuclear weapons; and the certainty of misperception and misunderstanding in the "fog of war."

What actions could the United States take to reduce these risks? We could assure a balance of conventional forces that deters Soviet attack and provides adequate defense; remove tactical nuclear weapons from the front line and reduce the vulnerability of theater nuclear forces (and NATO's reliance on them—even though these actions could increase the likelihood of conventional aggression); improve mechanical control over unauthorized firings; establish processes to reduce misperceptions and misunderstanding; and limit the interests of both powers in Eastern Europe or even West Berlin.

Though our framework is deliberately simple, we believe its application can help to identify actions that would actually reduce risks of nuclear war. Indeed, we believe one can identify many such initiatives.

This three-element framework can serve as a useful reminder in examining proposed weapons systems or measures for controlling arms. Rarely do proponents of such initiatives make a sufficiently sustained effort to assess the *net* effects of the proposal on the risks of nuclear war. For example: In 1982, the Reagan administration proposed in START that each side be limited to 5,000 nuclear warheads on strategic missiles (no more than 2,500 of which could be on ICBMs) and 850 launchers for strategic missiles. This represented reductions of about 33 percent in warheads for each side, and about 50 percent in strategic launchers for the United States and 62 percent for the Soviet Union. But under this proposal, the number of warheads *per ICBM* on each side almost certainly would have increased, thereby increasing the incentives of both sides for surprise or preemptive attack. On balance, implementation of this proposal might well have increased rather than decreased the risks of nuclear war.

Similarly one should question the actual effects of "raising the nuclear threshold in Europe"—an objective now espoused by virtually every political and ideological faction. The recent report of the

European Security Study Group, *Strengthening Conventional Deterrence in Europe: Proposals for the 1980s*[7], for example, argues that NATO must employ a wide variety of new weapons systems, based on emerging technologies, that can accomplish with conventional explosives certain military tasks (such as rapid destruction of airfields, aircraft, and missile launchers) that previously required the use of nuclear weapons. These proposals are intended to reduce the risk of nuclear war. But would they? If NATO were better able to fight and perhaps even to win a war in Europe with conventional weapons, it might well be less likely to resort first to nuclear missiles in the event of a conflict. But how would the Soviet Union react to such new NATO capabilities? If NATO could destroy Soviet theater nuclear forces with a preemptive conventional attack, what would be the effects on Soviet incentives to preempt in a time of crisis? Or on the chances of accidental or unauthorized nuclear use? Or on the NATO decision-making timetable? These questions must be addressed if the *net* effect of specific improvements in NATO's capabilities is to be correctly assessed.

By encouraging the analyst to stand back from a particular weapons system or scenario or arms control proposal, and to take a broad view of the forest, our framework helps keep us focused on what we are all trying to do: avoid major nuclear war. In using the framework for sustained analysis of proposed actions for reducing the risks of nuclear war, as we do in the following chapters, the reader will find it helpful to keep some general guidelines in mind.

First, remember that the general paths have been separated only for analytic purposes. The real world jumbles the various paths and the factors that affect likelihoods down each path. Actions that reduce risks on one path have implications for other paths as well. Deeper background factors, such as changes in the strategic balance, or likely political changes in Eastern Europe, or instability in the Third World, have implications that reach across all the paths.

Second, in assessing risks of nuclear war, never focus on a single scenario, or even a single path, in isolation. Net assessment requires *cross-path analysis*. Such analysis is difficult, and will often cloud or confuse an argument focused on a single scenario (for example, the vulnerability of U.S. land-based ICBMs to a Soviet first strike). But without a full cross-path analysis there can be no net assessment.

Third, recognize that the risks of nuclear war increase as one considers *multipath scenarios*. For example, a crisis in Eastern Europe can lead to a major nuclear war through various combinations of paths. If U.S. and Soviet forces were to confront each other in the Persian Gulf, there would be a risk of horizontal escalation to Europe, Korea, or elsewhere. Scenarios that compound the paths, especially those that include accidents or unauthorized use in the midst of an ongoing crisis, are thus especially worrisome.

Fourth, the highest-probability scenarios for nuclear war between the United States and the Soviet Union involve interactions between two different "logics of action." The first is the logic of deliberate, rational government choices such as characterized the onset of World War II. The second is the logic of inadvertent, accidental, and irrational events, which played a major role in the onset of World War I. We believe that one can develop not-implausible scenarios in which governments acting rationally—that is, deliberately calculating the expected value of the consequences of their actions—could at the end of the game find themselves in a nuclear war. But such scenarios become strikingly more plausible if one allows for the possibility of accidents, misperceptions, and irrationalities. Governmental choices that are rational in their own terms can trigger sequences of events that then pose choices under circumstances in which accidents are even more likely; together, such interactions can lead to consequences that no government would have chosen in the first instance. We will return to the interactions of these two logics when we look at the combination of paths in the conclusions.

Developing Priorities: Levels of Causation and Types of Response

This book addresses not just short-run or immediate causes of nuclear war. As the reader will see in the chapters that follow, we have tried to look back along the chain of causation. Nevertheless, many important causes and dimensions of war are deliberately ignored here. We have chosen to focus on areas where there is some hope that policy intervention could reduce risks.

Analyses of complex events often distinguish precipitating, contributory, and deep causes. For example, the assassination of the

Austrian archduke and the inflexibility of mobilization schedules precipitated World War I; the Austro-Russian competition in the Balkans and Serbian adventurism contributed to the onset of war; and the increased inflexibility in European alliances caused the war in a deeper sense. Or to use the simple metaphor of starting a fire: a match is a precipitating cause, kindling is an intermediate cause, and piling up of logs is a deep cause. Risk-reduction measures can also be classified in these terms.

Some of the steps that might be taken to reduce the risks of nuclear war are related to deeper causes. Examples include measures designed to remove some of the primary or most dangerous sources of potential U.S.-Soviet conflict. Peaceful settlement of regional disputes—with or without Soviet cooperation—can be of profound importance in reducing the risks of nuclear war. In a world where nearly a hundred countries suffer from poverty, rapid social change, and fragile political institutions, this may seem an impossible task. Certainly one must establish priorities. Some Third World crises are more likely to provoke superpower conflict than others. Among the most dangerous are those where both sides have high stakes but where their relative interests are ambiguous or uncertain. Policies that encourage effective communication about such issues can play a key role in crisis prevention and management.

Not all measures for crisis prevention need involve U.S. and Soviet discussions. The United States can take some actions unilaterally—for example, economic aid in the Caribbean, or peace efforts in the Middle East, or, more generally, prudence in the definition of its interests in Third World situations. Other measures may be multilateral, as with efforts to solve the Namibia conflict or to strengthen United Nations or regional peacekeeping capabilities.

The potential for unilateral measures to prevent nuclear crises points to the importance of domestic political factors in a strategy for nuclear risk reduction. Indeed, some might say that policy measures can be accomplished most easily in the domestic sphere.

Domestic factors are included in all the paths to nuclear war listed in table 1. Domestic politics could increase the odds of surprise attack in at least two ways: If a nation is lulled into complacency it might let its defenses atrophy, inviting attack; alternatively, domestic politics might be dominated by groups that felt they had "no acceptable alternatives" to attack. The likelihood of a preemptive strike in a crisis might be increased by domestic debate that suggested the imminence of a first strike, or by psychological stress that led to a misreading of signals. Escalation of conventional war could be affected by domestic political pressures in the losing state; increased military demands and rigid military procedures during war; a leadership struggle; or psychological breakdown under stress—to name just a few factors. Psychological stress or poor control procedures could make accidental war more likely. Risks of catalytic war are affected by intelligence capabilities for discriminating among attackers and procedures for dealing with terrorists.

In short, many of the measures for reducing the risk of nuclear war do not require negotiation with the Soviet Union but involve domestic and unilateral actions. A sensible strategy for nuclear risk reduction must look at all types of possible actions and give priority to those where policy intervention seems likely to accomplish most.

The Plan of This Book

The next part of this book examines each of the general paths to nuclear war. Paul Bracken's chapter discusses accidental and unauthorized use of nuclear weapons. The second and third paths, surprise attack and preemption in a crisis, are covered in a chapter by Richard Betts. Fen Hampson examines the possibility of escalation of conventional war in Europe, and Francis Fukuyama considers escalation in the Middle East. Henry Rowen examines ways in which the actions of third parties, including a use of nuclear weapons, might catalyze war between the superpowers.

Each of these chapters addresses three key questions: (1) How could the superpowers reach a major nuclear war? (2) What are the deep, intermediate, and precipitating factors that affect the probabilities of a major nuclear war down that path? (3) What are the principal actions that could be taken to reduce these risks of war along that path? The time frame for these analyses spans seven decades—drawing on lessons from the last forty years to suggest policies for the next thirty.

With this frame of reference, the authors have been asked to assume that some deep causes and factors—such as U.S.-Soviet ri-

valry, superpower interest in Europe, and Third World instability—
will continue unchanged. To consider changes in these important
underlying factors—and none is immutably cast in concrete—will
require another book.

Part 3 of the book puts the paths back together. In chapter 7,
Stephen Meyer summarizes the Soviet government's perspective on
each of the general paths and on the broader issue of nuclear war.
Chapter 8 presents our analytic conclusions, including our characterization of "Hawks, Doves, and Owls," and suggests ways to think
across all the paths. Chapter 9 proposes an agenda of specific policy
recommendations that we believe would reduce net risks of nuclear
war. This agenda is summarized in table 2.

Our principal purpose in writing this book is not to defend a
particular set of recommendations. Rather, it is to demonstrate an
approach to thinking about the nuclear dilemma that produces insights for action. This approach takes seriously President Reagan's
oft-repeated summary of the matter: "A nuclear war cannot be won
and must never be fought." The fact—a major nuclear war will have
no winners—motivates the imperative: it must therefore never be
fought. But how much risk of such a war should be accepted to protect
other values? This question has perplexed strategists and policymakers for decades past—and will, we believe, for decades to come.

Because "we are the first generation since Genesis with the capability to destroy God's Creation" (to quote the American Catholic
bishops), our society faces powerful temptations to utopian escape or
fatalistic resignation.[8] But the nature of world politics among sovereign states will not change quickly. Nor will man un-discover the
secret of the atom. Nor will human society be rapidly transformed.
The challenge is to move ahead with the many steps we can take to
reduce risks associated with nuclear weapons in the short term (a
decade), as well as the actions that can be taken to reduce our reliance
on nuclear deterrence over the long run (many decades). All such
actions must rest on careful causal analysis of the paths by which a
nuclear war might start and the factors that affect risks along those
paths.

TABLE 2
An Agenda for Avoiding Nuclear War

1. Maintain a credible nuclear deterrent.

    DO modernize the strategic triad.
    DO put alliance politics first.
    DON'T adopt a no-first-use policy.
    DON'T pursue a comprehensive freeze.
    DON'T confuse MAD with a strategy.
    DON'T assume that cities can be defended.

2. Obtain a credible conventional deterrent.

    DO strengthen NATO and the RDF.
    DO raise the nuclear threshold.
    DON'T provoke the Soviet Union.
    DON'T pretend that nuclear weapons deter only nuclear war.

3. Enhance crisis stability.

    DO take decapitation seriously.
    DO send a top leader out of Washington during crises.
    DO develop a survivable small ICBM.
    DON'T adopt a launch-on-warning policy.
    DON'T seek a first-strike capability.
    DON'T plan for a nuclear demonstration shot in Europe.

4. Reduce the impact of accidents.

    DO reduce reliance on short-range theater nuclear weapons.
    DO add safety devices and procedures.
    DO upgrade warning systems.
    DON'T use nuclear alerts for political signaling.
    DON'T multiply crises.

5. Develop procedures for war termination.

    DO plan for ending a war if it begins.
    DO develop survivable U.S.-Soviet communication.
    DO maintain civilian control over nuclear weapons.
    DON'T plan for early use of nuclear weapons.
    DON'T decapitate.

6. Prevent and manage crises.

    DO prepare decision-makers to deal with nuclear crises.
    DO work with the Soviets to prevent and manage crises.

TABLE 2 *(Continued)*

DO install bilateral hot lines between all nuclear powers.
DON'T engage American and Soviet forces in direct combat.
DON'T try to change rapidly the situation in Eastern Europe.
DON'T use nuclear weapons against third parties.

7. Invigorate nonproliferation efforts.

   DO maintain security guarantees.
   DO support the nonproliferation regime.
   DO explore sanctions against proliferators.
   DO protect against nuclear terrorism.
   DON'T be fatalistic about proliferation.

8. Limit misperceptions.

   DO meet regularly with Soviet leaders.
   DO encourage non-governmental contacts with the Soviets.
   DO expect the unexpected.
   DON'T treat nuclear weapons like other weapons.
   DON'T exaggerate military imbalances.
   DON'T cut off communications as a sanction.

9. Pursue arms control negotiations.

   DO preserve existing arms control agreements.
   DO pursue crisis stability through arms control.
   DO reduce uncertainties through arms control negotiations.
   DON'T oversell arms control.
   DON'T abuse bargaining chips.
   DON'T restrict arms control to formal agreements.

10. Reduce reliance on nuclear deterrence over the long term.

    DON'T assume that nuclear deterrence will last forever.
    DO intensify the search for alternatives to deterrence.

II.   Paths to Nuclear War

2 ACCIDENTAL NUCLEAR WAR

by Paul Bracken

ACCIDENTAL WAR has a large place in the lore of the nuclear age. Does public receptivity to stories of accidental war reflect a misunderstanding of the actual probability? Or is it a sign of common sense? Both views are true in important but different ways.

Most people doubt that any manmade system will work perfectly all the time, under all conditions. This is a profound insight that should be remembered when building weapons and plans for nuclear deterrence. Paradoxically, the conviction of many, perhaps most, strategists that nuclear war is a madness to be avoided may produce the very result intuitively dreaded by the public. Competitive operation of real nuclear forces is an enormously complex problem; our inability to comprehend its intricacies could lead inadvertently to war itself. If our behavior addresses only prewar events because deterrence is theoretically automatic, or if we fail to foresee what to do if there already is a failure or impending failure in deterrence, the public's insight will be especially compelling.

Inaccurate, even fanciful, descriptions of the everyday nuclear world have fueled fear of accidental war. Superficially, some accounts of things gone wrong are quite plausible—often more plausible than the convoluted logic of high nuclear strategy. In the early 1950s, for example, shortly after completion of the first air defense radar line, a flock of Canada geese that strayed into the beam's path did trigger alarms and indications of a Russian bomber attack. A few years later, the film *Dr. Strangelove* exploited the common-sense fear of an insane military leader by depicting a deranged Strategic Air Command (SAC) general officer who ordered his forces to attack the Soviet Union in an attempt to initiate a catalytic war.

Fail-Safe carried the fantasy of accidental war into the computer age. In this 1964 movie, a practice launch of the SAC bomber force goes almost perfectly. All but one plane returns to base. The lone aircraft is aimed for Moscow and eventually drops its nuclear charge on the Russian capital, but not until American fighter aircraft try to shoot it down en route, and not until the American military turns over its flight plan to the Soviet air defense so that *they* can try to shoot it down.

Sometimes reality has imitated art. When the new Ballistic Missile Early Warning System was finished in 1960, reflections of the radar beam bouncing off the moon gave the appearance of a Soviet missile strike on the United States. No one had anticipated this possibility. In 1979 and 1980 the failure of a single computer microchip, one of millions in present-day warning and alerting systems, triggered false alarms at the North American Aerospace Defense Command (NORAD). The chip failure created an image on the warning boards of Soviet attack with submarine-launched missiles.[1] Of course there was no attack, and all those involved in the incident now claim that they knew it was a technical mistake all along. But limited alerting actions were ordered, including the launch of some of our sensitive command and control aircraft in the Pacific.

The phenomenal popular success of the movie *War Games* showed that concern about unintentional nuclear attack remains fresh after thirty years of movies, novels, and apocryphal stories on the subject. In this 1983 film a computer brings us to the brink of war by confusing a game with reality. Although the plot is farfetched, the theme is not. In addition, this particular film contains what I believe are realistic portrayals of human operators who have been waiting for years to receive orders that never come, except in practice. When the real message does come, people balk, temporize, and find rationales to explain why it all must be a giant mistake. That they do not act illustrates the obverse of an accident that leads to war: an accident that *prevents* retaliation.

Since the nuclear age began in 1945, there have been no accidental or inadvertent nuclear weapon detonations or attacks. Yet fear of such events persists, and it is not difficult to understand why. Almost anyone living in the twentieth century is aware of the consequences of dysfunctional institutional behavior. A nuclear power plant comes close to melt-down despite repeated technical assurances; major electrical power blackouts occur not once but twice, again after experts have ruled out the possibility; the maker of a jumbo jet either ignores basic safety features or allows corrective orders to slip through the cracks of the bureaucracy, leading to repeated crashes and eventual discontinuation of the model; a major automobile-maker whose sales and reputation are on the line fails to notice that the gas tanks on one of its models have a tendency to explode; and an insurance company underwrites a bloc of fire policies without checking to find out that the properties in question form a large, combustible tract in the South Bronx. Stories like these describe the world seen by even the casual observer.[2] They may not happen often, but they certainly do happen.

The same pattern occurs in political and military affairs. The U.S. military claimed victory on the eve of the massive Tet offensive; repeated warning messages to the USS *Liberty,* to leave a war zone in June 1967, circulated around the command system randomly, going everywhere *except* the *Liberty;* the security of marines sent to Lebanon on a peacekeeping mission was breached by the lone terrorist driver of a truck bomb; and a carefully planned rescue of the U.S. hostages in Iran fell apart when aircraft crashed into each other because those in charge failed to seek expert advice on helicopter reliability and durability. Given the experience of history, it is hardly surprising that our public fears dysfunctional organizational behavior in the nuclear arena as well.

The strategic events of the twentieth century have been more closely tied to the dysfunctional behavior of institutions than to any calculated plan. The events after Sarajevo in the summer of 1914, the surprises at Pearl Harbor and on the Yalu River, even the astonishing failure of British diplomacy to come to grips with the dangers facing Britain in the 1930s, all testify to the ability of things to go wrong in spectacular ways. Designing perfect plans and systems is something far beyond the reach of twentieth-century man. Fear of accidental and inadvertent war arises from the belief that the mistakes and failures that have happened in familiar institutions could happen in the nuclear forces of the United States and the Soviet Union as well. To dismiss this possibility because popular scenarios lack knowledge of the inner workings of the system is to miss the point. The possibility of disaster will continue to haunt anyone who has observed how government and large organizations screw up in unanticipated but breathtaking fashion.

In fact, the particular fears of current movies, novels, and stories have virtually no validity today. Such disasters are not inherently impossible, but massive investments have been made to control and modify these dangers, which in the early days of the nuclear age were all too real. The persistence of fear may reflect intuitive folk wisdom about the dangers of our age. In the decade before 1914, the vision of a gigantic battle between Slavs and Teutons captured popular imagination. Something similar has happened in the nuclear age.

It is not just the public that is concerned about accidental and inadvertent nuclear war. Many strategic analysts also focus on the issue. Believing that nuclear war can have no rational justification, they view nuclear weapons as a necessary means of deterring attack on ourselves or our allies, rather than as instruments of policy to achieve political or military objectives. And indeed since 1945 deterrence has worked. At the same time the United States and the Soviet Union each maintain more than ten thousand-warhead strategic arsenals and routinely prepare for their use. In this environment one may well ask how a nuclear war could ever start, since its consequences would be so obviously devastating. The answer, at least for many analysts, is through some kind of unintended or unanticipated war. They examine the possibility of accidental and inadvertent war not because it seems particularly likely, but because it seems relatively *more* likely than a carefully planned premeditated nuclear war.

Political leaders are wary of accidental and inadvertent war. The superpower leaders and their allies in Europe have been more cautious than early theories of nuclear behavior predicted. Unlike strategists of the 1950s and 1960s, with their interesting brinksmanship theories of blackmail, chicken, and escalation, national leaders now see the danger in even appearing to begin any such process. No nuclear weapons have been used in anger since 1945; more impressive, there have been no full nuclear alerts on either side. At bottom, I believe, political leaders fear an unpredictable explosion in violence or some sort of complicated loss of control if they play nuclear chicken or even if they order their nuclear forces to full alert as a means to signal threat or resolve. Such signaling or tacit threat may seem convincing and workable enough on paper. The discussion of dysfunctional organizational behavior makes clear, however, how wide the gap between a plan and the real world can be. Political leaders may not be able to foresee the exact path of violent escalation, but they sense that such escalation is enhanced by nuclear sword-rattling.

Many analysts now recognize that the accidental/inadvertent nuclear war problem is far more subtle than was originally imagined. Thus the professional view is drawing closer to that of the public and the decision-maker: the systems we deal with are extraordinarily complex, and the policy choices of a national leadership are themselves likely to interact with these systems, not to be independent of them. There can be no clean, artificial separation between policy choices and technology.

We approach wisdom on the subject of accidental/inadvertent war when we consider accidents or inadvertent behavior during a tense high alert or limited war. There has been a tendency to think about the problem narrowly, under day-to-day peacetime conditions—that is, to wonder whether a stray Canada goose or failed computer circuit could trigger a nuclear weapon response.[3] Thus, we are misdirected from subtle, and probably more relevant, dimensions of the problem. When decision-makers believe that nuclear war is no longer unthinkable, and when the many peacetime obstacles to using these weapons are removed on alert, the true danger of accidental or inadvertent war becomes greatest.

Relevant Concepts and Language for the Discussion of Accidental/Inadvertent War

Purely *accidental war* starts without explicit decision by responsible leaders, perhaps through misunderstanding, equipment or system failure, or a subordinate's unauthorized action. *Accidental/inadvertent war,* on the other hand, flows from an escalation process in which each side keeps seeking an edge until the unintended "eruption" occurs.[4]

History offers few instances of purely accidental war. In legend,

King Arthur's last battle is one. As the opposing forces of Arthur and Mordred faced one another on the battlefield at Cam Lann, an asp threatened to bite one of Mordred's warriors. To kill the snake, he drew his sword. A glint of sunshine on the steel was seen by the other army, and Arthur's men fell on the enemy. In the carnage that followed, nearly all died.

While the lessons of this legend should not be ignored in a nuclear age, history records many more instances in which forces stood off from one another, and tension and stimuli did *not* lead to an accidental war. In many cases there *were* even accidents, but not war. Throughout World War II, Russian and Japanese forces stood eyeball to eyeball in Manchuria, and from time to time skirmishes between battalion-sized units broke out. In all cases, however, the fighting was contained until August 1945. The controlling factor was national interest, as analyzed by Tokyo and Moscow.

Examples of inadvertent conflicts are easier to find. World War I is most vivid. There, escalation involved ultimatums, precautionary alerts, counteralerts, and mobilizations. Despite efforts to halt the process after the downside risks became clear, it "exploded," producing the catastrophe of the Great War.[5] In hindsight, any European leader would gladly have accepted the peace he could have gotten in 1914, however humiliating the terms, in preference to the outcome of 1918. The treasure invested, in both men and money, outweighed the victory. Of course, the decision was never structured in this form, nor could it have been. Instead, it always seemed that more investment, say the offensives at the Somme and Verdun, would break the enemy.

The line between accidental and inadvertent war is sometimes hard to draw. World War I, for example, might be seen as an accidental war because it involved extensive misunderstandings among leaders. However, I prefer to use the term *accidental* in the narrower sense of involving equipment malfunction, subordinates' action, and so on. Similarly, it is not always easy to distinguish between inadvertent and deliberate war. For example, a conflict arising from two countries' mutual fear of surprise attack is in some ways a deliberate and in some ways an inadvertent war.

In analyzing the relevance of accidental and inadvertent wars in the nuclear age, it is important to drop a widely used element in definitions of accidental war. We ought not to restrict our analysis by assuming that accidents govern only the *initiation* of war. A major accident could occur in the course of a highly controlled conventional or nuclear war that had begun for other reasons. Consider the emphasis on limited nuclear war as a means to rationalize the use of these weapons. Strategists have postulated that limited nuclear attacks on an enemy would be met by limited strikes in return, thereby avoiding all-out destruction. But an accident, or series of accidents, during a limited war might upset any possibility of restraint and might even make limitation unlikely altogether.

German firebombing of Rotterdam in May 1940 illustrates the point. The Germans had warned the Dutch that they would bomb the city unless it capitulated by a specified deadline.[6] The defenders agreed to the German terms and informed the Germans of this decision before the time limit ran out. It was too late. Luftwaffe bombers were already airborne, dispatched early enough to reach Rotterdam at the appointed hour. The German plan allowed for redundant command and control over the bombers so that they would not strike the city in the event of a peaceful surrender. But delays in the German command system waylaid the message, and two additional independent controls broke down. The bombers were radioed to stop the attack, but the radios were either turned off or tuned to a wrong frequency, and the message was never received. A German signals unit on the ground at the outskirts of the city used a light-flashing device to order the bombers to halt the raid (this being a standard method used by ground units to communicate with airplanes in the early part of the war). However, the bombers missed the light signals, apparently because smoke from a nearby battle obscured visibility. The ensuing attack on downtown Rotterdam produced uncontrollable fires and many fatalities and marked the escalation of the war on the western front with air attacks on civil populations.

Clearly, World War II did not start accidentally. Had there been no war in progress, there would have been no attack on Rotterdam. Yet the example is interesting because it gets at why many people doubt the possibility of limited or controlled nuclear war, or even controlled conventional war, which might press upward against the nuclear threshold. Something may go wrong, and is far more likely to go wrong, once operations have started, or even once forces have been generated and put on alert. In other words, the risk of violent eruption is *sensitive* to the escalation process. The issue of sensitivity merits closer examination along with three other concepts necessary for a minimal understanding of accidental/inadvertent war: tradeoffs, reach, and reliability.

SENSITIVITY

Some situations and some systems have a very low shock tolerance. Even small accidents or inadvertent actions can induce failure and chaos. The German command and control over bomber forces at Rotterdam was disrupted by an inoperative radio and smoke, factors that might have been expected to accompany actual combat. In Manchuria during World War II, by contrast, repeated provocations failed to spark escalation to general war until a political decision was made by Moscow in 1945.

These contrasting examples illustrate the kinds of factors that can affect sensitivity to eruption from an accident or inadvertent action. Time pressures worked against Rotterdam, both in the imposed deadline and in the speed and limited flying time of the German aircraft. The fact that war had not been declared in Manchuria certainly restrained the numerous flare-ups there. And the consequences of accident in the two cases were different, with a city at risk in one instance.

It seems clear that nuclear weapons have raised the sensitivity of eruption to new and unprecedented levels for nearly all the contributing factors one can imagine. Time pressures are much greater than ever before. The consequences of an inadvertent launch or a targeting mistake need little comment. If intermediate-range missiles of the Soviet Union inadvertently hit French and British ports during a limited strike on Western Europe, either or both nations might launch a general retaliatory response, if their doctrines are to be believed. Such a response might have been preprogrammed in the belief that any initial blow would be a precursor attack intended to paralyze retaliation. Or suppose reconnaissance aircraft stray into Soviet airspace and lead to the use of nuclear air defense missiles and attacks on American carrier battle groups offshore. This first use of nuclear weapons might compel the United States to make its own nuclear response if only for defensive purposes. The result would be a regional nuclear war.

One *dampening* factor on sensitivity to an eruption in violence is the likely absence of a declared state of war. A declaration of war requires time on both sides, and in the Western democracies it requires coordination with legislative branches of government. Even if time *were* available for these actions, a war declaration might still be undesirable because it usually signifies a lack of restraint in military operations. Nuclear crises are unlikely to be characterized by complete abandonment of restraint, at least prior to the execution of nuclear attacks, and a fear of annihilation may well drive one or both sides to unusual levels of restraint in order to desensitize the escalation process.

TRADEOFFS

The accidental/inadvertent war problem must be considered in relation to other alternatives. The terrorist car bomb attack on the U.S. Marine compound in Beirut in October 1983 succeeded in part because of orders that perimeter guards not have live ammunition in the chambers of their weapons.[7] This order had been motivated by a wish to protect innocent bystanders in the event of small-arms firing. This fear of accident increased the chance of a successful surprise attack against the camp.

The knotty question is clear. How should the tradeoff between uncertain possibilities be managed, when choice itself may favor one possibility over another? In Europe, a full dispersal of battlefield nuclear weapons might minimize their vulnerability to attack and demonstrate steadfast political resolve—or it might trigger a preemptive attack.[8] And what of preparing the Pershing IIs for firing in a crisis? Although American political leaders may be confident that Pershing missiles have insufficient range to strike Soviet command centers in Moscow, it will quickly dawn on them that it is the *Russian* estimate of their range that is the key variable affecting preemption. Such tradeoffs are difficult and cannot be evaluated without looking at problems from both sides' perspective.

The systematic examination of tradeoffs in accidental/inadvertent war may define the freedom of maneuver for dealing with crises in the nuclear age. In arms control, moreover, it may be important to trade off military capabilities for increases in command stability, say through confidence-building measures. Stationing our Trident submarines farther from the Soviet shoreline may decrease our ability to strike their command centers rapidly, but it also conveys that we are not interested in doing so.

REACH

By *reach* I mean a political leadership's ability to control or influence military actions in the field. In theory, political leaders of most Western nations have absolute command authority. Several factors, however, interfere with the principle of civilian control.

First, the physical apparatus of command may be insufficient to the task. Ironically, World War I—a conflict noted both for crisis instability in the summer of 1914 and for the waste of human lives in futile attempts to break the deadlock of trench warfare—was the first war fought with the methods of modern communications and control. Telegraph lines connected the major capitals of Europe, railroads transported the mobilized armies, airplanes supplied surveillance information, and radios permitted instant control between field armies and political leaders. But improvements in communication and physical control were not enough for crisis management in 1914, and intuitively we recognize that they shortened the time available for decisions. In the ensuing military operations, the physical mechanisms of command (the telegraph, telephone, airplane, and radio) offered greater political control over field activities than ever before, but that control ended abruptly in the immediate combat zone. Artillery fire cut telegraph and telephone lines even when buried underground, and radios of the day were too bulky to be supplied below division level. Offensives could be carefully planned by high levels of authority, with detailed specifications on advance rates, the weight and timing of artillery fires, and logistic resupply levels. But once the battle began, the high command above battalion level, including the political command, had absolutely no control.[9]

A different kind of problem can also interfere with political control of military operations. The conduct of war can be determined by the goals, incentives, and operating practices of the armed forces as much as by the choices of the political leadership. In Vietnam, for example, the U.S. Army undertook battalion-sized search-and-destroy sweeps. Those were what the army had built itself to undertake in the preceding years.[10] Political leaders in Washington never chose a search-and-destroy strategy, nor did they do much to overrule it once its defects emerged. Despite superlative communications, their actual reach into field operations was minimal, although the military often complained about civilian "micromanagement" of the Vietnam War. In any case, the chief effect of search-and-destroy was a rise in U.S. casualty rates.

For various reasons, then, political reach into field operations is limited. Many choices will necessarily be made by the military on the spot. Furthermore, the fact that different parts of an organization may have different objectives, criteria, and routines reinforces the likelihood that authority will devolve downward, as it did in the Vietnam War.

Differences in information levels and objectives would almost surely emerge as control problems for nuclear forces. Indeed, these differences between parts of an organization in a nuclear crisis environment would probably be much greater than in non-nuclear precedents.

RELIABILITY

The complex of men and machines that manages nuclear deterrence is very unwieldy. Because these deterrents must be extremely reliable, they are cloaked in redundancy and proliferation. At the same time, short reaction times and a dangerous environment mean that our forces must be tightly coupled to warning and intelligence sensors. Together these factors create a potential for *malevolent redundancy,* that is, a redundancy of communication channels, command lines, and processing centers that creates new control problems of its own.

More redundancy may mean more reliability. But not always. Redundant systems have to be coordinated by carefully managing information flows.[11] However vast information transmission capacities may be, not all information can be sent to every user. Because military organizations must necessarily keep information from the enemy, they compartmentalize their internal information flows, attempting to ensure that each particular piece of information goes only to those with a legitimate need to receive it. The information routing problem contributed greatly to the *Liberty* and *Pueblo* debacles of the 1960s. In both cases messages were misrouted or blocked by organizational barriers.

Communication systems pose other problems as well. Because of component failures or a subordinate's error, messages may *not* be sent when they should. Peacetime training exercises may, understandably, overemphasize the need to avoid hitting the button when one shouldn't, rather than the need for appropriate action. Unauthorized button-hitting is a separate problem. Both are endemic in complex communication and command systems, and both demand a delicate balance of political and military control. Clearly, disaster can result from focusing attention on only one type of failure, for deterrent reliability is not measured by its average performance, but instead by the *variance* of its performance in response to different threats and to different types of internal failure.

To some extent such problems of internal failure have existed in many military organizations. What is unprecedented in nuclear command and control systems, however, is the possibility of failure caused by sensors, computers, or command posts sending *conflicting* information to different parts of the system. Political and military commanders must agree upon the nature of the threat or of the attack if one occurs. Additionally, they must agree upon a common response. Redundant systems of command and control may react "raggedly," that is, produce different versions of the threat. Ragged response, or partial paralysis of the system, could arise because two redundant command centers transmitted different orders or assessments. For example, one might indicate a small attack, the other a large one. A system-coordination mechanism must decide among conflicting information. Systems with little redundancy have a correspondingly small coordination problem. Coordination problems increase in geometric proportion to the level of redundancy. Very redundant systems, like those used for nuclear command, often experience declines in reliability, that is, *malevolent redundancy*.

Malevolent redundancy is most problematic where a demand for high reliability leads to a proliferation of backup computers, communication lines, and command centers. Procedural rules for information handling are designed to coordinate conflicts in the overwhelming flood of data these backups produce. For example, if there are redundant sensors for early warning, one rule might be to judge an attack as real only when *all* of the sensors indicate attack. This particular rule seems prudent in peacetime when no attack is expected. However, once deterrence has already broken down, it may be excessively prudent, leading to paralysis if failures occur in one of the sensor systems. Other wartime procedural rules must anticipate a disrupted information environment caused by enemy attack, both direct and indirect through the radiation effects of nuclear weapons that attack communication systems. In general, the malevolent redundancy problem works in favor of a first striker, because of the chaos induced in a victim's command system.[12]

Scenarios of Accidental And Inadvertent War

One cannot specify exactly how an accidental or inadvertent nuclear war might erupt. Even so it is useful to categorize a broad range of possibilities, referred to here as canonical scenarios. Such an approach will help us to devote greater attention to those routes to nuclear war that seem most plausible. Table 1 shows four canonical scenarios of accidental/inadvertent war. There is a fundamental distinction between wars and crises that start by some kind of inadvertent action or accident (scenario 1) and those that start on their own but escalate or explode because of unintended actions (scenarios 2–4). Scenarios in the latter category all include some precipitating events that make the overall situation more sensitive to the occurrence of an accident. While none may be especially probable, any of the latter three is more likely than scenario 1.

Scenario 1 includes situations generally considered as "pure" accidental nuclear wars. Examples include the flock of Canada geese that flies across a radar line, triggering a retaliatory launch of missiles or bombers, and the failed computer chip that lights up a warning board. Another instance is the "mad major"—or perhaps four-star general in charge of SAC—found in so many movies and novels.

In scenario 2, an actual war is under way, involving military

Table 1

Four Canonical Scenarios for
Accidental/Inadvertent War

1. ACCIDENT ——————→ NUCLEAR WAR

2. WAR ——————→ ACCIDENTS ——————→ UNCONTROLLED
   EXCHANGES

3. CRISIS ——————→ ALERTS ——————→ ACCIDENTS ——————→
   NUCLEAR WAR

4. ALERTS ——————→ ACCIDENTS ——————→ NUCLEAR WAR

Note: On this figure the terms *accidental* and *inadvertent* war are used in the broad interchangeable sense.

operations and exchanges of weapons—perhaps conventional, perhaps nuclear or chemical. Some accidental event then leads to uncontrolled exchanges. This scenario would include the hypothetical nonnuclear Soviet attack on Europe, whether premeditated or arising out of some political disturbance that spills across the NATO-Warsaw Pact divide. Escalation from a conflict in the Middle East or Northeast Asia would also fall into this category, if an eruption were triggered by an accident or inadvertent action.

In scenario 3, some nonwar crisis has prompted one or more nuclear powers to place their forces on a heightened state of alert; an accident then leads to war. A critical element of this scenario is the motivating political crisis. For example, if the Suez crisis of 1956 or the Cuban crisis of 1962 had led to reinforcing alerts, or to some unauthorized attack, then these situations would be included in this scenario. Distinguishing among causes can be problematic in scenario 3. High nuclear alerts may lead to major urban evacuations for civil defense reasons and would almost surely lead to stronger interactions between Soviet and American forces at sea. Under these conditions it may be difficult to identify any single action as the precipitating reason for a major eruption to nuclear war. What one side regards as a prudent precautionary measure the other may see as highly threatening, requiring preemption or at least more drastic "precautionary" actions that further drive up the spiraling interactions. Here we have inadvertent war at its most insidious, for we may be misled by the widespread conviction that crises in the nuclear age are controllable so long as no nuclear weapons are actually fired. Though this comforting belief has been borne out by experience so far, there is no guarantee that it will always hold true.

Scenario 4 describes a specialized situation in which an alert is not preceded by any sort of political or military crisis. The exceedingly quick-reacting nature of current nuclear forces requires that critical decisions be made in a matter of minutes. It is logically conceivable that some elaborate test of nuclear forces, coupled with other unpredictable factors, could make it appear that an attack was forming where in fact none was intended. This appearance might induce counteractions, such as a sudden emergency order to launch the entire SAC bomber force and associated command and control aircraft. Such sudden changes might reinforce each other even in the absence of a political crisis between the superpowers if there were accompanying "incidents" involving naval forces, the blinding of satellites, or the jamming of sensitive communication systems. Nothing like this has ever happened, but those responsible for monitoring nuclear warning and indications centers have complained of being "nervous" during elaborate tests of Soviet forces or during multiple test launches of Soviet missiles.[13]

The probabilities of the four canonical scenarios listed here have changed significantly over the course of the nuclear age.

SCENARIO 1

The "pure" accidental war of scenario 1 is a virtual impossibility today. In the 1950s, however, when the superpowers had little operational experience, the dangers were considerable. And although pure accidental war is sometimes dismissed out of hand, it is highly unlikely only because of large investments to eliminate the problem made during the late 1950s and 1960s. These investments involved not only hardware, such as electronic locks and better early warning systems, but important improvements in software, operational procedures, and organizational coordination. Checks and balances exist within the command system, along with mechanisms for minimizing the need to go to war because of spurious or ambiguous warning.

The dangers of scenario 1 were especially acute in the early 1950s, when SAC bombers were based on a small number of airfields, easily monitored by Soviet intelligence. U.S. intelligence of almost all kinds was primitive compared with today's, so that on alert SAC had to be placed on a hair trigger to avoid destruction.[14] President Eisenhower probably had few real nuclear options even on paper, because intelligence and postattack command and control were so poor that there would be little information available on which to base a choice among alternatives.

In the middle and late 1950s, America's nuclear arsenal grew considerably and was widely deployed outside of U.S. territory.[15] The Army and Air Force received nuclear weapons in Europe and the Pacific. The fleets were also getting their own supplies. Political supervision over these weapons was minimal, for geographic and security reasons. Armed nuclear weapons were freely moved about in exercises, even on the immediate borders of the Communist bloc.

In those early days of the nuclear age, the civilian control mechanisms over nuclear weapons had not been worked out. Virtually the only form of real political control was the accepted principle of civilian authority over the military, a principle that can be distorted. While this may have been a safe way for President Roosevelt to run World War II, it was hardly an adequate political command structure for the nuclear age. The problem of accidental war was eventually driven home to Washington through a series of accidents that involved the dropping of an H-bomb and the crash of airplanes with nuclear weapons aboard. No detonations took place, in part because of sheer good luck. On Inauguration Day 1961, a B-52 from El Paso, Texas, flying to Utah exploded en route. Four days later another B-52 crashed south of Goldsboro, North Carolina, while carrying two high-yield H-bombs. One bomb's high explosive charge detonated, while all but one of the safety interlocks on the other were triggered. Had the final interlock been thrown, the nuclear weapon would have detonated.[16] Although safety improvements were made in the following months, it is sobering to remember that a year and a half later this same B-52 force was placed on airborne alert during the Cuban missile crisis, in what was the highest overall nuclear alert the U.S. has ever reached.

The Defense Department had begun in the late 1950s to take the accidental war problem seriously and to spend lavishly to bring it under control. More reliable warning systems were built, and bombers were dispersed to more airfields so that SAC need not be placed in such a hair-trigger posture. Special procedures were developed so that SAC bombers could take off and fly to airborne holding positions without advancing to their targets inside the Soviet Union. At first known as fail-safe launches and later as positive control launches, the procedures allowed SAC to respond to ambiguous warnings without going to war. It was also decided not to place nuclear bombers or missiles near major command centers, such as Washington, D.C., or SAC headquarters in Nebraska.

Other major changes were made in the 1950s to reduce the probability of accidental war. The North American Aerospace Defense Command was created in 1957 to centralize warning information about potential nuclear attack on the United States. The intercontinental ballistic missile (ICBM) was much faster than the bomber, putting new stresses on the military command. Integration by organizational checks and balances between the warning (NORAD) and the response (SAC) functions was a major step in minimizing the chance of accidental or inadvertent nuclear war. Certain actions were allowed only if particular alert levels had been declared by an independent institution. The power to launch World War III was to be spread among several actors in the decision process in a model that resembled the checks and balances system of the Constitution itself.

By the early 1960s the development of the solid-fuel, hard-silo-based Minuteman missile gave the United States the option, if it chose, to *ride out* a Soviet attack. That is, it was no longer necessary to order a retaliatory strike on an ambiguous warning. Now, waiting and making a studied deliberate decision would not risk the survival of the retaliatory force. The Polaris submarine force also contributed to U.S. ability to ride out an attack, because it too was survivable.

Additional safeguards against accidental war were placed on U.S. nuclear forces, as shown in table 2. Beginning in the early 1960s, permissive action links (PALs) were placed on all U.S. tactical nuclear weapons. These electromechanical locks prevent a deranged military officer or a terrorist from launching or detonating a nuclear weapon. The Hot Line (formally known as the Direct Communication Link) was installed in 1963. Originally a teletype land line, it has since been upgraded to a satellite communication system. Although the decision to install the Hot Line was precipitated by the 1962 Cuban crisis, considerable thought had earlier been given to such a mechanism. A direct line of communication would enable the United States and the Soviet Union to explain any accident that occurred or to

TABLE 2

Department of Defense Initiatives to Minimize the
Chance of Accidental/Inadvertent Nuclear War

1950s

Reliable warning systems (DEW, Pinetree, etc.)
SAC positive control tactics
NORAD activated
Alerting system integrated with check and balance control system

1960s

Invulnerable second-strike forces acquired to ride out attacks
PALs (Permissive Action Links)
Hot Line
End of airborne bomber alerts
Principle of separating force generation from force application

1970s

Modernized Hot Line (satellite communication)
Incidents-at-sea agreement
Accidental-war agreements
Improved intelligence reconnaissance of threat areas

1980s

Updated Hot Line
Initiatives on confidence-building measures

describe why seemingly provocative military actions were being taken. For example, if an American bomber accidentally went off course and dropped its bomb on Russian soil, the president could use the Hot Line to explain that the affair was an accident, not the beginning of a general attack. Many potential uses of the Hot Line seem far-fetched, but its cost is low, especially compared with the cost of *not* having it should it be needed.

Certain strategic conceptions about the political command and control of nuclear forces also crystallized in the 1960s and contributed to the reduction of the chance of accidental and inadvertent war. In particular, the principle that force generation should be separated from force application emerged as a criterion for evaluating nuclear weapon systems. This meant that military forces that depended on mobilization for use, and particularly those that could not *stay* at heightened mobilization levels for long, were considered destabilizing. Analysts considered that a major reason for the uncontrollable outbreak of World War I was that armies could not stay mobilized for very long: once such a mobilization was begun, it was strongly disadvantageous to back down, that is, to demobilize. Thus arose the temptation to strike first as the least bad alternative.

In the 1960s, this principle led to a conscious deemphasis of manned bombers in favor of ICBMs and the Polaris-submarine-launched ballistic missile (SLBM).[17] Bombers had to escape early from their bases in order to survive, or to prepare for attack. While they could be called back to base, they would then be vulnerable, especially because of their mechanical and fuel requirements. ICBMs and SLBMs could be held at high alert for weeks, even months. Bombers had to return to bases after at most a few hours.

Some operational steps could be taken to mitigate the problems inherent in relying on bombers. One possibility was to keep some of the planes armed and in the air at all times, but this practice would raise the risk of accidental war by substantially increasing the probability of an airplane crash with loaded weapons aboard. The airborne alert also raised command and control fears, because the bombers (unlike ICBMs and SLBMs) could not ride out an attack without being committed quickly to war.[18] For these reasons, airborne bomber alerts were cut back in the 1960s and eliminated altogether by 1968. The B-47 bomber force, which had no airborne alert capability, was eliminated, and the entire role of bombers in the U.S. arsenal was deemphasized.

The first twenty years of the nuclear age thus saw a remarkable achievement: the probability of scenario 1, pure accidental war, was reduced from dangerously high levels to almost zero. Since then it has been made even more improbable, but the back of the job was broken in the 1950s and 1960s. It is useful therefore to see if any generalization about this early period is worth remembering. Significantly, the net effect of the actions listed in table 2 (along with some other actions) was to make the world safer almost independent of any likely policy choices of the superpowers. Driving down the probability of pure accidental war lost the United States no flexibility and no safety; by all accounts deterrence strengthened over this period. Although analysts of complex strategic problems often emphasize the need to make tradeoffs, this experience illustrates that improvements in one area are not necessarily offset by equally bad problems in another. Sometimes the structure of a problem is such that intelligent leadership can make net overall improvements without sacrificing anything.

During the 1950s and 1960s, everything done to lower the risk of accidental war could legitimately be called arms control. It was not the kind of arms control we know today, with official delegations meeting in conference rooms. Nonetheless, it did control arms. Moreover, except for the Hot Line, every action shown in table 2 for the 1950s and 1960s was unilateral and unverifiable. The United States' decision to place PALs on its nuclear weapons in Europe was not negotiated with the Russians. They could not verify that we had done so. The Russians could not be certain, either, that we would not reinstitute airborne bomber alerts in a future crisis, or that we would not place B-52s at National Airport in Washington as a deterrent to attack. I believe that effort to eliminate the chance of accidental war represents a greater arms control achievement than the SALT II agreement or any likely development in the START talks. The lesson may be that the most effective arms control measures will be improvements we make independently of the Russians. Perhaps we should look harder for unilateral actions and worry less about whether the Russians "give up" something too.

Finally, it is worth noting that these gains in reducing the probability of accidental war were made during a period of very poor

Soviet-American political relations and of direct confrontations in Berlin and Cuba. Apparently day-to-day political relations were less important than other factors, at least on this issue. We should remember this early experience and recognize that not all efforts to make the world safer need wait for improved political relations with the Soviet Union. Indeed, the worse the political relations, the more important it is to design measures to prevent major nuclear war.

Actions undertaken in the 1970s and 1980s further reduced the chances of pure accidental war (see table 2), so that today virtually anyone familiar with America's nuclear forces would conclude that no flock of geese, failed computer chip, or even crazed military officer could start a nuclear war.[20] In effect, the buttons and wires that launch missiles or bombers are not even connected in noncrisis, nonalert situations. Far more difficult, unfortunately, is the problem of preventing nuclear war in a threatening situation of crisis or alert.

SCENARIOS 2, 3, AND 4

What other systems, through accidents and inadvertent actions, can have trouble?[21] Air traffic control systems are extremely complex. They include radar networks, sophisticated radios, beacons, transponders, air traffic controllers, computers, and the airplane and crew whose behavior the whole system is trying to organize. The object, of course, is to prevent crashes and collisions. In the United States and other advanced nations, air travel has become consistently safer over the past thirty years, thanks to technical advances in air traffic control and the motivating pressure of public concern.

Maritime accidents are a different story entirely. There has been little reduction in the number of collisions among freighters, tankers, and other large seagoing craft, even though the technical sophistication of maritime control systems has increased greatly. Ships now carry radar and advanced communications. Their operations are supported by shore-based computers, overhead satellites, weather prediction systems, and navigational radio beacons. New ship designs have made hulls more damage-resistant.

Attempts to explain the disappointing rate of maritime accidents have noted a lack of public or elite concern about this issue; responsible international organizations have no real enforcement power; pressure to meet delivery deadlines is far greater than for airlines; and little emphasis is given to monitoring safety considerations. A more fundamental explanation, the relative danger of the sea as an operating environment, sheds light on the difficulty of controlling inadvertent escalation to nuclear war in a crisis.

Ships sail as independent entities. When one suddenly comes near another and a collision becomes possible, no single decision-maker is responsible for both. In an analogous situation involving planes, the air traffic controller on the ground is unambiguously in charge. Another difference between the air and maritime systems is the long tradition that a captain has rigid control over his ship. One result of these practices is that incompetent captains may remain on duty, whereas their counterparts in the air would be grounded. Rigid centralized control can produce many pathologies not adequately countered by the obvious remedy of holding individuals accountable for their actions.

Finally, no matter how safe and well-operated a ship may be, it can always be rammed by an unsafe vessel commanded by an untrained captain from a country that cares little about marine safety. In short, the variation of performance levels is higher at sea than in the world's jetways. One organizational theorist has described the marine system as "error inducing" compared with the "error damping" air traffic system.[22]

The maritime accident problem is analogous in many respects to the accidental/inadvertent war problem. Our governments' efforts to avoid war reflect at least an intuitive sense of the need for some higher-level system to govern the independent actions of the two sides. The Hot Line, I believe, arose from the hope that a last-ditch effort by political leaders to reach agreement in a crisis might avert disaster. In agreeing to consult each other in the event of an accident, rather than turning the problem over to military "captains," the superpowers recognized that a crisis cannot be left to its internal logic.

Whereas unilateral accidental war reduction measures were emphasized in the 1950s and 1960s, most of the initiatives and proposals of the 1970s and 1980s required some *bilateral* cooperation. In many respects the American and Soviet strategic forces have merged into a single gigantic, complex whole. The task ahead involves establishing rules of the road to steer, control, and govern this fantastic system.

The considerable difficulties of this task have received little attention. I believe that the collective likelihood of scenarios 2, 3, and 4 has *increased* since the mid-1970s and that these scenarios are more probable than other paths to nuclear war examined in this book. We are less likely to experience a surprise attack out of the blue or a catalytic war than an intense crisis or limited war in which an accident or unintended eruption brings on a nuclear war. It is difficult to distinguish the risk of inadvertent war from the general paths of escalation (described in chapters 4 and 5 for Europe and the Middle East) simply because any escalating conflict would be rife with possibilities for accidental and inadvertent war.

The problems of avoiding nuclear war in a time of crisis or alert have become more difficult, and they have not yet been taken seriously. Both the Soviet Union and the United States have developed quick-reacting nuclear forces tightly integrated with warning and intelligence sensors. This tight coupling makes it relatively easy to manage simple crises affecting only a single region, but difficult to manage intense crises. In a limited crisis, our systems will allow us to feel reasonably confident that a general attack is unlikely, because most of our warning and intelligence channels will indicate little activity except in the particular region affected by the crisis or war, whereas a general attack would presumably involve many parts of the Soviet military establishment. However, when a crisis spills across many geographic areas and Soviet nuclear forces are alerted, the reassurance that there is no imminent danger vanishes.[23] It is then that the nuclear establishments of the two sides may interact in complicated and complex ways, reinforcing the perception of danger and driving up the alert level still further.

Technical developments have also made the war-avoidance problem harder to manage. The accuracy of missiles is greater; flight times are made shorter by the positioning of Pershing II missiles in Germany and Soviet submarines off the American coastline; and fixed weapons and command centers are less survivable because of more accurate and deadly weapons. The development of "stealthy" systems compounds the problem because weapons that are hard to "see" with warning and intelligence sensors effectively reduce warning time to zero.

The doctrines of the United States and the Soviet Union are

especially troubling in this regard. Each makes little secret of its intent to attack command and control centers in order to paralyze the adversary temporarily until the full weight of attack can be brought to bear against its forces. This message is also clearly conveyed by the development of antisatellite weapons (to blind a victim) and the provocative peacetime patrols of submarines within short flight-time range of national command centers. Despite any high-level denials about these strategies, the military in each nation sees the actions and reads the talk of command structure attack as if it were official doctrine. These middle-level officials may have more reach into a future crisis than their political leadership. Consequently, their peacetime perceptions are crucially important.

For several reasons we have not yet faced up to the increasing risk of accidental/inadvertent war in an ongoing crisis or conflict. As nuclear arsenals have grown, and as the horror of nuclear war has increased with knowledge of "nuclear winter" and other phenomena, the tendency to ignore nearly all operational aspects of strategic and theater operations has also grown. There is a general assumption that for nuclear weapons only *prewar* moves are of interest, and that deterrence at these awful levels of destruction is automatic. As Herman Kahn pointed out, it is almost impossible to get people interested in the tactics and strategy of what to do at high alerts or when deterrence has already broken down. The notion that nuclear war is unthinkable, and that an ability to destroy Soviet society solves the strategy problem once and for all, has left many indifferent to the problems of dealing with accidental and inadvertent war at very high alerts or in war itself.

Concerted action has been taken to deal with the pure accidental war problem of scenario 1, for that risk just could not be ignored. It endangered every moment of our peacetime existence. In contrast, we have little experience at high alert levels in an intense crisis. As a result, less senior level political attention is given to the problem. Together, the increasing difficulty of the problem and its neglect *raise* the likelihood of this particular path to major nuclear war.

A rough subjective indication of the overall dimensions of the problem of accidental and inadvertent nuclear war is shown in figure 1. Because of the uncertainties involved in this characterization, a range of probabilities is shown in the figure. During the 1950s the risk was high, because of the danger of both accidental and inadvertent war. By the late 1960s, as the risks of purely accidental war were reduced, the situation became relatively safe, almost independent of the policy choices of either the United States or the Soviet Union. By the 1970s, however, the growing complexity of Soviet and American nuclear forces and their tight coupling with warning and intelligence systems, together with the widespread assumption that only prewar moves were relevant when deterrence was "automatic," began to increase the likelihood of some kind of disaster.[24]

This curve is an estimate of a major national security "disaster" caused by an accidental/inadvertent nuclear war, or by the *fear* of such a war. Tradeoffs between these twin dangers must be considered in any realistic discussion of the problem. For example, at some point the prospect of loss of political control over nuclear alerts or operations may be so great that leaders refuse to take needed action to stand up to a provocation. In effect, we may be afraid to put nuclear rounds in the chambers of our weapons for fear of loss of control; because of danger to Allied bystanders; or because we want to avoid provocation. This could ultimately contribute to a Munich-style capitulation, or even a nuclear Pearl Harbor.

Some Policy Implications

It must be admitted that as long as things remain peaceful, reliance on current controls will work well enough. That is, if the United States and the Soviet Union can avoid direct confrontations, then the initiating causes that underlie scenarios 2 and 3 will not occur, and inadvertent war will be avoided because conflict by pure technical accident has been eliminated as a serious problem. Scenario 4, war brought on by some complicated technical interactions between the two sides' forces, remains a problem, but it seems much less likely than scenarios 2 and 3.

Two policy approaches follow from this observation. First, it may be best to concentrate our energy on *preventing* confrontations, by diplomacy, wise foreign policy, and the fostering of a cooperative relationship between the United States and the Soviet Union. This was

FIGURE 1

Subjective Estimate of the Probability of a National Security Disaster in the
Next Decade or So (a NATO Failure in a Crisis, a Nuclear Sarajevo, Munich,
or Pearl Harbor, or Mutual Homicide)

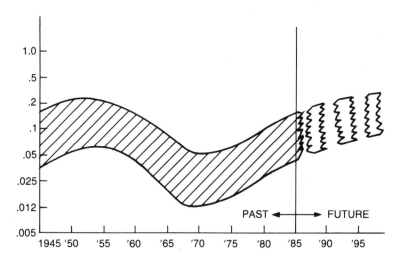

the rationale for the policy of détente followed by the United States
in the 1970s. In the future we might use START-type negotiations to
build a framework of cooperation between the two nations.

The second policy approach is to reach into the structure of the
problem itself, that is, to establish design principles and rules of the
road so that if an intense crisis involving high nuclear alerts does
occur, or if deterrence actually does fail, an eruption to large nuclear
war because of accident or inadvertence is rendered less likely. This
will not be easy, because it requires striking a balance between the
twin dangers of accidents, which lead to a loss of control, and overly
cautious actions that could compound the security problem. But the
obstacles may not be any greater in the long run than those involved
in restoring a cooperative relationship between the United States and
the Soviet Union.

These two policy approaches should not be seen as competing
alternatives. Talk of "setting priorities" or establishing an agenda of
importance presumes that there is an underlying standard of compari-

son between alternatives, whereas in this case the two approaches are working at very different levels of the problem of avoiding nuclear war.

Some may interpret any attention given to scenarios 2 and 3 as an indication of a war-fighting, rather than a deterrent, doctrine. Yet it is this attitude that has left the problem of inadvertent war to narrow military staffs without broader political review of alerting operations, dangerous strategies, and foolish military assumptions. And exclusive focus on deterrence may reinforce the danger of inadvertent war because it encourages unrealistic and even sloppy planning.

As an illustration of unrealistic thinking, consider the complicated release procedures for tactical nuclear weapons in Europe. The U.S. Army has estimated that it will take twenty-five hours to work through all the NATO committees and American layers of command to get permission to fire a small package of nuclear weapons at an advancing Warsaw Pact force.[25] This complicated command mechanism certainly achieves the goal of minimizing the chance of purely accidental war, but it also encourages ad hoc unwritten understandings about what to do in a war or crisis when it begins to dawn on everyone that there may not be twenty-five minutes left, let alone twenty-five hours.

There are broader reasons still for tackling the inadvertent war problem directly. As in the 1960s, when the system became safer almost independent of the likely choices of the superpowers, we should attempt to build security institutions whose success in avoiding nuclear war does not depend on crisis avoidance and a cooperative political spirit. What is needed is a system capable of withstanding adverse political relations and variations in the political stripe and the competence of leaderships—and perhaps even gross stupidities. We have designed our deterrent against direct nuclear attack on this basis and should put our accidental/inadvertent war avoidance system on as firm a footing. However difficult the problems, we should be thinking about long-term nuclear policies, anticipating that we are not likely to achieve general nuclear disarmament even by the early twenty-first century.

A first step in this process is to recognize that the problem of accidental/inadvertent war will be difficult to resolve if we attribute it all to incompetent people. Leaders have made mistakes in past crises and the military has not always carried out its orders suitably. But it is unproductive to speak of stupidity, the use of invalid mental models, or the introduction of "biases" in crisis decision-making as if we somehow understood how to overcome these obstacles. Our understanding of human behavior and its modification is far too shallow to accomplish this worthy objective. Instead of trying to change people, it will be more effective to change the premises of their decisions through better organizational design, better information flows, and removal of the threats that compel them to make irrevocable choices without due consideration of alternatives.[26] For example, trading deployments of Pershing II missiles in Europe for the Soviet submarines near the American east coast would give both sides precious minutes to take such steps as searching for corroborating evidence of attack or even translating messages sent over the Hot Line. Similarly, Robert McNamara has proposed that second use of nuclear weapons not be authorized until it is absolutely certain that an attack has taken place. The deployment of reliable satellites and ground-based warning systems can make this possible, and progress is being made on this front.

To help change the premises of decision-making, we need to develop realistic simulations that introduce members of the political high command to the problems of intense crisis and even the breakdown of deterrence. Nothing of this sort exists today. The tendency is to conduct stylized political exercises that do not introduce the fog of war, the breakdowns of command that occur in the real world, or the complexities of coalition defense. At the White House level there is a real need for continuity of people who understand the alerting process and its possible consequences. A serious study of a simultaneous Soviet-American nuclear alert has never been undertaken anywhere in the U.S. government. This is all the more remarkable given our fondness for fantastic paper studies of fine-tuned nuclear strategies that the military has not the remotest ability to carry out.

At the other end of the command hierarchy there is a need for more realistic exercises of a sort that would require White House initiative. Today military training exercises have to go by the book, although everyone understands that this will be impossible in a crisis where the threats are real. Dispersal of nuclear weapons in Europe can go smoothly when the exercise is done on paper; when there is no danger of an imminent attack that would disconnect hundreds of weapons from the command authority needed to employ them; and when our allies impose no last-minute restrictions on their use. Things may work differently in a war or crisis, and unless realistic exercises prepare people for what to expect, the chances of dangerous accidental or inadvertent actions increase.

In our peacetime planning we can search for "firebreaks," steps that are likely to provoke an escalated response from the other side. In our alerts we may not automatically want to sail our nuclear submarines close to enemy shorelines at a certain alert stage. And we may well want to let the Soviets know that they should not automatically reinforce their forces in Eastern Europe from their bases in western Russia if they have any interest in containing a crisis. We may not be able to prevent the Soviets from acting in a particular way, but we can make sure they realize the dangers involved. There is good reason to talk about these issues with the other nuclear powers, Britain, France, and China, as well. My hunch is that their governments have given even less thought to these issues than the United States has. Yet they may be forced into catalytic alerts that they cannot control politically. Can French, British, and Chinese nuclear bombers launch on ambiguous warning without advancing to their targets? What procedures have been established to ensure that the U.S. Navy does not mistake French nuclear submarines for Soviet submarines when all sides are on high alert? And what constitutes an effective deterrent to a Soviet threat to attack the French nuclear command structure? All of these questions could prove important in a crisis.

The list of suggested improvements and questions could go on, and the answers may be unpleasant or infeasible for various reasons. The goal of this exercise, however, is not to construct bizarre scenarios or even a list of arms control measures for its own sake. The purpose is to reduce the increasing probability of accidental and inadvertent war. Unless a more sober attitude to this problem emerges, the world may be edging toward an institutionalized nuclear showdown, one which admittedly is contingent on an external political shock to set it in motion, but one which may demonstrate how irrelevant many of our strategic and arms control ideas are to the security needs of the late twentieth century.

3 SURPRISE ATTACK AND PREEMPTION

by Richard K. Betts

IN THE POPULAR LEXICON, *surprise attack* and *preemption* are thought to be synonymous, and the adjective *preemptive* is often applied to any sort of first strike at all. In technical terms of military history and among professional strategists, however, the concepts are different. Surprise attack, in the popular sense of the term, is the least likely starting place for a nuclear war, and preemption is more likely. Although preemption is most likely to occur after conventional war has begun, this chapter focuses on nuclear surprise or preemption as the initial act of war. Other chapters examine escalation to the use of nuclear weapons in the course of a conventional war.

Dimensions of the Issue: Logic

Surprise refers to the difference between the victim country's actual military readiness at the time of attack and the degree of readiness it planned to have if given warning.[1] Thus a nuclear surprise attack (1) would be launched before the outbreak of conventional war; (2) would catch the victim's forces in their day-to-day posture, rather than in a full "generated" alert; and (3) would catch the country's leaders in Washington or Moscow, before they could be evacuated to airborne or alternate command posts.

A related question is whether effective warning of attack is received. In nuclear war there is a particular problem that *strategic* warning (evidence that the enemy is preparing its forces for war) is more certain than usable *tactical* warning (evidence that the attack is under way). Geography makes this a marginally greater problem for the United States than for the Soviet Union. Modern sensors can detect large-scale alerts and coordinated military preparations in time to take preparatory counteraction. Certain attack options, however, could conceivably make tactical warning so short that U.S. authorities and forces would be unable to react effectively before nuclear detonations severed critical communications links. This is because of the short flight-time of submarine-launched ballistic missiles (SLBMs) launched against Washington, D.C., the possible effects of electromagnetic pulse (EMP) from high-altitude bursts, and the potential for attacks on facilities for command, control, and communications (C³) that could prevent tactical warning nearly altogether—for example, Soviet sea-launched cruise missiles might evade radar detection and strike targets near the coast quickly.[2] The Soviets claim that they are similarly vulnerable to U.S. Pershing IIs and ground-launched cruise missiles (GLCMs) in Europe, although the U.S. government claims that the Pershing II lacks the range to hit Moscow, and the long flight-time of GLCMs makes it almost certain that they would be detected before detonating on Moscow.

DEFINING PROBABLE PATHS

In the popular view, surprise attack would be an unprovoked bolt from the blue, a strike with virtually no political or strategic warning. This contingency has been the first priority of U.S. strategic planning and nuclear force posture, in part because of Pearl Harbor's searing effect on a generation of leaders, and in part because it is the most demanding scenario. A posture that can meet surprise attack can also handle lesser contingencies. The Soviets, however, have appeared to worry less about a bolt from the blue. Historically they have kept their forces on lower levels of day-to-day alert than has the United States.

Surprise attack is technically possible, and given an insane leader in full control of a nuclear force, it is conceivable. Even an insane leader, however, would be blocked by checks and balances in the two superpower systems. The Soviet Union's leadership is collective; the only plausible situation in which a group of leaders could agree to strike would be a severe crisis, which is inconsistent with the notion of a bolt from the blue. There are fewer constitutional restraints on the American commander-in-chief, but in reality informal ones would operate, as suggested by a piece of anecdotal folklore: Lyndon Johnson is alleged to have said, "Some people wonder what would happen if I just woke up on the wrong side of the bed one day, decided I'd had it with the Russians, called the commander of SAC, and said 'General, go get 'em!' You know what the general would say? 'Screw you, Mr. President.' "

There are no grounds in history or logic to indicate that an unprovoked surprise attack, in a period of calm, is plausible. None of the notable conventional surprise attacks of the past half-century have occurred without either political warning (severe tension or crises) or strategic warning (evidence that the attacker was preparing its forces for war). Moreover, the astronomical risks and costs—both material and moral—make it almost inconceivable that leaders of either superpower would undertake a surprise nuclear attack except *in extremis* — in which case the political situation would not be placid.

PREVENTIVE WAR

Even if not truly a bolt from the blue, an attack may still be a surprise, because victims often fail to reduce their military vulnerability much even when crisis makes war possible. Moreover, an attacker could strike in a period of comparative calm, in the quiet aftermath of crisis, if it judges that the political conflict with the adversary is ultimately beyond peaceful resolution, and that the only alternative is war at a later date on less favorable terms. Therefore, nuclear surprise attack poses its greatest threat as a form of *preventive* war.

A nation might launch a preventive nuclear war if it decided that a continuation of the trends inherent in the status quo was certain to be intolerable, and that waiting longer before resorting to nuclear force would only allow the enemy to inflict greater damage later. The motive would be the prospect of *eventual,* not imminent, defeat or destruction by the enemy. In the nuclear age it is hard to envision either side's being so certain of a hopeless future that it would elect the quite possibly suicidal option of nuclear war. This path is plausible only in the presence of two developments: (1) a situation of tension following severe crises of unprecedented magnitude, in which the post-1945 international order is undergoing major and apparently uncontrolled change, and in which trends appear to be decisively and unalterably in the enemy's favor; and (2) technical changes in the balance of capabilities or calculations about a victim's resolve that make it seem possible to limit the damage from its retaliation.

Neither condition alone would suffice. If the first alone prevailed, nuclear attack would clearly be a case of suicide for fear of death, as Bismarck once defined preventive war. Even the high probability of political defeat should be preferable to the high probability of physical annihilation. The second condition in itself would be insufficient because the absolute damage from even weak retaliation would outweigh all but the most dire costs of maintaining peace.

The probability of preventive nuclear attack has been close to zero, as far as we can know from available evidence, since the end of World War II. A few U.S. officials spoke vaguely about such an option in the late 1940s, but they never reflected thinking dominant at any level of the government. Moreover, the United States then had few nuclear weapons and could not have destroyed the Soviet Union. Of course we have no way of knowing whether Soviet leaders ever considered the option, but they lacked the means to execute it for an even longer time.

PREEMPTIVE ATTACK

In strict meaning, preemption refers to striking first when one believes the enemy is about to try to strike—beating an opponent to the draw, not shooting him in the back. This is a more likely nuclear path, because it is the only situation in which the initiator would have reason to believe that starting a nuclear war could cost less than waiting to try other options. Even in this case a decision to preempt could not be rational unless certain technical preconditions were met. One relates to counterforce options—the capability to destroy an adversary's military assets, especially his nuclear forces, before they can be launched. There must be a "first-strike bonus"—the prospect of suffering less damage from retaliation if one strikes first. Such a bonus may not exist. If both sides have equal capabilities, for example, but it takes 90 percent of one's forces to destroy 50 percent of the enemy's forces, then the victim of a first strike would have five times as much reserve capability to destroy the attacker's cities as the attacker would have to destroy the victim's. (In actuality the difference would be less, since the initial counterforce attack would inflict appreciable collateral damage—destruction of civil infrastructure in the vicinity of military targets—but the theoretical difference is still significant.) If accurate MIRVs (multiple independently targeted reentry vehicles), which allow a small number of warheads to destroy a large number, had never been invented, it is possible that a first-strike bonus would not have been available to either superpower since the end of the 1960s. Except for a few years before MIRV deployment, however, some first-strike bonus has been available to the United States throughout the nuclear age, and lately to the Soviets.

Some observers believe that severe nuclear imbalance might also give the inferior side an incentive to preempt in a crisis, lest the superior side eliminate its retaliatory capacity altogether. In this instance, however, the inferior side would not have any option to limit damage to itself; it would have to strike first against cities, guaranteeing annihilation of its own cities in return. If annihilation seemed inevitable anyway, and the weaker side wanted to prevent the enemy's grandchildren from inheriting the earth, this is remotely conceivable. Capitulation without nuclear war, however, would probably appear preferable. However galling that would be, it would leave some hope for immediate survival and eventual political resurgence.

The theoretical probability of preemption as a path to nuclear war was probably highest from the mid-1950s to early 1960s, when the United States had massive superiority and the Cold War made the possibility of hot war evident. Preemption was probably least likely from the mid-1960s to late 1970s, when the Soviet Union secured a powerful deterrent and détente reduced the incidence of military crises and the perceived danger of war. In the mid-1980s, we are somewhere between these extremes; the possibility of war has become more apparent again, but neither side can escape powerful retaliation. Despite these relative variations, the overall probability of nuclear preemption has been very low, with the possible exception of the 1962 Cuban missile crisis.

INEVITABILITY AND CREDIBILITY

Given the apocalyptic consequences of nuclear war, even devastating political losses in the international arena would probably be preferred if one had a choice. Starting a nuclear war becomes less unthinkable if there appears to be no choice or if the attacker believes that limited war is possible—that the enemy will be "self-deterred" into capitulating after being struck, keeping its surviving nuclear forces leashed.[3] Thus the essential questions are how one decides that war is virtually inevitable (at whatever point that occurs, the opponent's nuclear force is automatically transformed from a deterrent into a target, which must be attacked to limit the damage that will be suffered from the inevitable exchange), or that the victim will surrender rather than retaliate.

In reality, war can never be inevitable, and neither side can be certain that the victim of a counterforce attack will not release its surviving forces against the attacker's military forces, cities, or other valued assets. Moreover, these two conditions are unlikely to coincide. If war seems inevitable to one side because it believes the other side is about to strike, the first side could hardly believe that the other would be too timid to retaliate after being struck itself. The gamble on self-deterrence therefore is relevant only in two situations: (1) where the attacker is recklessly confident or prone to take extreme risks; or (2) when a conventional war is already under way, in which case nuclear escalation could hardly be a real surprise.

Thus the crux of the problem for surprise attack is the determination that war is inevitable. A cool and rational decision to this effect by a collective body is hard to imagine, because the more people are involved, the more likely that some will argue that other alternatives are available and that deterrence can hold. The danger lies rather in a less than fully rational process of deliberation, if stress or panic make the alternatives seem black and white and encourage "groupthink" in a pessimistic direction. Irving L. Janis, however, notes that U.S. decision-making in the Cuban missile crisis was an exception to the pathological form of groupthink—decisions were made in sober reflection, not panic.[4] Given the high stakes involved in a decision for nuclear preemption, group decision-making is as likely to lapse into paralytic debate as to lurch toward preemption, unless there is unambiguous evidence that the other side is about to strike. To rational decision-makers, however, nothing but tactical warning would be unambiguous, and in that case it would be too late to preempt. Strategic warning would show only that the other side was alerting its forces for action, which would be just as consistent with the readiness to retaliate or launch-on-warning as with intent to strike first. Panic, or false technical explanations of indicators by experts to untutored political leaders, could obscure this ambiguity and feed the urge to preempt.

Thus there are few plausible circumstances in which striking first could seem to make sense—at least for the superpowers, which have redundant and survivable forces, hyperdeveloped command and control constraints, highly institutionalized and at least moderately pluralistic decision-making processes, animosities based on ideology and the balance of power more than on visceral hatred, and long experience in cultivating the principle and lore of mutual deterrence. In a world of greater nuclear proliferation, one or all of these conditions could be missing among other contestants—for example, between Arabs and Israelis, or Indians and Pakistanis. In such cases the potential for surprise attack or preemption would be much higher.

Paths to First Strike: Past and Future

What can we learn from history about surprise attack and preemption as paths to war, and the hypothetical circumstances that might lead a nuclear power to strike first in the future? Different elements of past cases overlap the theoretical distinctions between preventive and preemptive attack, and there are few pure cases of either.

Historical analogies have very limited applicability. Most obviously, there are no nuclear war case studies, and there is only one episode (the Cuban missile crisis) that might remotely be considered a "near miss." Moreover, no past decision for conventional attack involved potential costs at all comparable to those in a nuclear world (although many led to outcomes far worse than the initiator anticipated). One tentative and partial exception to these points is the Arab decision to strike into Israeli-occupied territories in 1973. A few observers have argued that the Egyptians and Syrians limited their aims and passed up a chance to penetrate farther toward Israel proper for fear that the Israelis might assemble and use nuclear weapons.

PREVENTIVE WAR

In some respects preventive motives figured in World War I, the Japanese attack on Pearl Harbor, the Middle East wars of 1956 and 1973, and the U.S. quarantine of Cuba in 1962. In some of these cases, particularly World War I and Pearl Harbor, the attacker's decision was affected by militarist constituencies that had a positive desire for war, which was only reinforced by the pessimistic view of alternatives. The political systems and cultures of today's superpowers, as well as the nuclear danger, make this an unlikely element in U.S. or Soviet calculations. (It could figure, however, in decisions by some future Third World authoritarian countries with nuclear weapons.) To understand how a superpower might choose preventive war, we should focus on the historical actors' reasons for desperation about the consequences of refraining from attack.

In each case the status quo, or what seemed bound to flow from it, appeared intolerable (or less tolerable than a gamble on war); war at some point in the future, with declining prospects for victory, seemed inevitable (or almost inevitable); and there appeared to be no satisfactory diplomatic or other alternative to change the situation (or none more palatable than war).

In the nuclear world, however, the qualifications noted in parentheses above would rarely obtain, and they constitute the key difference between a strong impulse to lurch into war and an irresistible one. In the past, two considerations allowed leaders to believe that war was preferable to the apparent alternatives: first, meaningful victory at tolerable cost was militarily possible; second, even defeat in war would not annihilate the nation. The existence of a nuclear retaliatory capability requires the attacker to place an exceedingly high bet that either (1) damage from the opponent's retaliation can be limited to "acceptable" levels, or (2) the enemy will be self-deterred from executing its option to wage total war and to inflict unacceptable damage in retribution.

Japan's decision in 1941 seems to have rested on the latter gamble. Knowing that total war would be disastrous, leaders in Tokyo hoped that initial Japanese success in limited war and the prospect of costly effort to roll back Japanese advances would deter effete Americans from the sacrifice of all-out war. Considering the applicability of this calculation to a future case, one finds that the mutually suicidal costs of general nuclear war cut both ways. The attacker would face much graver consequences should the gamble fail; at the same time there would be more reasons to believe that the gamble could succeed. In 1941 Washington did not have to fear that the continental United States would be incinerated if it waged total war after Pearl Harbor; today, it would face such a prospect if it responded with full force to a Soviet counterforce attack.

A major question is why the victims of past attacks did not act before the fact to convince the initiator that acceptable alternatives to war existed. Occasionally the victim shared the view that conflict in some respects was inevitable, or felt there was no way to reassure or satisfy the opponent without entailing unacceptable political losses, or believed that the moment of decision was not yet at hand and that it was not urgent to undertake risky conciliatory initiatives. It is easier for the stronger party to make concessions (the weaker is more likely to fear that concessions would only offer the opponent an opening wedge), but strength also tempts one to press his advantage. An example of prudent concession was Kennedy's *tacit* deal to withdraw U.S. missiles in Turkey after the Soviets withdrew theirs in Cuba. But this was not a formal or explicit concession (indeed, if it had been, U.S. deployment of Pershing IIs and GLCMs in Western Europe two decades later might be cited as a circumvention), and it was something Kennedy wanted to do anyway—so it was hardly a painful choice.

Failure to do enough to defuse the attacker's anxiety is to some extent logically inherent in the nature of political conflict severe enough to make war an attractive option. Intense conflict of interest by definition ensures that the contestants will have different perceptions of stakes, threats, legitimate aims, and acceptable alternatives to violence. But while these perceptions cannot be identical, the existence of nuclear weapons shows contestants that their *risks* may be identical.

For several powerful reasons, then, adversaries will be more likely to squelch an urge to preventive war in the nuclear world than they have been in the past. Under what circumstances could one nation nevertheless launch a preventive war?

It is hard to distinguish deep causes from intermediate ones, except to say that the deep cause is the enduring confrontation of interests and power itself. Two intermediate causes seem possible. First, the attacker might decide that the adversary, always dangerous and threatening, had stepped onto a new plane of hostile intent and become implacable, irrational, undeterrable, and bent on destruction of the attacker's regime. Such a conviction could emerge from a combination of steadily worsening trends in policy and the advent of new and more aggressive leadership. Second, the attacker might come to believe that the adversary's relative capabilities were improving and that countering them would become progressively more difficult. Technically, these capabilities would include the quantity and quality of the enemy's military forces; politically and economically they could mean an expanding and more cohesive enemy coalition, and a declining and increasingly fractious alliance of one's own: in short, negative trends in what the Soviets have called the global correlation of forces.

POTENTIAL PRECIPITANTS

A precipitating cause of preventive war could be a megacrisis in which long-term trends were rapidly and dramatically intensified— with multiple serious reverses in the immediate balance of global influence, several of them close together in time (with active involvement of the adversary), matched by rhetoric and actions of the adversary indicating immediate intent to challenge not just peripheral interests but core security. In theory such a pattern could threaten either of the superpowers. The United States, however, is inherently less vulnerable to collapse of its core security zone (unless, hypothetically, hundreds of thousands of Soviet troops poured into a newly Marxist Mexico). The following sequence illustrates one hypothetical impetus for the Soviet Union to launch preventive war.

Suppose the following events occurred within two or three months. A coup in Libya installs a pro-Western government; Israel punishes Syrian provocations by marching to Damascus with the apparent green light and logistical support of the United States; Iraq breaks diplomatic relations with Moscow. Overlapping with Middle East developments, centrifugal forces in the Soviet empire explode. Rumania withdraws from the Warsaw Pact; the United States reconciles with a revisionist Cuban government that expels Soviet advisers; the Polish government crumbles into catatonia as a reborn Solidarity runs wild. Meanwhile, the United States signs a mutual defense treaty with China and begins to transfer large numbers of modern weapons; the U.S. president announces plans to station ballistic missiles in Turkey; several American armored brigades and a wing of tactical aircraft are sent to Pakistan; and Western aid to Afghan insurgents increases visibly. Finally, a "Prague Spring" breaks out in the German Democratic Republic, and the U.S. president announces that deployment of a large ballistic missile defense (BMD) system will begin the following month. Soviet leaders caucus, agree that the handwriting on the wall is unambiguous and that delay in action risks precipitous implosion of remaining buffers, and decide to launch a full-scale counterforce attack on the continental United States, U.S. bases abroad, and NATO.

Although this sequence is not particularly plausible, it suggests the dangers of a concatenation of crises. Fewer crises, more widely separated in time, would be more readily handled by non-military or at least non-nuclear means. The probability that a more limited set of precipitants could provoke preventive attack would rise if the Soviet Union had reverted from collective to individual leadership (à la Stalin), and especially if technical options for significant damage-limitation seemed available. The latter could emerge from a break-through in air defense combined with either an effective BMD system or a breakthrough in antisubmarine warfare (ASW).

Alternately, a preventive nuclear attack could take the form of a limited strike meant to cow or jolt the opponent into reversing course and coming to terms. For example, the Soviets might attack only U.S. tactical or intermediate-range nuclear forces in Europe or at sea, or only U.S. ICBMs. The latter type of attack would inflict less collateral damage than striking submarine bases and all the bases and dispersal airfields for bombers, a wider scenario given prominence by James Schlesinger and Paul Nitze in the mid-1970s.[5] Similarly the United States could launch a demonstration attack against a token number of Soviet missiles.

It is not clear whether a limited attack is more or less risky than an all-out strike; depending on the reaction of the victim, it could result in either more or less retaliatory damage to the initiator. On balance, limited attack appears the worse option. A limited attack would keep most of the victim's assets hostage to the initiator's reserve forces, and by sparing the leadership would leave open the possibility that the victim could maintain control of surviving forces and prevent them from striking back at all. If not self-deterred, however, the victim would be able to visit greater destruction on the initiator than if the first strike had been comprehensive. Although self-deterrence—or tit-for-tat limited retaliation—might be the rational course, it is hardly what one would expect from a power so threatening that it had made continuation of peace seem impossible (the premise for any type of first strike). In particular, the Soviets would have little reason to strike U.S. regional nuclear forces alone unless they really believed that—contrary to long-standing NATO policy—they were decoupled from intercontinental forces. Either a purely conventional attack on Europe or a full attack on all U.S. nuclear capabilities would be less risky. For the United States, a selective attack on Soviet ICBMs could not accomplish much militarily (it would not dent the Soviet conventional threat or significantly reduce Soviet nuclear options), but it would be far too provocative to allow any confident predictions of the Soviet reaction.

Preventive nuclear attack threatens most when compelling political incentives and apparently permissive technical options coincide. Even then, the awesomeness of nuclear war remains a powerful reason to choose another option—*conventional* attack under the shield of the nuclear deterrent held in reserve. A nuclear first strike at the outset, as opposed to escalation in a war already under way, is more conceivable when it appears that there is not only no alternative to war but no alternative to nuclear war.

PREEMPTION

In practice the distinction between preventive and preemptive attack is often blurred. In World War I, for example, both motives figured in German strategy.[6] There are relatively few cases of pure preemption. Perhaps Chinese intervention in Korea in 1950 and the Israeli attack in 1967 come closest. We do not know why the Chinese attacked. They may have feared the U.N. forces approaching the Yalu would cross the river and carry the war to China. (On the other hand, the motive could have been preventive—to preserve a Communist North Korea as a buffer, lest the West be positioned to attack China at a future date.) In 1967 Israel faced Arab actions that appeared to be clear preparation for war in the near future; given the imbalance of populations and territorial depth, Israeli military doctrine had developed a commitment to preemption, and it was implemented on June 5.[7]

Only one crisis between the superpowers ever raised a hint of the possibility of preemption. In October 1962 U.S. nuclear forces went to DEFCON 2 alert (the level of alert just below wartime conditions), and President Kennedy is said to have estimated (in what must have been hyperbole) that the chances of nuclear war were between one in three and fifty-fifty. He announced that if a missile from Cuba were launched against a country in the Western hemisphere, a full U.S. "retaliatory" attack would come down on the Soviet Union. At the time, the United States enjoyed its greatest capacity for limiting damage by an attack on Soviet forces. Moreover, the military leadership of the Strategic Air Command (SAC) appears to have been oriented to preemptive doctrine since the mid-1950s.[8] There is *no* evidence, however, that U.S. political leaders discussed preemption in the Cuban crisis, or that any U.S. president ever endorsed preemption as a strategy for SAC, even indirectly. Finally, the very fact that the U.S. capability for damage limitation dwarfed that of the USSR in 1962 meant that Soviet preemption was highly unlikely: the Soviets could not hope to limit damage by striking first. Thus few U.S. leaders really believed they might strike first, and *mutual* fear is the prerequisite for preemption by either side. Missiles in Cuba posed a long-term threat. In the short term of the crisis, the only sensible thing for fearful Soviet leaders to do would have been to prepare their forces for launch-on-warning rather than for a first strike.

The causes of preemption in the pure sense are almost all technical and involve indications of capability. Political causes make war possible, but a decision that the enemy is preparing an imminent strike hinges on monitoring the status of its military forces and communications. A political cause would be powerful only if the enemy issued an ultimatum that it would attack by a certain date if concessions were not made. Indications of intent could be intermediate causes, establishing the context that would make preparation of capabilities more threatening.

Under current conditions of nuclear parity *and* vulnerability of forces sufficient to offer both sides a first-strike bonus, technical incentives for preemption have increased. This technical situation could constitute an intermediate cause of preemption in a future crisis, depending on the size of the bonus. But without dramatic increases in the vulnerability of forces or in strategic defenses, marginal differences in the balance of forces could only be a straw to break the camel's back—something that would tip a decision that was already only a millimeter away from being made for other reasons.

The precipitating causes of preemption would be intelligence indicators that the enemy was preparing to strike. These signs would be ambiguous because they would be identical with preparation for defense, enhancement of deterrence or signaling of resolve, or generation of forces and command networks to maximize retaliatory capability. Such indicators would include evacuation of leadership; high alert status for military forces in general; dispersal of bombers to additional fields, flushing of ballistic missile submarines (SSBNs) out of port, and dispersal of regional tactical nuclear forces; surges in coded communications traffic to nuclear commands (especially the appearance of new or unusual codewords or ciphers); and civil defense preparations. In the midst of a crisis such indications would be alarming to either side. They might, however, be more alarming to Washington. The United States has alerted its strategic forces a few times in the past, and they are kept at relatively high levels of day-to-day alert in normal times.[9] Neither is true of the Soviets. Thus even moderate increases in Soviet alert would appear significant, and full alert would be unprecedented.

Risk Reduction Options

Ways exist to trim the danger of nuclear strike through misperception, miscalculation, or panic. But three related considerations fundamentally limit what we can hope to accomplish through new ideas. First, because deterring such an attack has been the overriding priority of both superpowers' strategies for many years, most of the unimpeachable solutions have been discovered and implemented. Second, most solutions pose tradeoffs in other objectives; this is particularly true of ideas that have not yet been implemented. Third, deterrence depends to some degree on cultivating uncertainty about intentions and rationality (because the threat of retaliation might not be credible otherwise). Uncertainty highlights the possibility of miscalculation, which provides incentives for prudence.

DOCTRINE AND POLICY

Preemptive attack would be less attractive if both sides eschewed counterforce targeting in operational doctrine and if each *believed* that the other had done so. As long as *capability* for counterforce exists, however, it will be almost impossible for whichever side faces it to be confident it will not be used. An alternate solution is to adopt a policy of launch-on-warning. This might be desirable for deterrence, but its potential dangers, such as false alarms, have been widely noted. In practice it probably could not be accomplished anyway, unless the crisis already had the president keeping one eye on the button.[10] Thus this "solution" is more relevant to potential preemption than to a surprise preventive attack.

Foreign policy and grand strategy are the major influences on the incentives for preventive war; preemption becomes an issue at a later stage, when it no longer seems possible that diplomacy might avert war, and is most affected by military doctrine and posture. How then can we reduce the political risk that war could ever come to appear inevitable? There are two obstacles to answering this question. First, it is part and parcel of the overall problem of managing superpower competition, finding ways to preserve or gain an advantageous position in the correlation of forces—the balance of political, economic, diplomatic, and military power and influence—without provoking a dangerous response. This means that recommendations will be either a litany of familiar generalities with ambiguous operational content or a set of specific recommendations that pose controversial challenges to long-standing aspects of high policy.

In precrisis times the most certain way to prevent tension is to give in to the opponent, but this approach can be counterproductive if the other side takes advantage of relaxed inhibitions to expand its influence. If neither side wishes to revise the international order, and they can make their willingness mutually credible, tension can be reduced through détente. New détente in the 1980s and 1990s might require much greater measures of superpower activism or passivity than characterized détente in the 1970s. The U.S. and USSR must demarcate and manage spheres of influence—a collaboration that verges on condominium. Or they must reciprocally disengage from spheres of influence and volatile peripheral areas, which amounts to promoting the diffusion of power and voluntarily relinquishing the role of a superpower. Either alternative is a fundamental matter of high policy and national objectives, which are decided by elections and leaders, not analysts. Policies that reduce perceptions of threatening intent include non-intervention within the opponent's spheres of influence (especially countries on its border) and declaration of a nuclear no-first-use doctrine. The first places major constraints on strategic competition (for example, Pakistan and Afghanistan border the Soviet Union), and the second compromises deterrence of conventional war if it is credible and has no reassuring impact if it is not.

The second obstacle to prefabricated *political* measures for risk reduction is inherent in the causes and dynamics of crisis. In a situation so severe and unprecedented that either side contemplates deliberate resort to nuclear war, the parties will almost by definition have passed the point at which signals of political intent or cooperative measures for reassurance will be either feasible or credible. Moreover, it would be particularly difficult at that point to distinguish between action taken to bolster deterrence or defense and offensive actions taken to prepare an offensive. The key would be to demonstrate innocent intent toward a party that feels so absolutely threatened that it would consider starting a nuclear war that it might well not survive. But if suspicion, fear, or panic are intense enough to have raised this possibility, what gestures of intent would suffice to defuse it, short of a dramatic concession? Reassuring rhetoric carries little weight in itself in a near-war situation—indeed, it is likely to be viewed as deception. Voluntary concessions are possible but unusual for countries that feel themselves benefiting from a growing and favorable momentum. Measures of reassurance concrete enough to reassure leaders who perceive their core security to be crumbling will be unattractive to the side that is gaining advantage unless it realizes that it is close to pushing the other side into war. Such a realization is possible but requires a degree of prudence and empathy rarely consistent with crisis. If it had been possible for diplomacy to demonstrate convincingly that aims were limited, the near-war situation should not have erupted; if the crisis is near the point of war, reassuring diplomacy cannot easily be made credible. At this point, to use Robert Jervis's distinction, "signals" of intent (which are only gestures or assertions) are less meaningful than objective "indices" (which contain inherent credibility).[11] Apart from clear concessions to political demands, indices mostly relate to postures.

FORCES

Military changes that would reduce incentives for *preventive* war relate primarily to overall force structure, size, and perceived capability; they are discussed in this section. Measures that would reduce incentives for *preemptive* attack relate primarily to nuclear forces and to procedures for their alert and generation; most of these are discussed in the following section.

The notion that stability is a technical quality and is inherent in certain configurations of force structure has dominated published American thought on nuclear strategy, which has generally developed in a nonideological frame of reference. (In the Soviet Union, by contrast, where scientists and academics have less to do with strategy, this notion has been less prevalent.) There is little evidence in history that technological factors determine the origins of war. As Stephen Rosen writes, "It is difficult to find even one war caused by [technical military] instability."[12] The revolutionary significance of nuclear weapons, however, places a higher premium on stability, because it radically increases the dangers of risk-taking or miscalculation.

Eschewing offensive forces and development programs that appear to threaten offensive action against core security interests might help to signal that war need not be inevitable. The simplest hypothetical way to do this would be to construct an international order in which defensive capabilities dominated offensive ones at all levels. In the nuclear sphere, this could mean the combination of (1) deployment of highly effective air and ballistic missile defenses; (2) reduction or elimination of offensive forces and of the production base that could break out and build enough forces to overwhelm the defenses; and (3) credible bans on research and development of countermeasures or new offensive options. The solution in its most ambitious form requires unprecedented levels of overall cooperation, commonality of strategic conceptions, and synchronization of programs on both sides.

Incremental moves in some of these directions are desirable (though some—such as only moderately effective BMD—would be wasteful or counterproductive).[13] But progress in this direction entails strategic as well as financial costs.

Even if technically and politically feasible, greater stability at the nuclear level would aggravate instability at the conventional level. The United States and NATO in particular have long relied on the threat of nuclear escalation to deter conventional attack by the Warsaw Pact. The closest thing to conventional stability would be establishment of an equal balance of forces, with "offensive" components minimized and "defensive" ones maximized. But it is difficult to assess the relative offensive and defensive characteristics of complex conventional force structures whose evolved capability has never been tested in war. Before World War I, the offensive was prevalently and mistakenly believed to be dominant; before World War II, the offensive potential of tanks and submarines was prevalently underestimated. And history provides scant support for the hope that equality in the balance of forces will deter a decision to attack.[14] In essence, the dilemma of Western strategy since the Cold War began has been that the goal of eliminating the possibility of nuclear war conflicts with the goal of reducing the danger of conventional war.

The alternative that has appealed to strategists is also more technically feasible: to retain nuclear retaliatory capability while eliminating significant counterforce capability. A deliberate nuclear first strike would presumably not be chosen if it could not destroy a significant amount of the victim's ability to inflict destruction in return. At the same time a nation contemplating a deliberate conventional first strike against the adversary's core interests could not be certain that the stricken victim's response would be rationally restrained. Thus nuclear weapons, in this situation, would offer no rational appeal as instruments for starting a war, but would retain some credibility as instruments of reprisal—and thus of deterrence. The cooperative solution would be to negotiate force structures in which a counterforce attack by either side would leave it with reserve forces smaller than the surviving forces of the victim. This involves (1) minimizing the proportion of launchers that are vulnerable to attack; and/or (2) equalizing the number of counterforce-capable launchers that are vulnerable and restricting them to single-warhead loadings, so that the side striking first would expend more than it would destroy.[15]

The first goal could be accomplished by replacing fixed ICBMs with mobile ones, but this would raise command and control problems and would also make it difficult to verify numbers, and therefore to ensure equality of forces. The second goal could be accomplished by destroying MIRVed ICBMs and filling silos with equal numbers of single-warhead missiles on both sides. But unless old missiles *and* silos were destroyed, and the new silos and missiles were very small, this solution would be more vulnerable to reversal, as MIRVed ICBMs could be phased back in during a period of deteriorating relations. And to protect the balance from breakout (the rapid installation of capabilities that overturn the basis of stability), the numbers of single-warhead fixed ICBMs on both sides would have to be very high (when Paul Nitze discussed this option, he usually spoke of several thousand for the United States).

Improved protection of command, control, and communications (C^3) is a high priority for all circumstances but is more relevant to the problem of preventive surprise attack than to preemption. C^3 is most vulnerable in noncrisis times, when political leaders and military forces are not in a state of alert. Preemption in the pure sense presupposes mutual alert, in which case backup systems (such as airborne communications links and command posts) may already be activated and leaders primed to react quickly, perhaps by authorizing launch-on-warning. This, indeed, aggravates the danger of preemption, since such precautions can be misread as preparations to strike.

The ideal solution for C^3 is one that does not require precipitous changes in posture or provocative actions. It is hard to devise a means to this end, however, because fixed assets are inherently vulnerable—especially in the United States, where the capital city is on the coast —and C^3 functions are too complex to be relegated to constantly mobile mechanisms. It would help to eliminate systems with very short flight-times to target—that is, the Pershing IIs in Europe and Soviet SLBMs near the Atlantic coast (the U.S. government says the Pershing II cannot reach Moscow, but the Soviets claim that it can). Either weapon system could be reintroduced on short notice, however, and if the withdrawals had been negotiated and were violated, the repositioning of the weapons would make matters worse than if no agreement had existed.

The potential escalatory effects of violation might be modified (or deterred) by declaring in advance that any violation would trigger reciprocal reintroduction of the comparable system. The United States would still be at some technical disadvantage since submarines can be deployed more quickly. An option would be to declare that detection of a submarine within the forbidden range would prompt immediate launch of airborne communication links (which would mitigate the paralyzing effect of a decapitating attack on leadership in Washington, since subordinate commanders would have more chance of coordinating retaliation). Such a declaration, however, could only be a temporary solution to deter immediate attack unless a larger, redundant fleet of these airborne posts were developed, so that a sufficient number were constantly rotating on station. The launch of airborne communication links could also encourage preemption, though if it has been declared in peacetime to be an automatic response it is less likely to elicit a preemptive response than if it is undertaken without prior explanation. Moreover, without such restraints, intensified U.S. tracking of Soviet submarines during a crisis would be necessary (especially those deployed close to U.S. shores), and this would alarm Moscow.

On balance, agreement to withdraw such short-warning delivery systems would be advisable, but it would only marginally modify incentives for preemption. In practice, moreover, agreement on such limits would be dominated by considerations about the aggregate balance of forces (for example, intermediate-range nuclear forces in Europe) more than by considerations of how the two specific systems might affect stability in a crisis.

PROCEDURES

To ensure consistency between political aims and military signals, political leaders at cabinet/Politburo level and above—and their personal staffs—should be thoroughly educated in the dynamics of military alerts and crisis deployments. The briefing process should involve diplomats and political advisers as well as military professionals. The latter, even when fully sensitive to potential counterproductive side-effects of precautionary mobilization, face three problems: (1) their professional ethos forbids them to express opinions on political matters; (2) they have a conflict of interest: their primary responsibility —to maximize capability to wage war—can conflict with diplomatic crisis management, which is the responsibility of civilians; and (3) historically, virtually all military leaders have tried to prevent "meddling" by policy authorities in operational matters.

The best way to revise operational procedures to eliminate incentives for preemption would be to institute clear distinctions between the types of alert and mobilization necessary for defense and retaliation and those necessary for an offensive first strike. It is hard to see how this distinction can be made, however, because whichever motivation prevails, the task for physical capabilities is the same: to be ready to launch instantaneously on receipt of an order.

Avoiding alerts in a crisis would reduce chances of provocation and escalation. One suggestion is to proscribe full simultaneous alerts.[16] But forces cannot be kept permanently deployed at full readiness, and crises are what alerts are for—if forces do not go on alert in crisis, they might as well never do so. Avoiding readiness for combat would appear to compromise deterrence at just the point when deterrence is most needed. In a crisis in which each side suspects the other of aggressive intent, the line between deterrence and provocation becomes dangerously blurred. Minimizing risk of provocation is desirable, but doing so by institutionalizing restraints can also limit political options, military flexibility, and adaptation to unforeseen circumstances. Imposing operational restraints on an ad hoc basis, however, can be dangerous—more likely to be done in a bumbling way or to be misunderstood.

The potential ratcheting effect of alerts might be softened by prior exchanges and consultations in which both sides explain the circumstances in which they might undertake alerts for precautionary reasons, to clarify the innocence of intent in advance. The credibility of this "signal" of intent, however, would remain less certain than the "index" of capability revealed by the alert in practice. In any case, one desirable operational option could be encouraged: a rolling or partial alert that can be sustained indefinitely. For example, instead of bringing bombers from 30 percent to 90 percent readiness, or having all serviceable ballistic missile submarines surge out of port, the preferable move would be to an intermediate level—say, 60 percent of bombers and 70 percent of submarines.[17] Otherwise, maximum alert aggravates incentives to strike, because at some point readiness must erode (crews tire, equipment runs down, logistics blows a fuse), and so a difficult choice could emerge whether to move forward or stand down —use the alert or lose it. The pressure to act quickly if at all could tilt a close decision.

Another option, although extremely expensive, is to raise the level of day-to-day alert by 10 or 20 percent. A permanent increase would mean higher annual operating costs, personnel problems, and earlier replacement of aircraft and submarines (high operating rates reduce their life span). But there would be less perceived need to ratchet up in a crisis, because the marginal increase in deliverable destruction would be relatively slight. Day-to-day alert forces already cover most targets of significance; a generated alert (readying almost all forces for launch, rather than just the proportion normally ready) would add mostly minor ones, which professionals refer to as "trash" targets. Higher day-to-day alert could thus comfortably suffice even in crises. This change would require a greater adjustment for the Soviets, because they keep very few of their SSBNs deployed in normal times. Even a unilateral U.S. increase in normal alert levels, however, would improve the situation because it would then not be necessary to respond to a Soviet alert and thereby give a signal that could aggravate Soviet incentives to preempt.

Finally, to reduce the payoff from a surprise first strike, either side could institute a policy of responding automatically to strategic warning by evacuating the chief executive or designated successor to a location that could survive attack (probably airborne for the United States, or a secret hardened facility for the Soviets). Such a policy would reduce the attacker's chances of limiting damage from retaliation by destroying the leadership. It is, however, not very realistic politically, especially because what constitutes real strategic warning is ambiguous. Declaring the policy in advance, however, might at least mitigate the escalatory impact if it were ever implemented.

COOPERATIVE MEASURES

Diplomacy can play a useful role in preventing surprise attack or preemption by (1) reaching arms control agreements on configuration of forces that would reduce first-strike incentives by eliminating a first-strike bonus; and (2) improving communication and common standards for judgment to avert misperception in crises.

In practical terms, arms control should aim to reduce MIRVed ICBMs, prevent deployment of highly accurate SLBMs unless vulnerable ICBMs are eliminated, and minimize active strategic defenses unless they are developed concurrently with severe and reliable limits on offensive forces. Otherwise, competition between offense and defense would only divert resources without sufficiently reducing vulnerability, and the competition would be destabilizing because developments on the two sides would be uneven or unsynchronized. In the absence of fundamental breakthroughs in negotiation on forces, the most significant arms agreement would be to limit antisatellite warfare (ASAT) to protect capabilities for tactical warning and strategic communications.

To foster common understandings on crisis behavior, it would be helpful to institutionalize consultations on operational procedures and actions that each side would consider threatening, but this would be difficult. It would essentially amount to a mutual educational process in two dimensions: between the political and military establishments within each nation and between the two sides. The institutional and sociological obstacles to movement in either dimension are substantial. And in dealings between the sides, improved understanding of military options is a two-edged sword, since one side's understanding of the other's options can mitigate the usefulness of that option for improving wartime capabilities. What is good for averting war is unfortunately not what is good for fighting the war if it comes nevertheless. On balance, however, even incremental improvements in mutual understanding are valuable enough to justify the establishment of institutionalized centers for ongoing exchanges between professionals on both sides, to reduce risks of miscalculation.[18]

Conclusions

Observers in the United States have generally overestimated the danger of Soviet nuclear surprise attack and underestimated the danger of Soviet preemption (in the strict sense of a strike launched in anticipation of U.S. attack). From the limited indications available, Soviet views are a bit closer to the mark. They appear to have more confidence in political and strategic warning of an impending American strike, and more sensitivity to the delicacy of the issue of preemption (a subject that in its strict definition is virtually never discussed in American professional military writings). As Stephen Meyer discusses in chapter 7, however, Soviet writings on this subject are usually cautious or elliptical, and there are few other good sources on Soviet policy, so my discussion focuses on American approaches.[19]

American strategists have been most sensitive to the danger of surprise attack during periods of tension and perceived increases in Soviet capabilities. (Top Air Force professionals, however, were sometimes less concerned than civilians, because they were more oriented to the offensive and more willing to consider American preemption. When Albert Wohlstetter and other Rand Corporation analysts were crusading to reduce the vulnerability of SAC bases in the mid- to late 1950s, SAC was not immediately responsive.)

Concern about the danger of Soviet nuclear surprise has usually been future-oriented. During the "missile gap" controversy, the issue was whether the Soviets might achieve superiority a few years later. In the late 1970s the raging controversy was whether the "window of vulnerability" would open by the early 1980s. (When the early 1980s arrived, and the actual operating balance of intercontinental launchers and warheads had moved further in Soviet favor, U.S. concern evaporated because Reagan's *plans* for strategic modernization and buildup had mollified most hawks or pulled their talons.)

Apart from academic theorists of deterrence, Americans have been less sensitive to preemption for three reasons. First, until the mid-1960s U.S. strategic superiority was so great that the Soviets could ill afford to expend their arsenal in a counterforce attack. Second, the NATO doctrine of extended deterrence disposed Western leaders to believe that the nuclear initiative would belong to the United States. Third, most Americans take it for granted that their country's lack of aggressive intent is obvious to the Soviets, and that a Soviet first strike would necessarily be willful rather than the product of fear of unprovoked attack by the United States. The problem of incentives for preemption has worsened with the advent of strategic parity. Imbalance leaves the weaker party with a less apparent option to limit damage by striking first (rather than launching on warning).

The principal arguments of this chapter are that (1) the pure model of unprovoked surprise attack is the least likely path to nuclear war; and (2) preemption is a more likely path, but preemption before the onset of conventional war (as opposed to escalation) is still less likely than the other paths discussed in this book. Nevertheless, protection against surprise attack has been the first priority of strategic planning. Perhaps this bias has helped to make the problem the least worrisome of the various paths. U.S. policy has been less effective in negating the possibility of Soviet preemption, in part because of its success in minimizing the danger of surprise. Alerting and deployment of forces and command networks are a hedge against surprise in a crisis, but such measures could contribute to a Soviet perception that Washington was about to strike—thus igniting incentives to preempt.

Some reforms (within the context of overall nuclear parity) would mitigate the danger of both surprise and preemption on both sides: (1) reducing the proportion of launchers that are vulnerable to attack; (2) shifting the "exchange ratio" (through reduction of MIRVed ICBMs) so that an attacker would have to expend more warheads than it would destroy; (3) reducing the vulnerability of command, control, and communications. The third objective is most crucial, but also hardest to accomplish. Military communication links can still be improved at the margins, but the vulnerability of the president in Washington remains the most critical problem. Little is known, from open sources, about unique vulnerabilities of the Soviet command and communication system. While improvements of the sort described above are desirable, they may be less likely in coming years than developments in the opposite direction: further centralization of C^3, advances in stealthy options for attacking national command authorities, more antisatellite capabilities, confidence in counterforce options, less redundancy of forces (if arms control succeeds in achieving reductions), and uneven strategic defenses.

The most promising recommendations are those that modify operational procedures to reduce preemptive incentives at the margin. Incentives for preventive attack are less technical, more political and visceral, and thus less susceptible to a priori prescription. All of the major measures that might mitigate either problem impinge on fundamental policy objectives, large sunk costs (such as vulnerable counterforce capabilities—especially Soviet ICBMs, the bulk of their force, deployed at great expense), or alliance cohesion.

Potential benefits and costs of many risk-reduction measures are closely balanced because it is often difficult—especially in crises—to distinguish between deterrence and provocation. For example, Soviet missiles deployed in Cuba in 1962 and U.S. missiles deployed in Europe since 1983 were deterrents to the side deploying them and provocations to the side facing them. Moreover, deterrence is based on threat, and the two sides often disagree about which types of weapons and deployments are inherently retaliatory rather than first-strike threats. In crises mistrust and commitments harden, making it more difficult for leaders to be confident that they can discern or demonstrate the differences between enhanced communication and deception or between restraint and weakness. The best solution to these tensions is to install sober and careful statesmen in both capitals —a vital but lofty goal.

If this analysis appears pessimistic about the probability of marked improvements in our capacity to avoid surprise attack or preemption, it nevertheless reflects optimism: strategy and doctrine have already done much to institutionalize caution and erect sturdy barricades across these paths to apocalypse. The barricades should be reinforced, but perhaps it is even more important to strengthen the obstacles across other paths.

4 ESCALATION IN EUROPE
by Fen Osler Hampson

NOT FOR ALMOST half a century has Europe been engulfed by war. This relative peace since 1945 testifies to the strength of extended deterrence, the credibility of U.S. nuclear guarantees, and the success of collective security. The existence of clearly designated spheres of influence and the superpowers' respect for each other's vital interests have also contributed to stability and peace. Most observers would agree that the probability of war—conventional or nuclear—over Europe is now low. But few would say that the threat of war has been removed forever. Indeed, the recent tide of public protest against nuclear weapons in NATO and the demand, by some, for greater accommodation with the Soviet bloc suggest a deep-seated pessimism about the ability of deterrence to last.

Postwar history supports these concerns. Since 1945, war in Europe has seemed likely if not imminent on several occasions. In the three Berlin crises (1948, 1958–59, and 1961), for example, the prospect of military confrontation that could have escalated to a nuclear war loomed large.[1] In both the Korean War and the Cuban missile crisis, Western leaders also feared that conflict might spill over to the European theater.[2]

The risks of war in Europe were lessened in the early 1960s by informal understandings over Berlin, and later by a general improvement in the overall East-West relationship: first with Brandt's *Ostpolitik* and then the Nixon-Kissinger détente.[3] Still, Europe remained vulnerable to the possibility of horizontal escalation from superpower confrontation in another corner of the globe. The worsening of U.S.-

Soviet relations since the 1970s may have increased the dangers of war significantly. As we look forward thirty years, there are reasons to believe that the situation could deteriorate in Europe as well.

Deep Causes

The deep causes of conflict lie in the U.S.-Soviet rivalry—intense ideological and military competition that has yet to be channeled into more cooperative forms. These causes are a necessary but not sufficient condition for war in Europe, however. If the superpowers perceive each other's political commitments in Europe as strong and the costs of changing the status quo as high, the situation will remain stable despite these profound political differences. If these commitments were to weaken or to change in some fundamental way, however, the likelihood of conflict could change as well. The reasons why lie at the heart of the concept of deterrence.

Deterrence links military capabilities to political interests and objectives, and says so, loudly, to the adversary.[4] In contemplating any action, the aggressor must calculate not only the opponent's military capability, but also his willingness to defend his interests. Deterrence makes the aggressor shoulder the burden of risk when he gambles on changing the status quo. Only if the opponent's capability or resolve is weak will the gamble seem acceptable.

Current military capabilities of the United States and the USSR ensure that war in Europe would be costly. Modest changes in the current balance of forces would not significantly change this calculation. But this is only one side of the equation, for deterrence could fail for political reasons having little to do with the military balance. A perception of weakened commitments or resolve could increase the likelihood of a challenge. How might this occur? It would probably come about through a general loosening of the Western alliance that created opportunities for Soviet adventurism, or a deterioration in Eastern Europe that tempted the United States to reverse the Yalta accords, or, more likely, some combination of the two.

The NATO alliance could falter if the United States withdrew, or reduced the level of, its troops in Europe; if Germany became independent or neutral; or if the Europeans formed an independent defense community. A combination of these could also emasculate

NATO; there are currently pressures in all three directions.[5] For example, there have been various proposals in Congress to reduce troop levels in Europe. Some of these simply reflect a desire to prod our European allies to contribute more to their own defense, but sentiment grows in some quarters that the United States should consider pulling out of Europe altogether.

The Europeans have always been uneasy about their dependence on the United States. There is now, however, active discussion about reducing this imbalance by strengthening military cooperation within Europe, perhaps through creation of a European defense community.* This is an old idea, restored to new life. The fragile consensus within NATO is also threatened by divergent U.S.-European views about a number of issues: the meaning of Yalta and the Helsinki agreements, arms control and détente, East-West trade, the gas pipeline, the neutron bomb, and deficits and interest rates. The NATO marriage has had its rocky moments. At present, U.S.-European differences extend over an unusually wide range of issues. The most drastic and ultimately dangerous source of change, however, may lie in public attitudes toward NATO. Europe's youth do not share the older generation's attachment to the alliance, a worrisome trend that bodes ill for NATO's long-term survival.

The health of the Soviet alliance in Eastern Europe is also in doubt. Polish disaffection is well known, and there are similar signs in East Germany and Rumania.[6] How much to make of these developments is a contentious issue. The Warsaw Pact is not about to unravel, but it could be significantly weakened by internal political change in Eastern Europe, including such factors as the emergence of restive popular sectors that oppose Communist authorities; a general erosion of the political "legitimacy" of the Communist parties of Eastern Europe; and the emergence of pro-Western leaderships.

---

*Although a common European defense might be a sufficient deterrent to the Soviets, it would probably be weaker than the one now provided by NATO. The transition to such an arrangement could also be enormously destabilizing as the Soviets sought to exploit rifts among the various partners to prevent its formation. Unless the Europeans were to pool their nuclear capabilities and develop some sort of joint institutional mechanism for their use, the nuclear components of European defense would be weak and would encourage each member of the community to develop its own nuclear deterrent force.

None of these things will necessarily happen. NATO and the Warsaw Pact probably will remain intact for a while to come. Clear vital interests and spheres of influence will continue to invite restraint and contribute to political stability. However, since the political situation will change over time, it is important to anticipate the long-term consequences of political change. Obviously, much depends on the speed and magnitude of the shift. Some weakening in the Warsaw Pact is obviously in NATO's interest: a divided, partially fragmented alliance poses less of a military threat than a cohesive, politically integrated one. But too much internal division and unrest in the Pact would greatly complicate relations between East and West. Some major European wars have flowed from the breakup of empires. Europe was engulfed by the Thirty Years' War following disintegration of the Holy Roman Empire. The weakening of the Austro-Hungarian Empire was an important factor in the origins of World War I, as was the collapse of the Ottoman Empire, which encouraged Great Power competition for the spoils and led to a rash of war scares at the turn of the nineteenth century.

A dramatic weakening of Soviet hegemony over Eastern Europe would contribute to greater political competition and conflict between the United States and the Soviet Union as the perception (or misperception) of weakened commitments encouraged the West to action. Although the West was relatively restrained during the Polish crisis, the costs of antagonizing the Soviets in that situation were high. A major transformation in Poland would not have been possible without direct military support and intervention. Even so, some favored a much tougher policy toward the Soviets than that of the Reagan administration.[7]

What should the West do if the situation in Eastern Europe should start to unravel? The obvious danger of an activist policy is that the Soviet Union might at some point decide to reverse the erosion by force to prevent collapse of its empire. Even if the governments of the West chose to do nothing, in the interest of political stability, they might nevertheless be drawn along by powerful transnational social and political forces. If East Germany rose up as Poland did, and Soviet attempts to restore order resulted in large-scale civilian casualties, would West Germans sit idly by? Might not vigilante groups spring up in West Germany to support resistance in the East? How would the government of the Federal Republic of Germany respond to Soviet efforts to seal off the border, especially if there were forays into West German territory and West Germans were killed? The ties of family, culture, and nation between the two Germanies are still very strong and unlikely to weaken. These centripetal pressures could be an important catalyst for conflict between East and West.

An erosion of the NATO alliance might also cause severe problems and lead to political conflict if the Soviets tried to exploit the situation. The Soviets made a not-so-subtle bid to exploit cleavages in NATO and to manipulate Western European public opinion in an effort to prevent the INF (intermediate-range nuclear forces) deployments. Although their efforts failed, they would not hesitate to pursue a similar opportunity in the future.

Growing political competition might not lead to military conflict. It is difficult even to know the direction of change. For example, while a weakened NATO would probably incite Soviet adventurism and raise the risks of war in Europe, it might actually lower the risks of a nuclear war between the superpowers if the United States were no longer committed to the defense of Western Europe. But even if the alliance were severely weakened or dissolved, the United States might still come to Europe's defense in time of need. The absence of formal treaty commitments did not prevent the United States from joining its European allies in both world wars.

Some believe that a formal disengagement of the superpowers from a new neutral and nuclear-free zone in central Europe would reduce the likelihood of military conflict. This notion lay at the heart of the Rapacki plan, initiated by Poland's foreign minister in the late 1950s.[8] It was an idea espoused in a somewhat different form by George Kennan and most recently resurrected by the German peace movement and the Greens.[9] But there are tremendous uncertainties in the creation of a neutral zone in Europe. Superpower withdrawal from Central Europe would probably lead to German reunification—a situation that the Soviets would find intolerable and would seek to reverse. A neutral Germany would no doubt take military steps to preserve and defend its "neutrality." Germany's idea of defense could easily look like provocation to Europe.

Ambiguity and political uncertainty are the seeds of military conflict, especially when one side tries to exploit a situation to its own advantage and miscalculates the degree of the other's commitment to prevent that loss. Conceivably, if the situation in Eastern Europe deteriorated further, countries might appeal for Western assistance and get it—from official or unofficial sources. Military confrontation might follow if the West underestimated the Soviet Union's willingness to use force to reestablish its political control and prevent the loss of its empire. Either side, not just NATO, might fail to understand the other's commitments and resolve. A more fluid and vaguely defined set of alliance commitments in Europe will increase such ambiguity and the likelihood of misperception and miscalculation. Given the basic dynamics of the U.S.-Soviet rivalry, the probability of military confrontation and a major nuclear war could increase. The Soviet Union's vitriolic reponse to President Reagan's statements that the United States no longer fully supports the Yalta agreements indicates its considerable sensitivity to this problem.[10]

Intermediate Causes

ESCALATION OF OTHER WARS

A war in Europe need not have its political origins in Europe or in a weakening of alliances. It might emerge from superpower conflicts in other parts of the world. Such conflicts could infect the European theater because of the way military operations were conducted or through deliberate horizontal escalation.[11] There are some historical precedents. World War I began on the fringes of Europe (the Balkans), but the main locus of conflict quickly shifted to Central Europe. The Seven Years' War between France and Britain began as a competitive struggle for influence in the then "gray area" of the world, North America, but rebounded to Europe. These conflicts were rooted in Great Power competition in Europe, but the examples are suggestive for the future. In both cases, conflicts in the periphery were extremely important catalysts for war in central Europe. This may, in fact, be the most likely scenario for war in Europe.

Military conflict in the Middle East could spill northward. If the Soviets invaded Iran by way of Turkey, the rest of NATO could be dragged into the conflict.[12] The Soviets would probably surmise that

NATO would abandon Turkey, but if NATO intervened—to prevent the dissolution of the alliance—the war would escalate to Central Europe very quickly.

A conflict in the Middle East or some other Third World region could invite horizontal escalation if either superpower tried to compensate for its military inferiority in one arena of conflict by attacking in another, thereby forcing the opponent to distribute his resources more thinly. Under such conditions, a weakening of the alliance in Europe that made it seem there were real opportunities for gain would provide a further incentive for horizontal escalation. In previous crises when horizontal escalation seemed possible, such as the Cuban missile crisis, the superpowers have drawn back from the brink. There is no guarantee that they would exercise such restraint in the future.

CHANGE IN BALANCE OF FORCES

The forty-year peace in Europe testifies to the stability of the current military balance. Both sides possess an array of forces, from conventional to tactical, theater, and strategic nuclear, but neither has decisive superiority in any one of them. The evolution of these forces and the balance on each rung of the escalation ladder have been important to poltical and military stability. But certain trends could bode ill for the future.

NATO depends on U.S. commitment to defend Europe with strategic forces. Recent trends in the strategic balance, however, make this extended deterrence (under which the United States extends its security umbrella to other nations) look less dependable.[13]

Over the past two decades U.S. strategic superiority has eroded and rough parity between the superpowers has emerged. The significance of this change is controversial. What are its implications for extended deterrence? Some believe that as long as the United States has assured destruction capabilities and could respond to a Soviet first strike with an attack on Soviet population centers, it can effectively deter the Soviet Union.[14] These analysts admit that strategic superiority was a good thing as long as the United States had it, certainly preferable to the situation now. But they argue that efforts to redress the balance and reestablish U.S. superiority will be counterproductive, especially if the United States competes in a costly arms race with the Soviet Union. They believe that the danger of any nuclear exchange and the latent risks of escalation in conventional conflict are important constraints on Soviet behavior, particularly in Europe, where the United States has clearly defined vital interests.

Others, however, assert that assured destruction capabilities are not sufficient for extended deterrence or, for that matter, for deterrence of "limited" counterforce attacks against U.S. ICBMs, bomber bases, submarine bases, C^3 (command, control, and communications), and other military installations and facilities, short of all-out nuclear war.[15] Some within this second group want the United States to strive for strategic superiority and acquire damage-limitation capabilities to remedy current deficiencies.[16] Still others feel it is impossible for the United States to regain superiority.[17] Instead, they argue that extended deterrence requires building a countervailing capability that will enable the United States to deny the Soviet Union a favorable shift in the nuclear balance and to put Soviet forces, C^3, and industrial economic base at risk.

There is merit in each viewpoint. However, it is probably wrong to assign too much importance to "bean counts" of each side's forces.[18] The objective state of the balance is less important than Soviet perceptions of U.S. willingness to defend its commitments.[19] Deterrence would fail if the Soviets believed that the United States and its allies would not act on their commitments. In this respect, current rhetoric about the weakening of extended deterrence and the inability of the United States to defend its allies may become a self-fulfilling prophecy. Although there is much in the current administration's rhetoric and policies to suggest the contrary to the Soviets, some influential spokesmen have come close to saying that extended deterrence is no longer credible.[20] If this skepticism were to become widely shared within the American strategic community, the United States might decide to back off from its commitments under extended deterrence. If the United States came to believe that it did not have effective parity with the Soviet Union, the Soviets themselves would start to wonder about U.S. credibility.

Discussions of the balance of conventional forces in Central Europe echo many of the themes of the debate about nuclear arms. A great many strategists believe Soviet conventional superiority would force NATO to an early use of nuclear weapons in a conflict.[21]

But they argue that it is unlikely that NATO would have the political will or ability to authorize an early first use of nuclear weapons, and it is probable that NATO forces would be overrun before a decision about nuclear use could be made. The threat to use nuclear weapons in NATO's defense therefore lacks credibility. A further worsening of the conventional balance would encourage Soviet adventurism and perhaps even lead to a conventional war if the Soviets came to believe that they could quickly defeat NATO in a conventional offensive before the war had a chance to go nuclear. We could solve this problem by boosting NATO's conventional defense expenditures.

The fate of extended deterrence ultimately depends on both the nuclear and the conventional balance, and, more importantly, on Soviet beliefs about NATO's ability and will to defend itself. If the Soviets felt that the balance had decisively tipped in their favor, this would undoubtedly affect their political and military calculations in a way harmful to NATO. Thus a further deterioration of the strategic and conventional balance, either real or perceived—or the belief that the balance was soon to tip decisively and irreversibly—could be an important intermediate cause of conflict.

TRANSITION FROM A MAD TO A DEFENSE-DOMINANT WORLD

Technological developments in ballistic missile defenses (BMD) could also affect the likelihood of a nuclear war over the next thirty years.[22] The Soviets have deployed a crude BMD system, and the United States is embarking on a major research effort on a variety of defensive systems under President Reagan's Strategic Defense Initiative. Given the limitations of current and future technologies, however, neither superpower is likely to become a strategic sanctuary in the foreseeable future.[23] Nevertheless, it is quite conceivable that new, if imperfect, missile defense systems will be deployed by the United States and the Soviet Union before the end of this century. It is therefore important to consider the implications of these systems for extended deterrence and the likelihood of a nuclear war.

Some believe that the deployment of ballistic missile defenses would erode extended deterrence.[24] BMD would make the United States less vulnerable to Soviet attack but would leave Europe as vulnerable as ever.[25] European anxieties would increase. Fearing that the superpowers might confine a war to Europe to avoid escalation, the Europeans might try to withdraw from NATO or seek a separate accord with the Soviets. It is not at all clear that the weakening or dissolution of NATO would increase the likelihood of nuclear war. It could encourage Soviet adventurism, thereby increasing the likelihood of war in Europe, but the probability of a major nuclear war would depend on whether the United States decided to come to the defense of Western Europe.

Others believe that BMD would strengthen extended deterrence.[26] With BMD the United States would feel more secure and therefore would be more prepared to defend its commitments, not less. The risks of escalation to a nuclear war between the superpowers, and the costs of damage from such a war, would be lower than they are now. BMD would undeniably strengthen coupling (that is, U.S. willingness to defend Europe with its forces), but in terms of the alliance, much would depend on *political* circumstances and on the Europeans' view of BMD deployments. If they saw them as a positive development, the likelihood of a nuclear war would be reduced: the Soviets would be more, not less, persuaded of the U.S. commitment to defend Europe.

More important than the actual capabilities of a BMD system would be American national security decision-makers' perceptions of those capabilities. If the president and his advisers lacked confidence in the system and still believed that the costs of a limited counterforce or countervalue attack with imperfect defenses would be prohibitively high, BMD would probably do little to encourage the United States to act on its treaty obligations. Matters would remain much as they are now. If, however, the president believed in the system's ability to limit damage to the United States from a counterforce and perhaps even a countervalue attack, then BMD probably would strengthen extended deterrence. An American president would presumably then have less to fear from a nuclear war between the superpowers. But the uncertain factor in either case would be European perceptions of BMD, and they could see it either way.

The other major uncertainty is whether the Soviets would deploy new defenses and how effective they might be. If the Soviets deployed an extensive and sophisticated system and had confidence in it, they would be less worried about the prospects of going to war with the

United States. If the United States could not credibly threaten the Soviets, extended deterrence would no longer exist. In such circumstances, the deployment of defenses by both of the superpowers might significantly raise the risks of both conventional war and a nuclear war confined to Europe. Neither superpower would have very much to fear from an escalation to the homelands, which could invite adventurism.

BMD might not be a net gain for NATO, especially when the political context and the reaction of our allies to deployments are taken into account. Soviet BMD deployments could effectively neutralize American offensive strategic capabilities and would further weaken, if not completely undermine, extended deterrence. They would also reduce, perhaps eliminate, the deterrent value of British and French nuclear forces. On these grounds alone, the allies might well oppose the deployment of active defenses by the superpowers.

While the *consequences* of a nuclear war would go down with the deployment of even imperfect defenses, the *probability* could rise if the superpowers then felt they had less to fear. These probabilities would be significantly affected if BMD deployments led to a weakening or dissolution of the NATO alliance that spurred Soviet adventurism in Western Europe.

Precipitating Causes

A nuclear war over Europe would, more likely than not, start with a limited use of nuclear weapons. How would the nuclear threshold be crossed and how would a limited nuclear war escalate to an all-out nuclear war? Last, how could major conventional war in Europe explode into all-out nuclear war without this intermediate step?

Any discussion of the precipitating causes of war depends on the particular scenario under consideration—more so than a discussion of "deep" or "intermediate" causes, which are unrelated to specific events. The following scenarios are intended to be suggestive rather than predictive.

At the political level, a war between NATO and the Soviet Union could begin in many ways. But it would follow one of the two general patterns described above: (1) a dissolving NATO and/or political change in Eastern Europe; or (2) a conflict that began in some other area of the world and spilled over to the European theater. At the military level, a nuclear war could begin with either (1) a deliberate use of nuclear weapons by NATO or the Warsaw Pact; or (2) inadvertent use, without the foreknowledge of responsible political authorities. Inadvertent use would include situations in which one side's forces did something that provoked the other to use nuclear weapons for reasons that were not fully grasped beforehand. These political and military scenarios can be mixed in different ways.

SCENARIO 1. WAR IN THE ATLANTIC

The United States and the Soviet Union are involved in a conventional war in the Middle East. Fearful that the war may escalate, the Soviet Union mobilizes its troops in Eastern Europe. NATO decides to counter the Soviet threat with a mobilization of its own troops. The United States air-and sea-lifts its forces to Europe. As NATO's naval forces move into position to protect sea lines of communication (SLOCs) across the Atlantic, a carrier task force and several antisubmarine warfare (ASW) hunter-killer groups are sent northward to seal off Soviet submarine traffic through the Greenland-Iceland-United Kingdom gap. To protect its own SSBN (nuclear-powered ballistic missile submarine) and SSN (hunter-killer attack submarine) forces, the Soviet Union disperses some of them to the Norwegian Sea and the Atlantic, where they threaten SLOCs. Western sensors pick up this rush of activity and NATO hunter-killer submarines sink blockade-running Soviet SSNs and an SSBN. Perhaps to demonstrate the risks of escalation, a Soviet SSN destroys a NATO surface vessel and severely damages several other ships with a nuclear torpedo.

How plausible is scenario 1? Nuclear weapons might well be fired first at sea rather than on land. Soviet doctrine on nuclear weapons in theater warfare appears to have shifted somewhat in recent years; on land, the Soviets would probably prolong the conventional phase of a conflict as long as possible and would use nuclear weapons only if nuclear war appeared imminent.[27] At sea, however, this is apparently not the case: the Soviets have long viewed nuclear weapons as a way to overcome an adversary with general naval superiority.[28] Lacking naval parity, they believe that to use nuclear munitions against an unprepared opponent would be to their military advantage.

Given their current logistics, if Warsaw Pact forces did not reach the Rhine within two weeks they would find themselves in serious trouble. NATO reinforcements would then play a decisive role, and the battle at sea would determine the outcome of the battle on land. If NATO shipping were getting through and Soviet submarine losses were heavy, they would be greatly tempted to go after these forces with nuclear weapons. In addition, the risks of collateral damage at sea are much lower than on land, and nuclear weapons would prove a reasonably cost-effective way of destroying a group of ships (such as a carrier task force). Of course, such action would have to be weighed against the costs and risks of escalation, which would be enormous. The Soviets might also do the job with precision-guided air-to-surface weapons, which proved lethal in the Falklands War. But if the Soviets thought a demonstration use of nuclear weapons against NATO's naval forces could deescalate a conflict by directly raising the specter of escalation, this could change their initial calculation of the costs and risks of first use. Such use might also occur accidentally. American submarines do not have permissive action links (PALs).[29] If Soviet submarines also lack these controls, an unauthorized first use of nuclear weapons at sea is possible.

A first use of nuclear weapons at sea might also start with NATO. NATO might use nuclear depth charges and torpedoes against Soviet submarines, especially those that are difficult to destroy with conventional munitions. The urge to do so would grow if shipping losses were high.

SCENARIO 2. WAR IN EUROPE

Domestic political troubles in Poland have rippled over into East Germany and Czechoslovakia. Political authorities in both these countries have appealed for Soviet help to quash labor unrest and restore economic activity after a series of crippling national strikes. NATO warns the Soviets that "intervention will be viewed most gravely." The Soviets ignore these warnings and send troops into Czechoslovakia and East Germany. Efforts to restore order lead to a confrontation in which several hundred workers are killed and thousands arrested and imprisoned. The West responds with a complete economic boycott of Eastern Europe and the Soviet Union. The Soviets then impose a land and air blockade around Berlin. Several aircraft attempting an emergency airlift of food and medicine are "accidentally" shot down. NATO invades East Germany to regain Berlin. NATO and Soviet forces become involved in serious fighting and the conflict quickly expands along much of the inter-German border. NATO is able to hold its own in the initial stages because large numbers of Soviet divisions are tied down in Eastern Europe, but as additional reserves are brought in from the Soviet Union, NATO finds its defenses crumbling in the northern sector of the Central Front.

2a. NATO warns the Soviets to withdraw or "suffer the consequences." To signal its resolve, NATO fires several nuclear-tipped cruise missiles at key bridges and choke points along the Elbe River. The Soviets return fire with SS-21, SS-22, and SS-23 missiles against Pershing II and other nuclear weapon sites in West Germany.

This NATO "demonstration shot" case might alternatively involve the detonation of a nuclear weapon at sea or in a place where the potential for collateral damage was low. In any case, however, NATO's leadership would have to reckon the benefits of first use against the costs and risks of escalation. There are other imponderables: a pure demonstration shot might signal fear of nuclear war rather than resolve, conceding advantage rather than gaining it.

A first use of nuclear weapons by NATO could also occur inadvertently. Once NATO's nuclear weapons are dispersed from their storage sites to their launching platforms, their use—particularly in the case of short-range weapons—might be delegated to units in the field.[30] Elaborate command and control mechanisms should prevent a field commander from firing without authorization from political leaders. But a field commander could conceivably shoot on his own, if his forces were about to be overrun and he already had the firing codes.

Scenario 2 might also develop along the following lines:

2b. As NATO finds its conventional defenses crumbling, orders are given to prepare dual-capable systems for nuclear combat (these are systems such as aircraft and artillery which can be equipped with conventional or nuclear weapons). Soviet intelligence picks up the activity as nuclear warheads are dispersed from their storage sites and other preparations are made for nuclear combat. Moscow decides to preempt with its own nuclear forces.

There are strong reasons for believing the Soviets would try to preempt before NATO had dispersed its weapons.[31] Preemption is openly contemplated in Soviet doctrine, as Stephen Meyer argues in chapter 7, and it would be more cost-effective than attacks after nuclear weapons had been dispersed, since NATO's nuclear weapons (with the exception of Quick Reaction Alert forces) are kept in a limited number of targetable storage sites (fifty or so). Whether the Soviets would preempt with nuclear, chemical, or conventional munitions is an open question.

2c. As NATO's defenses crumble in the northern sector—even though NATO is holding its own in the central sector—the French become fearful not only of a Soviet sweep and encirclement that would cut off NATO from the rear and jeopardize their own ground forces in the Rhineland, but also of a continued Soviet thrust through Belgium into France. The fall of Hanover and Göttingen confirms those fears. The French decide to slow down the Soviet advance by attacking Soviet follow-on forces, as well as key airbases in Eastern Europe, with their new, land-based Hades missiles.

The French have their own nuclear strike force.[32] It is likely that France's leaders would use nuclear weapons if national security and survival were threatened—presumably before French forces were overrun and the country invaded. While Britian's nuclear forces are formally "integrated" with NATO's and the British would likely not use them before consulting their allies, the same may not hold true for the French.

These scenarios are not exhaustive. Escalation at sea is also possible in the Mediterranean, where Soviet and NATO naval forces regularly sail across each other's bows and modern weaponry creates strong incentives for preemption. Although most military forces, and the largest share of tactical and theater nuclear forces are stationed on the central European front, war might begin, for example, if the Soviets tried to position themselves in a Middle East crisis by taking their forces through Turkey. The incentive to use nuclear weapons would be high if NATO's conventional capabilities were insufficient and nuclear weapons were viewed as the only alternative to halt a Soviet advance and to prevent the defeat of an ally.

How likely are these scenarios? Are some more likely than others? The designation of probabilities has important implications for policy and the allocation of attention and scarce resources. Unfortunately, there is no easy answer to these questions, as continuing policy debates make clear.

NATO would probably not deliberately use nuclear weapons unless hostilities had begun and NATO appeared to be losing the conventional conflict. *When* NATO would be forced to use nuclear weapons, however, is a contentious issue. Some believe that NATO could blunt or halt a conventional attack by Warsaw Pact forces and sustain itself for an extended period of time.[33] Others believe that NATO's defenses would crumble quickly in the face of Warsaw Pact superiority.[34] Ultimately the question of whether or when NATO would lose depends on the mobilization scenario (that is, what forces NATO and the Pact could mobilize in a given period of time), how each side's forces actually perform in war, and attrition rates. In all these areas, there is much uncertainty. The issue of "losing" is also problematic since the NATO line of defense might not collapse all at once. The front would probably become quite ragged during the actual conflict: while NATO might hold its own or actually appear to be winning in some sectors, it might simultaneously be losing in others.

As some scenarios suggest, the nuclear threshold might be crossed independently of the anticipated outcome of the conventional conflict in Europe and perhaps even before actual hostilities on land had begun. These are the inadvertent scenarios for first use of nuclear weapons in the European theater.

Inadvertent escalation would have its roots in the way U.S. or Soviet forces performed when hostilities began, or were about to begin, and in various "standard operating procedures" developed to deal with particular contingencies. For example, the U.S. Navy's mission to protect sea lanes in the North Atlantic could precipitate a Soviet first use of nuclear weapons, especially if the Soviets believed their key strategic assets were at risk.[35] Preparation of dual-capable systems in the theater for nuclear missions could also precipitate a Soviet preemptive attack against NATO—and one that might be nuclear. There is no real historical analogue to these cases, although the inability of the Great Powers to halt mobilization just before World War I was an important precipitating cause of that conflict.

A breakdown in the political-military chain of command (in NATO or the Warsaw Pact) could also precipitate first use of nuclear weapons as, for example, in the case of a field commander fearing the imminent overrun of his forces. Although PALs and various "dual key" arrangements are designed to prevent this, it is difficult to predict how they would work in the "fog of war," or once the weapons had been dispersed and military authority for their use had been granted. Thus again, it is difficult to assign probabilities to these scenarios.

TRANSITION TO A MAJOR NUCLEAR WAR

How might a war in Europe lead to an all-out nuclear war? On the basis of purely rational calculation, such escalation could occur in any of the scenarios described above. For example, scenario 2a might evolve as follows:

NATO has just conducted a limited nuclear attack against several targets in Eastern Europe in an effort to halt a Soviet advance and terminate hostilities. All U.S., British, French, and Chinese forces are on high alert, and the Soviets perceive that there is a very high risk of: (1) a premeditated attack on all of their forces and C^3, including their land-based strategic forces; (2) a deliberate escalation by NATO and the Chinese to a higher level of nuclear conflict; or (3) an inadvertent launch of nuclear weapons due to the very high alert levels.

The United States finds itself in the same position with Soviet forces on a similarly high level of alert. Fearful of the devastating consequences of an all-out nuclear war, the American president sends an urgent message over the Hot Line that both sides should agree to cease hostilities. The Soviets, however, believe that there is a real risk that the United States will preempt, and their estimate of the probability of a U.S. attack is raised even higher by the sinking of one of their SSBNs in the North Atlantic. Before the American president can communicate that the sinking was an accident, the Soviet military informs the Politburo that nuclear war is inevitable, and unless they are allowed to preempt immediately, the Soviet Union will be destroyed. They point out that although the costs of going first may be very high because NATO will still have a surviving second-strike capability, the outcome will be far worse if the Soviet Union waits and absorbs a first strike. There is also a slim chance that a successful counterforce attack against NATO and the Chinese will be so disruptive to the other side that the expected retaliation will be greatly attentuated. The Kremlin bows under this pressure and orders a major counterforce attack against the United States, its NATO partners, and China.

The situation would be enormously unstable if one or both sides believed that preemption might work. Generated alerts or accidents would raise fears of impending attack. If nuclear war appeared likely, perhaps inevitable, the incentives for preemption would greatly increase. Launching a major nuclear attack might seem "rational," even though the costs, under the best of circumstances, would be enormous.

Nuclear war need not be started by the Soviets. U.S. decision-makers might also decide to strike first if they believed that they could knock out a large percentage of Soviet strategic nuclear forces (approximately 75 percent of which are land-based) in a first strike and further weaken (if not eliminate) the Soviet ability to respond by attacks on their leadership and C^3. Again, as Richard Betts argues in chapter 3, such a decision would only be "rational" if a major nuclear war appeared virtually inevitable—which it might if the United States and the Soviet Union were already at war and had put their nuclear forces on a very high state of alert.

This same calculation could be made under other, quite different conditions. All-out nuclear war would *not* have to start with a deliberate, limited first use of nuclear weapons. It could arise directly out of a conventional war without the intermediate step of a limited use of nuclear weapons on the battlefield. If the Soviets believed that preparation of NATO's battlefield and theater nuclear weapons (scenario 2b) was a signal for nuclear war—and if this conclusion was reinforced by the preparation of Pershing II missiles capable of attacking targets within the Soviet Union—they might decide to preempt with a major nuclear attack. The Soviets could draw the same conclusion from an inadvertent use of nuclear weapons, a French nuclear attack (scenario 2c), or the catalytic use of nuclear weapons by a third party. The United States could draw similar conclusions from a Soviet first use and might also decide to preempt.

Which of these situations would most likely precipitate all-out nuclear war? Inadvertent use is probably a greater danger than demonstration or limited use on the battlefield. But the risks would be substantial in the latter case as well. Diplomatic signaling and communication of intent would help to lower the risks of escalation in a demonstration use, but they could also create a false sense of limits to the conflict.

The enemy could easily mistake the inadvertent firing of a nuclear weapon for the first salvo in total war. If one side fired a weapon after nuclear forces had been dispersed and placed on alert, the other would have a very strong incentive to preempt. Efforts to apologize for a mistake would probably come too late.

Preemptive strike also begins to look good when one's own strategic forces are vulnerable—because of the opponent's technological advantages, such as ballistic missile defenses or special antisubmarine warfare capabilities—or are simply being outgunned. If escalation to all-out nuclear war appeared inevitable, a preemptive first strike would seem all the wiser.

"Nonrational" factors—misperceptions, stress, and the psychology of individuals or groups—would also affect a decision to preempt.[36] These factors helped bring about the Japanese attack at Pearl Harbor.[37] The Japanese navy feared that a British-American alliance would tip the scales against Japan in the Pacific. The navy hoped an attack on the U.S. fleet at Pearl Harbor would successfully eliminate the American presence and that strong isolationist tendencies in American public opinion would keep the U.S. government from retaliating. The Tojo government was blind to the way an attack would change American attitudes toward war. The Japanese also ignored President Roosevelt's promise to intervene if Japan took the Philippines. In the end, cultural misperception, fundamental misunderstanding of American politics, fractionation of political councils in Japan, and intense rivalry between the Japanese navy and the other armed forces all contributed to the Pearl Harbor attack.

These same factors can also invite miscalculation and lead to an escalation of conflict during the actual course of a war. During World War I, for example, German Chancellor Bethmann-Hollweg reluctantly caved in to pressure, extending German submarine attack to Allied and U.S. shipping in the Atlantic. Bethmann-Hollweg did this even though he had been warned by Germany's ambassador to Washington and other officials that it would draw the United States into the war and lead to Germany's defeat.[38] Why did Bethmann-Hollweg act against his own instincts and Germany's best interests? The navy believed that a blockade would bring Britain to its knees within weeks. In the face of an enormous toll in German lives and matériel, eroding public support for the war, and military pressure from quick action, Bethmann-Hollweg relented—a decision he subsequently called one of the greatest blunders of the war.

During any war, political leaders will confront enormous military pressure to sanction the quick decisive blow at the enemy's most vulnerable spot.[39] Military organizations dislike wars of attrition: the economy of violence dictates speedy, overwhelming attack. This was just as true in World War I as it was at Pearl Harbor, in MacArthur's advance to the Yalu River in the Korean War, or in the U.S. Air Force's unhappiness about limits on bombing North Vietnam (one case in which the military was overruled).

Intense psychological pressures can derail decision-making. During the Cuban missile crisis, for example, at least one participant in the Executive Committee of the National Security Council was unable to endure the intense strain of the crisis and had to withdraw from the deliberations.[40] Despite President Kennedy's efforts to structure decision-making procedures and processes in the best way, by the end of the crisis all the participants were suffering from the enormous stress.

A large conventional war in Europe would undoubtedly pressure the president and the Kremlin's leadership to use nuclear weapons to end hostilities. These pressures would be very strong if NATO or the Warsaw Pact appeared to be losing a conventional conflict. A fractionation of the decision-making group, either during a period of intense crisis or during the actual course of a war, could have adverse consequences for decision-making on either side.[41] Stress and fear might force decision-makers to take faulty actions and to underestimate costs and risks in the actual conduct of war. They might also lead decision-makers to a false belief in limits and encourage them to underestimate the dangers of escalation. A political leader's irrationality under pressure could also lead to a major preemptive nuclear attack. Decision-makers might see windows of opportunity, as the Germans did in World War I or the Japanese at Pearl Harbor, when in fact there were none.

Actions to Reduce the Risks of a Major Nuclear War

Recent policy debates have offered many recommendations to reduce the risks of a nuclear war. Virtually all these proposals, and indeed the general character of the debate itself, are preoccupied almost exclusively with precipitating or intermediate causes. Remarkably little thought has been given to the problem of deterrence after fighting starts and how it might fail—in particular, how a (limited) first use of nuclear weapons could lead to an all-out nuclear war.

Risk-reduction measures can be divided into three major categories: doctrine and policy, forces, and cooperative measures. I will discuss briefly the pros and cons of each.

DOCTRINE AND POLICY

No-first-use. Some believe that a formal change in NATO's declaratory policy could reduce the risks of a nuclear war in Europe. The most important recent proposal has been for no-first-use—a formal commitment on NATO's part not to use nuclear weapons unless the Soviets used them.[42] The key issues in this debate are:

1. How will a change in declaratory policy affect Soviet perceptions of NATO behavior?
2. How will it affect U.S.-allied relations?
3. How will it affect NATO's forces and central command over them?

A change in NATO's declaratory policy is unlikely to have any effect on Soviet behavior and war plans *unless* such a policy precipitates a change in theater nuclear deployments and capabilities. Of course, changing Soviet behavior might not be the objective of a no-first-use policy. Perhaps this should not be its prime objective. Even if most tactical nuclear weapons were removed from the European theater as part of a no-first-use policy, a change in Soviet behavior would still be unlikely because of the existence of intermediate-range nuclear weapons and delivery systems, which could be used for some, though obviously not all, battlefield missions.

No-first-use might, however, have a positive impact on our own military. It could induce a restructuring of forces and operations that reduced the risks of an early first use of nuclear weapons in a conventional war.[43] For example, a no-first-use declaration might encourage better control of battlefield and theater nuclear forces. Systems especially likely to be destabilizing in a crisis (such as short-range tactical nuclear weapons) could be removed. These actions, of course, might make sense even without such a declaration. NATO has already moved down this path; the Montebello decision of October 1983 calls for withdrawing 1,400 warheads during the next several years in addition to the previous withdrawal of 1,000 warheads. A leap of faith is required if one is to believe that political declarations will change the ways of large military organizations. History is not especially reassuring on this point. Those who have looked at the problem have argued that declaratory policy has tended to ratify the status quo in force deployments and employments rather than to lead the way.[44]

Advocates of no-first-use policy often argue that it will force NATO countries to build up conventional forces. But the allies' reaction to no-first-use has been lukewarm at best.[45] Conservative and moderate elements in Europe fear that without much-needed conventional force improvements, it would weaken deterrence. There is support for a no-first-use policy in the German Social Democratic Party, but without strong NATO support, U.S. pressures for a no-first-use policy would weaken the alliance.[46]

There are other ways of framing a change in NATO's declaratory policy. A no-*early*-use declaration would reserve to NATO the right to use nuclear weapons first in its defense but not early in a conflict. Such a policy would probably not meet with as strong opposition among the allies as no-first-use. Why? Because the more moderate version would involve less drastic change and would not be incompatible with NATO's current strategy of "flexible response." Such a declaration might achieve many of the same political and military objectives as no-first-use. It is fair to say, however, that the Europeans have traditionally been more wedded to early use than the Americans.

Strategy. A change in NATO's strategy could overcome some of the deficiencies in its conventional forces. Proposals range from area defense (favored by elements of the German left), to mobile/maneuver, to offensive and counteroffensive strategies and tactics.[47] Detailed discussions of these proposals would be outside the scope of this study. None of them, however, comes to grips with political realities and the extraordinary reluctance of our European allies to alter the current strategy of forward defense. Nor is it evident that many of these strategies could work without additional expenditures over and above what NATO spends now, or is likely to spend in the future. This is especially true for a genuine offensively oriented battle strategy, since new logistics and hardware would be required to conduct deep counterattacks into Warsaw Pact territory behind the front lines.[48] Although offensive and counter-offensive strategies are intended to strengthen deterrence, they are also recipes for escalation if deterrence fails.

Nevertheless, doctrinal innovations, like the U.S. Army's "Air-Land Battle," are provoking the development of more cost-effective ways for using new equipment on the battlefield and are encouraging ground commanders to think about the course of battle on both sides of the front.[49] They are also leading to a healthy discussion within the alliance about tactics in conventional warfare; in recent combined NATO field exercises, greater attention is being paid to maneuver tactics in forward-line defense.

FORCES

Nuclear Forces. The deployment of Pershing II and ground-launched cruise missiles (GLCMs) in Europe represents the most recent effort to strengthen extended deterrence and ensure coupling between NATO theater and U.S. strategic forces. The decision was marked by enormous controversy within the alliance.[50]

Some believe that these force improvements will strengthen coupling. For the first time, "theater-designated" nuclear weapons will be within reach of targets in the Soviet Union. The Soviets have made it clear that they would treat such attacks as they would an attack by U.S. strategic forces. Others have argued that the deployments would have little or no effect on coupling. No president would authorize the firing of these systems, because it would invite retaliation against the American homeland. Thus, if a nuclear war did occur, it would be confined to Europe. It has also been repeatedly pointed out that the systems are also quite vulnerable in their current basing modes and, in a crisis, would be likely targets for preemption.

Conventional Force Improvements. NATO can improve the balance of conventional forces in Europe by adding manpower and weaponry, strengthening reserves, and improving rapid mobilization capabilities—for example, through the acquisition of fast sealift, prepositioning of war reserve stocks, and improved communications.[51]

While some of these improvements are necessary and feasible (see below), the NATO countries currently lack both the financial resources and the political will to implement them. Most have had difficulty meeting existing defense spending goals. Even if these improvements were made, the Soviets might respond by matching, even exceeding, NATO efforts.

High-Tech Solutions. General Bernard Rogers and others (notably the Report of the European Security Study) have urged that NATO make use of so-called "emerging technologies" to remedy deficiencies in NATO's force posture.[52] Dramatic improvements in reconnaissance, surveillance, target acquisition, and interdiction capabilities have the potential to provide a wide variety of new opportunities in conventional warfare. Although some technologies are almost available, others cannot be deployed for five to ten years.

Short-range systems, such as third generation antitank guided weapons and multiple launch rocket systems equipped with smart warheads, would be used at the front. Longer-range systems (like conventional cruise and ballistic missiles) would be used to attack Soviet second echelon follow-on forces, airfields, and other key logistical transportation and communication choke points. It is expected that these systems could play an important role in support of tactical airpower whose mission is to attack Soviet follow-on forces and operate in the extended battle area behind the front—a mission that seems more and more difficult because of the growth of Warsaw Pact air defenses.

The faith in these new technologies, however, may be ill-founded. These technologies provide targeting information to battlefield commanders without a time lag—that is, in "real time"; but it may be very difficult to get these real-time capabilities to work at the interface between technology and military organizations. Organizational inertia will make it difficult to act promptly on new information since different echelons in the army work according to different definitions of real time, and the air force has its own definition as well. There are also enormous organizational and technical impediments to conducting coherent operations in a disruptive wartime environment. When decision loops operate in different time frames, real-time operation becomes next to impossible. To achieve the advertised levels of effectiveness of these emerging technologies, decision-making and operational loops will have to be very closely synchronized.

Conventionally armed missiles for deep-strike attacks may also destabilize crises.[53] How will the Soviets know the difference between a two-stage Pershing II missile and a one-stage Pershing II equipped with conventional munitions (one of the systems on the planning boards for deep strike)? Soviet intelligence might read the difference between conventional and nuclear systems through different basing modes, radar cross signatures, and so on.

The Soviets will take electronic countermeasures (ECM) to foil missiles equipped with homing devices, thereby degrading the general performance of these systems. Counter-ECM is obviously an important area for NATO development.

Dependence on these new technologies for surveillance, reconnaissance, and target acquisition could well increase dependence on existing C^3 vulnerabilities. Data processing and communication centers on the ground and in the air will be vulnerable unless they are hardened against attack and sufficiently redundant.

The Europeans will resist emerging technologies if they lead to increased dependence on the United States as a military supplier. In reconnaissance, surveillance, and targeting, where new computer systems play an enormous role, the overlap between civilian and military technologies may sharpen conflict between the public and the private sectors and within NATO as a whole.

COOPERATIVE MEASURES

Arms Control. Arms control also provides a potentially important way to raise the nuclear threshold. Persuading the Warsaw Pact to cut back its conventional forces could reduce the probability of a successful Pact attack against NATO. The history of the MBFR (Mutual and Balanced Force Reduction) talks, however, is not very promising.[54] Tentative agreements have been reached to reduce active duty ground forces in Central Europe to a common ceiling of 700,000 men for each side and to reduce the risks of misperception and miscalculation in a crisis through prenotification of troop movements. However, the talks have stalled on data issues and disagreement between East and West over the numbers of Warsaw Pact ground and air personnel in Central Europe. These disputes undoubtedly reflect deep-seated Soviet reservations about major troop and force reductions. The Soviets will always want to keep a surplus of forces in Eastern Europe because they are uncertain about their own allies. Their fears will grow as the political situation in Eastern Europe worsens. Superiority is also a hard thing to give up once you have it.

Force reductions could create new military problems for NATO as well. For example, lower force-to-space ratios would weaken NATO's ability to respond effectively to a Soviet surprise attack. Nevertheless, there are good reasons for continuing these talks, not only as confidence-building measures, but also because even modest agreements could help stabilize the arms race in Europe and reduce uncertainty on both sides.

Confidence- and Security-Building Measures (CSBMs). CSBMs include agreements on prenotification of troop movements; information exchanges on the structure, organization, and location of forces; on-site inspections; and restrictions on the size and location of maneuver. Modest agreement exists on some of these measures in MBFR, and the Stockholm Conference has become the focus of recent efforts to expand them.[55]

Many of these measures could build confidence and defuse tensions in a crisis. If CSBM agreements were broken, they would provide early warning of a possible attack and perhaps help to improve NATO's reaction times, especially at the political level. Critics, however, argue that the Soviets have already violated the spirit, if not the letter, of these agreements by not providing advance warning of troop movements just before the Polish crisis in 1981 and the invasion of Afghanistan in 1979.[56] Further evidence of Soviet bad faith is found in sightings of Soviet submarines that have trespassed into Finnish, Norwegian, and Swedish territorial waters. There is some justification for the view that CSBMs might lead to a false sense of security in a crisis if they were used as a mask to cover activities just before attack.

Other Proposals. The report of the Independent Commission for Disarmament (Palme Commission) urged the creation of a nuclear-free zone in Europe, along the inter-German border, as a way of raising the nuclear threshold.[57] Robert McNamara has also supported this recommendation.[58] However, the width of the zone would have to be defined more clearly than it has been so far, and there is some evidence that the Germans would find it extremely difficult to move nuclear weapons from their current positions because of public opposition to redeployments. Such a measure would not prevent the introduction of nuclear weapons into the zone in a crisis. The zone could always be fired into from outside, and such action might weaken deterrence along the inter-German border, especially if the Soviets sought to acquire a small strip of land for political bargaining purposes.

Net Assessment of the Alternatives

DEEP CAUSES

A nuclear war in Europe might trace its origins to a variety of factors. In considering how to avoid such a war, it is important not to lose sight of the deeper levels of causation, particularly the political factors. Uncertainties in the political realm and the obvious problems in any sort of long-range political forecasting, however, make prescriptions difficult. There is an additional problem: governments are not very good at long-term planning and management. This is particularly true of the United States government. Even if one were to come up with a list of policies for the long term, they would be difficult, if not impossible, to implement.

These institutional problems are compounded by real dilemmas in U.S.-Soviet relations.[59] Each of the superpowers has a vested interest in a weakening of the other's hegemony. Nowhere is this more true than in Europe. But as we have seen, the erosion of the spheres of influence in Europe is fraught with risk for both sides. Some weakening of Soviet hegemony in Eastern Europe is a good thing for the West, especially if it makes the Soviets less willing to use force or political blackmail. Too rapid a deterioration of Soviet influence in Eastern Europe, however, might tempt the West to accelerate the process, perhaps by military intervention. Empires are always lost more quickly than their owners are prepared to accept. Perceptions take time to become congruent with reality. Quite likely, the Soviets would use force to reverse a deterioration of their influence, especially if they felt the West was playing too active a role in manipulating political developments in Eastern Europe. The Soviets are capable of the same kind of behavior with respect to NATO. Perhaps the most likely route to war is a weakening of alliances on both sides that would exacerbate feelings of weakness and hostility and lead to paranoid and reckless behavior to preserve power and influence.

None of this may ever happen. There is little in current Soviet behavior to suggest that they are willing to make any significant concessions in Eastern Europe or release their grip on political processes there. But they cannot control all facets of political, economic, and social change, as Eastern Europe's current economic difficulties and recent events in Poland and East Germany indicate. Clearly, the NATO countries must think through their long-term political and economic strategies for dealing with Eastern Europe and anticipate the problems that might occur if the situation in the Soviet bloc were to unravel further.

It would be naive to expect a transatlantic dialogue on such matters, given the significant differences between the United States and its European and Canadian allies about how to conduct relations with the Soviet Union. These differences are based on fundamentally different perceptions of the nature of the Soviet threat, and they are unlikely to be resolved in the near future. But we must continue to try.

An important paradox in the management of East-West relations is reflected in the contrasting approaches of the United States and Western Europe. The confrontational approach of the Reagan administration has raised the level of tensions and, some believe, the risk of conflict. It has also complicated Western European efforts to develop a more cordial working relationship with the East. But the détente approach of the Europeans runs the risk of planting seeds of discord between East and West as well. Closer ties between Eastern and Western Europe, via aid, credits, and the like, could weaken Soviet hegemony. Demands on Eastern Europe for greater autonomy from the Soviet Union could grow. So could citizen dissatisfaction as they perceive that greater gains in their standard of living and their freedom are to be had from even closer relations with the West. Manifestations of some of these tendencies exist now, particularly in

Poland, East Germany, and Rumania. Thus, while détente and the development of closer ties between Eastern and Western Europe may lessen tensions over the short term, over the long term they might easily raise them. This paradox must be recognized as the United States and its European and Canadian allies work out their differences.

INTERMEDIATE AND PRECIPITATING CAUSES

Intermediate and precipitating causes are so linked that actions on one level are apt to be useful on the other. For example, bolstering the conventional military balance may strengthen deterrence (thereby reducing the intermediate risks of war) and, if fighting starts, forestall an early first use of nuclear weapons by NATO. What may be good for escalation control and preventing an early crossing of the nuclear threshold, however, may not be good for deterrence. Raising the nuclear threshold too high—say by eliminating all nuclear weapons from Central Europe—might increase the likelihood of conventional war. It is obviously important not to weaken deterrence in efforts to reduce the risks of nuclear war. Efforts to reduce the risks of nuclear war also have to be squared with other foreign policy objectives and goals.

The nuclear threshold could be crossed in a variety of ways. All contain possibilities for escalation. Strengthening conventional capabilities should reduce the likelihood of a deliberate first use of nuclear weapons. Prolonging conventional war-fighting would increase opportunities for political bargaining and diplomacy to end the war before it went nuclear. Strengthened conventional capabilities would also improve deterrence. But the nuclear threshold could also be crossed inadvertently. Forces and military operations should be structured so as to reduce the possibilities of inadvertent use. NATO should also address its vulnerable tactical and theater nuclear forces. It should not put itself in a position where it would be forced to an early use of nuclear weapons to avoid preemption by the Soviets (or a situation where it would invite the Soviets to preempt by getting ready to use them), although it should not eschew early use in the interests of deterrence. This poses some real dilemmas. Many of the least vulnerable systems are also the most dangerous from the point of view of inadvertent escalation.

These scenarios suggest that ambiguity in the preparation of nuclear forces should be eliminated. Preparation of these forces could lead the Soviets to believe—incorrectly—that a nuclear war was about to occur. That would invite a preemptive attack. This is as true of battlefield and theater nuclear forces as for strategic forces on high alert.

Central priorities in Europe should be:

- Increase NATO's conventional capability so as to achieve essential equivalence. This will preserve extended deterrence and maintain the credibility of flexible response.
- Reduce the risks of deliberate early first use by reducing deployments that threaten preemption or accidental launch. With its robust deterrence, NATO can trade a possible reduction in theoretical deterrence for a reduction in the likelihood of accident or preemption.
- Devise a long-term political strategy toward Eastern Europe. NATO has been lax in developing such a strategy. But it should be cautious in its efforts to promote change in Eastern Europe and recognize that important tradeoffs will critically affect the long-term stability of East-West relations.

The following agenda flows from these objectives.

DOCTRINE AND POLICY

A declaratory statement of no-early-use could have a positive effect on NATO's own forces. It would underscore the need to improve theater C^3 and ensure that NATO members go on trying to meet goals for conventional force improvement and modernization. It might also lead to a search for less vulnerable basing modes for short- and intermediate-range nuclear forces (thereby enhancing crisis stability). This would not have the adverse effects of a less discriminatory no-first-use policy (with respect to both deterrence and alliance relations), and would achieve many of the same goals.

"No second use against small attacks until careful study and efforts at communication" would reduce the risks of escalation, especially on the battlefield or at sea.

FORCES

Strategic Defenses. U.S. decisions about defense deployment are unlikely to be determined by its allies' feelings. Even so, it is essential that the United States inform its allies about its research plans for these new technologies and to show greater sensitivity to their needs and concerns. Failure to do so will further widen rifts in the alliance.

Nuclear. NATO should continue its current efforts to reduce the number of short-range tactical nuclear weapons in the theater (especially nuclear artillery and mines). Once these systems are dispersed in the possession of field commanders, they may be difficult to control. It may be possible to find less destabilizing ways to deploy them, so that the gain in operational control will not be offset at the level of deterrence.

Some medium-range theater systems can be used, if necessary, for a number of battlefield missions. The Soviets are well aware of this possibility. Thus, deterrence will probably not be significantly eroded in the interim. The U.S. Army might not view further reduction in battlefield nuclear weapons as a great loss since it has long held doubts about using them in a combined conventional/nuclear environment.

NATO should reduce ambiguity with respect to its dual-capable (nuclear and conventional) systems, especially Quick Reaction Alert forces. The critical issue of inadvertent escalation at sea has, until recently, received scant attention. It would be extremely difficult to regulate ASW activity in a crisis or to develop ASW "codes of conduct."[60] But there is an urgent and obvious need for civilian authorities to acquire a better understanding of the details of naval operations and warfare and to ensure that during a crisis overly provocative actions are not taken.

Chemical. Chemical weapons have also blurred the nuclear threshold. NATO policy is to use nuclear weapons if there is no available non-nuclear method of response to a chemical weapon attack by the Soviets. A verifiable agreement with the Soviet Union prohibiting production, stockpiling, and use of chemical weapons could make a useful contribution to raising the nuclear threshold.

Conventional. Strengthened conventional capabilities will reduce pressures on NATO to respond to a Warsaw Pact attack with early use of nuclear weapons. Prolonging the conventional phase of the conflict may also increase opportunities for negotiations to achieve a political resolution before a conflict goes nuclear. Although any sort of major sustained buildup of NATO's conventional forces is politically infeasible for the time being, several important actions could be taken to sustain conventional war-fighting capabilities at relatively low cost. Some actions could provoke the Soviets into an arms race (as, for example, if NATO acquired a new weapons system or purchased large numbers of an existing platform or weapons system). Others would not necessarily provoke the Soviets but nevertheless have important force-multiplier effects (for example, improved C^3 capabilities). Most of the following actions fall into this latter category.

These conventional improvements should not be pursued at the expense of alliance cohesion, however. Although NATO requires additional resources if it is to remain strong, there is an obvious danger that if the United States pushes too hard to get them, the alliance will be weakened by increased political tension and conflict as governments resist outside pressures because of countervailing pressures at home. The dilemma will be especially acute if countries are experiencing little economic growth and are facing domestic pressures to increase social expenditures.

Warning. NATO's ability to react to warning by mobilizing its forces could be an important force multiplier. The breaking of CSBM agreements about troop mobilizations and maneuvers would provide unambiguous warning in a crisis that an attack was under way. CSBMs are a double-edged sword because there is potential for ambiguity in any agreement that could serve as a basis for deception. But this is an argument for better agreements, not against CSBMs.

Sustainability. NATO has the goal of maintaining thirty days' worth of stocks, munitions, and other critical items. Nations have varied enormously in their ability to meet this goal. Some have stocks for only fifteen days or less. Improvement in stocks is critical despite the risk of dislocating the modernization programs of some countries.

Follow-On Forces. It is dangerous to assume that U.S. follow-on forces (ten divisions) would be ready when needed. The United States has serious airlift and sealift deficiencies. In addition, there are major shortages in airlift capabilities for moving forces and supplies once they arrive in Europe. There is an urgent need to complete prepositioning of matériel and equipment overseas.

Reserves. Reserve forces need to be improved. Although declining birth rates in Germany and Western Europe as a whole limit the reserve forces that can be created, further improvements are possible through the expansion in scope of the Wartime Host Nation Support Agreements between the United States and its European and Canadian allies. Such agreements are in progress or have been completed with Belgium, Canada, Denmark, Italy, Luxembourg, Norway, the Netherlands, Turkey, and the United Kingdom. There is ample room to expand the nature and scope of these agreements with great savings and improvements in efficiency in the use of manpower and resources.

C^3. Although awareness of the need to invest in C^3 has grown, remarkably little has been done and enormous vulnerabilities remain. At the moment the allies have severe communications problems. There is an urgent need to improve communications among the national units, to reconfigure hardware, make facilities less vulnerable to attack, and sort out protocols. Measures the Pact could take to interfere with or destroy NATO C^3 also create tough problems and need to be considered.

Air Defenses. The buildup of the Warsaw Pact's frontal aviation and missile capabilities threatens NATO's control of the air. NATO needs to upgrade its air defenses and to build additional runways and landing strips, along with shelters for aircraft, to reduce existing vulnerabilities. Deployment of the Patriot missile and upgrading of the Hawk missile are important steps in this direction.

Barriers. Barriers on the defensive line along the inter-German border would be an important force multiplier.[61] The Germans in World War II almost defeated a larger Allied force at D-Day with barriers. Continuous barriers would cause serious political problems in Germany today and evoke memories of the Maginot Line. Random-pattern barriers, which are laid in the path of the advancing enemy and rely on surprise, might avoid these problems, and rockets could be used to lay mines. Attention should also be given to the problem of deciding what stage of alert is necessary to set up barriers and how to do so in ways that are not provocative.

Emerging Technologies. Many of the so-called emerging technologies have the potential to strengthen conventional capabilities and deterrence. New technologies for reconnaissance, surveillance, and selection of targets could prove a very important force multiplier in support of traditional operations and tactics for forward defense. Third generation antitank guided weapons, remotely piloted vehicles, laser-guided munitions, and multiple-launch rocket systems equipped with front ends that can home in on targets should also be developed, for they will improve kill rates at the front. Many of the technologies for these systems are currently available or very close to being so. More research, however, is needed to determine whether long-range conventional ballistic missile systems are cost-effective for deep strike attacks (of 250–300+ kilometers) against Soviet follow-on forces. The implications of these systems for crisis stability should be carefully studied before they are acquired.

COOPERATIVE MEASURES

The United States should try to talk again with the Soviets on intermediate-range nuclear forces, either at the bilateral level or in some other forum. The central goal of these talks should be reductions that will eliminate systems that would erode crisis stability and dramatically escalate the level of nuclear conflict.

NATO should also continue its efforts to negotiate troop reductions in the MBFR talks and, more generally, seek to reduce tensions and improve relations with the Soviets. Undoubtedly, the Soviets face the same cost constraints as NATO. The likelihood of reaching an MBFR agreement is probably greatest if the goal is limited to freezing current manpower levels for both NATO and the Pact, or aiming for more modest reductions in combat forces than those currently contemplated.

Over the long term, arms control is a potentially important means of raising the nuclear threshold and creating a framework for evolving change in Europe.

CONTROLLING ESCALATION

NATO should eschew strategies of horizontal escalation, especially those that would escalate conflict from other areas to Europe. It is also important, in dealing with conflicts in other parts of the world, to manage forces so that the theater of conflict does not widen inadvertently. This is particularly true for naval forces and operations that could act like a chain of firecrackers in carrying conflict to other theaters, or to the nuclear level.

Once a war in Europe began, it would be difficult to control, particularly escalation in the nuclear realm. Given the dangers of escalation, however, especially if nuclear weapons are inadvertently used, attention must be paid to control through diplomacy rather than force. We should not over-rely on gimmicks like hot lines and crisis centers, but we must find ways of maintaining communications with the Soviets not only during a crisis period, but also after military hostilities had commenced.[62] Such channels, useful in diplomatic efforts to end conflict before it went nuclear, would also be a mechanism to talk with the Soviets in the event of an inadvertent use of nuclear weapons. A hot line between the Supreme Allied Commander of Europe and his Warsaw Pact counterpart or the Kremlin might not be the right solution, but it should be explored along with other mechanisms for wartime communication.

The deep causes are the most impervious to quick fixes. The effective management of alliance relations and the preservation of NATO should be top objectives of U.S. foreign policy, along with the development of an alliance strategy for dealing with Eastern Europe over the long term. A war in Europe would have its origins here, not in NATO's inability to strengthen its conventional capabilities by procuring a particular weapons system or meeting certain spending goals—although a severe deterioration in the balance of forces could affect Soviet decisions on whether to wage war. In coping with day-to-day problems, the political dimension of change should not be forgotten. Indeed, it should be paramount.

5 ESCALATION IN THE MIDDLE EAST AND PERSIAN GULF

by Francis Fukuyama

Introduction

The Middle East/Persian Gulf region is a likely place for U.S.-Soviet conflict to become nuclear war. High mutual superpower stakes, endemic political instability, and strong military forces in close proximity ensure insecurity. Within the region, stretching from Morocco to Pakistan, local conflicts abound, with correspondingly many ways the superpowers could be drawn into war. Of these regional conflicts, two stand out as serious enough to spawn nuclear war: a possible Soviet invasion of Iran and other parts of the Persian Gulf, and the Arab-Israeli conflict.

A superpower war over the Middle East/Persian Gulf is more than an abstract possibility. The United States and the USSR have confronted each other on this ground throughout the postwar period. One of the first major crises of the Cold War developed over Soviet refusal to withdraw from northern Iran in 1946. The United States alerted its strategic forces in response to Soviet actions during the 1958 Lebanese-Iraqi crisis and at the end of the October 1973 Arab-Israeli War. In addition, the United States sent Marines to Lebanon in 1958 and 1982 and deployed naval task forces to the eastern Mediterranean in response to wars in 1956, 1967, 1973, and 1982.

The Soviet Union has threatened to intervene with combat forces in Middle Eastern crises on six occasions. Three times, all during the Khrushchev era, the Soviets brandished nuclear weapons: during the Suez crisis of 1956, the Syrian-Turkish crisis of 1957, and the Lebanese-Iraqi crisis of 1958. In the first of these conflicts Soviet Premier Bulganin wrote to British Prime Minister Eden:

In what situation would Britain find herself if she were attacked by stronger states, possessing all types of modern destructive weapons? And such countries could, at the present time, refrain from sending naval or air forces to the shores of Britain and use other means—for instance, rocket weapons . . .

Moscow dispatched 20,000 air defense troops and other advisers to Egypt during the 1970 war of attrition, deployed another 6,000 to Syria in the wake of the 1982 Lebanon war, moved warships into the theater in response to a variety of other crises, and intervened in Afghanistan in 1979 with combat forces numbering over 100,000. Perhaps no single Middle East crisis has been as severe as those surrounding Cuba and Berlin, but the superpowers have collectively threatened and actually used force more often here than anywhere else.

Although the Soviets have not threatened to use nuclear weapons in the Middle East since the late 1950s, tensions have increased in the succeeding years. During the crises of the 1950s, for all the intensity of Soviet rhetoric, the Soviet Union never came close to using either conventional or nuclear weapons; all of its threats were in fact bluffs.[1] The United States then enjoyed a superiority in both strategic and conventional forces and had strong treaty commitments to several important states in the region. In the 1980s, by contrast, the Soviets speak more softly but carry a bigger stick: not only has the United States lost its nuclear superiority, but Moscow's relative ability to project force into the region has increased. At the same time, the U.S. stake in the Persian Gulf has increased. OPEC demonstrated the vulnerability of Western economies to oil shortages in the early 1970s.

Despite the real risks in this region, it may be counterproductive to overemphasize the danger of superpower war. So far, both sides have managed to control risk fairly well and have never come close to direct conflict.[2] This result has been achieved partly through negotiated and cooperative measures, but primarily through a sort of mutual deterrence that extends down through conventional forces. Deterring Soviet and other threats to U.S. interests in the Middle East, which in the short run often involves risks of confrontation and active preparations for war, has actually contributed to peace. In any event, while nuclear war would be catastrophic, the probability of its arising out of any particular crisis in the region is extremely low; the imperative of lowering the risk of nuclear war must be balanced against the multiplicity of other U.S. interests.

This chapter will seek an understanding of how nuclear war could arise in the Middle East/Persian Gulf region, drawing largely on historical precedents, and on this basis look more closely at the means of avoiding war.

Factors Affecting the Probability of Nuclear War

Let us analyze the deep, intermediate, and precipitating causes of war.

DEEP CAUSES

The most important deep cause of nuclear war flows from the long-term rivalry between the United States and the Soviet Union. While that rivalry originated primarily in the division of postwar Europe, it quickly spread to Asia and various parts of the Third World, including the Middle East. Its roots—ideological, geographical, economic, cultural, and historical—are deep and likely to persist. Since superpower conflict in any region is largely a symptom of the broader rivalry, one cannot hope to heal the deep causes of war by any actions specific to a particular theater.

A second deep cause, the endemic political instability of the Middle East, invites superpower intervention. Long-standing conflicts like the Arab-Israeli struggle and the rivalry between Iran and Iraq are accompanied by a host of smaller conflicts resulting from ethnic, class, sectarian, and ideological disputes. Policy changes may soften, even solve, some of these conflicts but most have deep historical and cultural roots and will not disappear within the timeframe of this study.

INTERMEDIATE CAUSES

The intermediate causes of war develop from the way a larger U.S.-Soviet rivalry is played out in a regional context.

A nation's willingness to risk war depends on the absolute value of its interests threatened by another power. Nations by and large do not go to war unless substantial interests are at stake, and the stakes must be particularly high to justify the risks of nuclear war. The United States and the Soviet Union both have interests in the Middle East/Persian Gulf that are potentially strong enough that the use of nuclear weapons might be considered, but these interests differ according to the specific subregion and conflict in question. America's stakes in Persian Gulf oil, in the survival of Israel, and in the western Sahara, for example, are very different. Thus our analysis begins by examining the hierarchy of interests of the superpowers as they are affected by developments in this region.

Wars arise less often where superpowers stakes are asymmetrical than where they are both strong and evenly balanced. For instance, the United States' interest in Polish independence and human rights is dwarfed by the Soviet Union's stake in preserving Poland as a security buffer. Consequently Washington has never contemplated a military challenge to Soviet hegemony over Poland. By contrast, the severe Berlin crises reflected the fact that *both* superpowers had high stakes in the future of that city, and of Germany.

The Middle East/Persian Gulf presents special dangers because the U.S. and Soviet stakes are both strong in absolute terms and relatively evenly balanced. I will argue later that the United States has had and will continue to have the larger stake in this region overall, and that the Soviets have generally respected this fact. Nevertheless, the frequency of tension in the Middle East largely stems from the mutual and conflicting interests of the two superpowers. Again, the balance of relative stakes varies among subregions and needs to be evaluated in greater detail.

To avoid the challenges that lead to war, the superpowers must *perceive and correctly evaluate* each other's underlying stakes. The most dangerous situation arises when one superpower takes an action that it believes will not provoke a response on the other side, but which in fact threatens a vital interest. Gauging stakes is much more difficult in the Middle East/Persian Gulf than in Europe because these interests have changed over time and are constantly influenced by local political developments whose strategic significance is often hard to interpret. For example, *both* the United States and the Soviet Union thought the outbreak of the Iran-Iraq war would be an opportunity for the other. The lines dividing East and West in the center of Europe have been clearly drawn for nearly forty years. In the Middle East/Persian Gulf, major countries like Egypt and Iran have been able to switch sides or hover precariously between the superpowers with highly ambiguous effects for their net interests. One can only imagine the consequences for Europe had West Germany broken away from NATO and tried to establish a foreign policy somewhere between the two blocs.

The United States. The United States has a major stake in seeing that Middle East states, beginning with Iran, do not fall under Soviet influence or control. President Carter proclaimed, "An attempt by any outside force to gain control of the Persian Gulf region will be regarded as an assault on the vital interests of the United States of America. And such an assault will be repelled by any means necessary, including military force."[3] Carter was not the first U.S. president to speak so forcefully. Nor has the American stake in the Gulf been limited to oil.

The United States in some sense is heir to Britain, who throughout the nineteenth and early twentieth centuries repeatedly blocked Russian attempts to expand southward into the Persian Gulf. The British believed that the area was vital to imperial communications, particularly with India, and that Russian control would be highly dangerous to the European balance of power.[4]

This same logic underlay U.S. policy in the 1940s as it filled the vacuum left by the British. The United States made repeated attempts to organize the states of the so-called Northern Tier (Turkey, Iraq, Iran, and Pakistan) into a series of anti-Communist alliances, including the Middle East Defence Organization in 1951, the Baghdad Pact in 1955, and subsequently the Central Treaty Organization (CENTO). Access to Persian Gulf oil was only one of several considerations. Until the late 1950s the United States needed access to the Northern Tier to support its strategic deterrent. At the time, this deterrent relied heavily on intermediate-range systems like B-47 bombers and intermediate-range ballistic missiles (IRBMs) and sought to create a series of interlocking defensive pacts around the periphery of the Soviet Union. The Eisenhower Doctrine of January 1957 declared that in the Middle East, "the United States is prepared to use armed forces to assist any nation or group of nations requesting assistance against armed aggression from any country controlled by international communism."

This Eisenhower-era concern with the Northern Tier diminished somewhat with the collapse of the Baghdad Pact in 1958 and the introduction of intercontinental nuclear delivery systems. These made it unnecessary to maintain bases on the periphery of the Soviet Union. The general American interest in Persian Gulf security took on a more specific and vital focus during the 1970s—access to oil. In 1977, just before the Iranian revolution, Western Europe imported 406 million metric tons of oil from the Persian Gulf, 65 percent of its total oil consumption and 35 percent of its overall energy consumption.[5]

The Western economies' vulnerability to oil shortages has diminished considerably since then through market forces and government efforts to seek alternative energy sources. The United States, moreover, receives a much smaller percentage of its oil needs from the Persian Gulf than does Western Europe or Japan. Nonetheless, U.S. policymakers agree that access to Gulf oil is a vital American interest, for several reasons. First, since the world oil market is highly integrated and oil is a fungible commodity, any major shortfall in Persian Gulf oil would mean higher prices for American consumers. Second, even if Western European and American interests in Gulf oil were separable, Soviet control of the Gulf could have disastrous political consequences if it split the Western alliance system, including U.S. ties with Japan. Successful Arab efforts to politicize the oil trade with Western Europe over the Palestinian issue illustrate the kind of leverage that might accrue to a Soviet Union in control of the Persian Gulf.

The United States has a highly complex stake in Israel. Concerned with Arab reaction, successive American administrations have denied Israel the protection of formal commitments of the sort extended to the NATO allies, Japan, and Korea. Nevertheless, it is clear that the United States is deeply committed to the survival of Israel. The U.S. stake is based on ideological solidarity with a fellow liberal democracy, a history of past commitment and invested prestige, and an emotional element whose strength is difficult to measure exactly but is undeniably large. Israel has also served as a *de facto* strategic asset because of its military predominance in the region and its reliable long-term alignment with the West. At the same time, Israel has also been a strategic liability, since it serves as a constant irritant in U.S. relations with the Arabs.[6]

The Soviet Union. Imperial Russia and subsequently the Soviet Union have always been interested in the Persian Gulf; much of Russia's southward expansion in the Caucasus and Turkestan during the nineteenth century came at the expense of the Persian Empire. Russian troops have occupied Iran twice in this century. Soviet interests in this region can be divided into three categories. The first concerns defense of the nation's southern borders. Since World War II, the Soviets have repeatedly fretted over developments in an area adjacent to the southern borders of the USSR. During the revolution and civil war, White forces under General Denikin attacked the fledgling Soviet state from this direction, and in the 1950s the Soviets were quite concerned by the deployment of strategic systems in the Northern Tier by the United States. These acute defensive concerns have probably diminished with the collapse of the Baghdad Pact and the final demise of CENTO by the late 1970s. Currently, the Soviets show political concern over developments in a weak and unstable border region, developments that could spill over into the Soviet Union itself. Many of the region's ethnic groups, most notably the Azeri Turks in northern Iran, also inhabit the Soviet Union. Soviet leadership may fear that the religious and nationalist currents of the Middle East/Persian Gulf will find a sympathetic echo in the Soviet Union itself.

The second Soviet interest in the Gulf revolves around strategic communications. Russia has long faced the problem of being "bottled up"; to reach the outside world, it must pass through choke points often under the control of hostile powers. The 1941 Soviet General Staff *Command Study* of Iran quotes Stalin in this regard:

The great importance of the Caucasus for the Revolution is not to be seen in its being a source of raw material, fuels, and food but rather its position between Europe and Asia and especially between Russia and Turkey and the strategic crossroads which pass through it . . . In the final analysis, that is what it is all about: Who will own the oil fields and the most important roads leading to the interior of Asia?[7]

This concern over strategic communications is broader than a "drive for warm water ports"; Moscow has an interest in air and land access as well, and in protection of the lines running between the European and Far Eastern parts of Russia through the Indian Ocean. These would be especially critical in the event of a war with China.

The third area of Soviet interest lies in oil and other natural resources. This interest is not tied directly to the Soviet Union's energy requirements—the USSR has not been and is not likely to be a large importer of Persian Gulf oil or natural gas—but rather to the value of these natural resources per se. Soviet influence over these resources would constitute a massive transfer of wealth, giving Moscow leverage over the Western alliance. Soviet leaders recognize the strategic value of Persian Gulf oil to the global balance of power; the 1941 Soviet Command Study, for example, notes oil-producing areas in Iran and Iraq as significant strategic objectives.[8]

The Soviet stake in its Arab clients is similarly complex. Moscow originally became involved in the Arab heartland in 1955 to gain a bargaining card in trade for the neutralization of the Norther Tier. Over the years priorities changed, and countries like Egypt and Syria became centerpieces of Moscow's courtship of the Third World. In the 1960s these countries also served a specific military objective by supporting the deployment of the Soviet Fifth Eskadra in the Mediterranean and occasional Indian Ocean task forces. Moscow's current stake in Syria does not match its former stake in Egypt during 1970–1973. But Damascus remains its principal Arab client and its primary source of influence in crucial eastern Mediterranean theater, the beneficiary of thirty years' and billions of dollars' worth of military and economic support.

The Soviet Union has consistently used great caution in directly challenging U.S. interests in the Middle East/Persian Gulf. All along, it has backed away at the prospect of a military clash with the United States, such as occurred during the Azerbaijan crisis of 1946 or the crisis over Iraq in 1958. The Soviets tolerated close military ties between the United States and Iran under the Shah. They might have done otherwise; the 1921 Soviet-Iranian Treaty gave Russia the right to introduce troops into Iran in response to a third-party threat originating there. In the Arab-Israeli theater, Moscow has watched while its clients suffered humiliating setbacks at the hands of Israel, usually at great cost to Soviet prestige in the Arab world. The most blatant case of Soviet nonsupport was the June 1967 war, when Egypt, Moscow's oldest and perhaps most important Third World client, was routed militarily and stripped of the Sinai.[9] When the Soviets have threatened to intervene in an Arab-Israeli war, it has always been after the peak of the crisis had passed and it was relatively clear that their threat would not have to be carried out. While the Soviets dispatched 20,000 air defense troops to Egypt in 1970 and another 6,000 to Syria in 1982, it was fairly clear in both cases that their intervention would not provoke a direct U.S. military response; when such a response has occurred, the Soviets have backed down.

Two reasons account for this historical pattern of Soviet caution. First, while the balance of superpower stakes may seem comparable, the Soviets appear to have tacitly recognized the superiority of the American interest throughout most of the postwar period, particularly its interest in oil. For example, Mohammed Haykal reports that in the midst of the 1958 Lebanese-Iraqi crisis Khrushchev told Nasser:

I want you to know what Eden told me and Bulganin when we were in London in 1956. Eden said that if he saw a threat to Britain's oil supplies in the Middle East he would fight. He was talking quite seriously, and what has just happened [i.e., the Anglo-American intervention in Jordan and Lebanon] shows this . . . Now, the revolution in Iraq is a threat to that oil. I don't know anything about the new leaders in Iraq, but it is most important that they should reassure the West that its supplies of oil will not be interrupted.[10]

Persian Gulf oil, it should be noted, was much less critical to the advanced industrialized world then than now.

Moscow's caution also reflects the U.S.-Soviet military balance and the relative ability of the superpowers to project forces into the theater. Haykal reports another interesting conversation between the Soviets and their Arab clients: when asked by Syrian President Shukri al-Kuwatly to intervene on behalf of Egypt during the Suez crisis, Soviet Defense Minister Marshal Zhukov

produced a map of the Middle East and spread it on the table. Then, turning to Kuwatly, he said, "How can we go to the aid of Egypt? Tell me! Are we supposed to send our armies through Turkey, Iran, and then into Syria and Iraq and on into Israel and so eventually attack the British and French forces?!"[11]

By the early 1970s the situation had changed considerably. The Soviet Union had achieved rough strategic parity with the United States. Even more, it had acquired substantial projection forces, including permanent Mediterranean and Indian Ocean naval squadrons, seven airborne divisions, and airlift capabilities.

We know little of the Kremlin's present evaluation of stakes in the Persian Gulf or the military balance. While they probably recognize the strength of the Western stake in oil, they may well feel that the gains of the Iranian revolution are long-lasting. In 1974 Soviet Foreign Minister Gromyko stated that "there is no question that can be settled without the participation of the Soviet Union." Soviet military power has burgeoned over the past two decades, however. The Soviets may now judge that some developments would be intolerable, such as another pro-American regime in Teheran, one that would welcome U.S. military facilities and access to Russia. The long-term Soviet force modernization has obviously increased Moscow's self-confidence. Its interventions in the Third World between 1975 and 1980 indicate that. If subjective evaluations of relative stakes are now uncertain and the force balance has shifted away from American predominance, there is now a new danger of superpower conflict.

PRECIPITATING CAUSES

The precipitating causes of war include local political conflicts that could trigger superpower confrontation. These conflicts must (1) be inherently plausible and (2) affect superpower interests enough to bring in combat forces. Clearly, there are a multitude of plausible local conflicts in the Middle East; not many, however, truly affect superpower interests.

Superpower conflict could arise in the Middle East/Persian Gulf without a precipitating local conflict. The Soviet Union could invade Iran in the context of a European war. Alternatively, it could undertake the first move in such a war, as a means of gaining decisive political leverage over the West. The first of these possibilities is a real one, but outside the scope of our present analysis, which focuses on how war could originate in the Middle East itself. The second is a rather unlikely event. As Richard Betts pointed out in chapter 3, few attacks come completely out of the blue, without some precipitating local cause; even the German invasion of Poland in 1939 loomed against the background of Polish-German conflict in Danzig.

This chapter focuses on two chief scenarios for local political conflict escalating into nuclear war: a Soviet intervention in Iran and an escalation of an Arab-Israeli war. These choices do not require elaborate justification. Both superpowers have contemplated, threatened, and on occasion carried out interventions in these subtheaters. Resulting crises have raised the possibility of wider war. What of other scenarios? Middle Eastern politics spews out new precipitating conflicts virtually overnight. In early 1978, for example, no one was predicting that Soviet troops would be fighting in Afghanistan and that a fundamentalist regime in Iran would be at war with Iraq within two years. The most dangerous superpower confrontations can occur over the least expected developments, which are problematic precisely because they were unanticipated.

In addition to local political conflicts, precipitating causes might include a number of military factors. Weapons by themselves do not cause wars, which can be fought at any level of armament. Certain military factors can, however, increase the likelihood of war, or at least of escalation to nuclear weapons.

The first and most obvious consideration is conventional military deterrence in the subtheaters of the region. War is less likely where the controlling power favors no change and has the conventional military capability to make it stick. The most dangerous situation will be when the status quo power finds its conventional options limited and is tempted to compensate through use of nuclear weapons or expansion of conflict outside the theater. Force imbalances between rival regional powers can also encourage attack. Iran's apparent weakness and internal disarray in part prompted the Iraqi attack in 1980. Superpower clients that lose wars are quick to call upon their patrons for help, as the Arabs have done in each war with Israel. Finally, many Middle East states have big military organizations that themselves invite, limit, or otherwise affect the superpowers' use of force.

Second are special incentives for preemptive or early use of force by the superpowers. When technical military considerations dictate prompt resort to force by the superpowers, time is shortened for decision-making and negotiation. Incentives for early use arise from a variety of conditions. As noted, asymmetries among superpower and local forces may lead one side to redress the balance by surprise attack. Could this happen in the Persian Gulf, to the U.S. Central Command (CENTCOM)? CENTCOM, established after events of the late 1970s as a rapid intervention force, has no forces based in the Persian Gulf and must deploy them on receipt of warning. The Soviet Union, by contrast, has roughly thirty divisions and accompanying air armies in three military districts bordering Iran.[12] Such imbalance puts great pressure on the United States to commit forces early and to escalate for lack of better conventional options. Another factor is the nature of the terrain in the combat theater. Iran is traversed from east to west by two mountain massifs, the Elburz and the Zagros, which confine Soviet military operations to six major axes of advance.[13] In the event of a Soviet invasion of Iran, there would be strong U.S. incentive to hit Soviet columns early with either conventional airstrikes or tactical nuclear weapons while Soviet forces were still moving through the mountainous and constricted terrain of the Elburz. Finally, characteristics of specific weapons systems (for example, the vulnerability of naval forces relative to ground forces) may invite preemption or accidental attack.

Routes to Nuclear War

In a small but plausible number of ways, conventional war could break out between the United States and the Soviet Union in the Middle East/Persian Gulf. It is harder to imagine how escalation to a first use of nuclear arms in the region would lead to major nuclear attacks on American and Russian cities—perhaps because this territory is (fortunately) less well charted in our actual experience. Even so, plausible escalation scenarios can be developed. Obviously, any of these scenarios could develop in unpredictable ways, or conflict could follow an unforeseen course. These scenarios are not intended, then, to predict, but to illustrate plausibility.

SCENARIO 1: SOVIET INVASION OF IRAN

Following the death of Ayatollah Khomeini and a power struggle among the senior ayatollahs, leftist groups that have been patiently building strength underground and abroad stage a coup d'état in the capital. Within a few months the new government in Teheran declares Iran a People's Republic. It signs a treaty of friendship and cooperation with the Soviet Union and receives Soviet advisers and military equipment. The professional army, seeing political order crumbling throughout the country, takes matters into its own hands and with significant popular support in the countryside marches to overthrow the new government in Teheran. In the face of the army's advance, the leftist government in a panic calls on the Soviet Union for "fraternal" assistance.

The Soviet leadership decides to stage a massive intervention in the northern half of the country. Twenty of the thirty divisions stationed in the Transcaucasus, North Caucasus, and Turkestan Military Districts cross the border. They are joined by the Group of Soviet Forces in Afghanistan. The Russians intend to occupy the country down to a line running through Hamadan, Qazvin, Teheran, and Mashhad. By consensus the primary objective is to support the pro-Soviet government, as in Afghanistan in 1979. A powerful faction within the leadership argues, however, that Iran presents an opportunity of historic proportions for the Soviet Union. It can seize a significant portion of Persian Gulf oil reserves and deal a decisive setback to the United States before the latter completes its long-term defense modernization plans. Thus Western Europe and Japan will be divided from the United States once and for all, it is argued. The risk and cost will be lower than those of a frontal offensive in Central Europe. This logic carries the Russian day. Military plans are made to seize not only the oilfields in southern Iran, but in Kuwait, southern Iraq, and northern Saudi Arabia as well.

Warned of a massive Soviet intervention, the United States deploys Central Command forces to the Persian Gulf. Along the way, however, unforeseen problems arise. The Gulf states with which the United States has contingency basing plans refuse to permit precautionary U.S. Air Force deployments before the actual Soviet crossing of the border; once the Russians cross, in a panic these small states seek to propitiate the Soviets by continuing to bar the United States. This means that air interdiction can be mounted only from bases in Turkey, by B-52s operating out of Egypt and B-1Bs from the continental United States, and from the carrier battle groups concentrating just south of the Straits of Hormuz. A second problem is that the United States can find no one in legal authority in Iran who will issue an invitation for U.S. forces to intervene; in fact, the provisional Islamic government still in power in the southern provinces denounces both superpowers and states that an American intervention would be opposed by force.

Soviet columns advance into Iran quickly along the six major axes in northern Iran and from Afghanistan. They meet little resistance from Iranian forces. The U.S. decides to interdict the Russian forces with conventional airstrikes while they are still in the constricted Elburz passes. Without access to land bases in the Gulf, it is impossible to launch a sufficient volume of sorties. Ground forces could be deployed in southern Iran only after a prolonged and costly amphibious landing along the Persian Gulf coast. Thus the president reluctantly accepts a Joint Chiefs of Staff (JCS) recommendation to launch a limited tactical nuclear strike against selected choke points in northern Iran with B-52s operating out of Egypt.

This decision is governed by two considerations: first, it is believed that the use of five or six weapons will impose significant delays on the Soviet advance; but more importantly, the U.S. hopes that this demonstration of resolve will force the Soviets to stop and reconsider their invasion before reaching the southern oil fields.

The strike is successful in slowing the Soviet advance and causes several thousand Soviet casualties. The Soviet leadership decides not to back down, however, arguing that the Soviet Union will look weak if American first-use is not met with a response in kind; that mounting domestic pressure in the United States and Europe will prevent further American escalation; and that they are in any event close to achieving their original invasion objectives. The Soviets launch selected nuclear strikes with Backfire bombers against the U.S. carrier battle groups concentrating in the Persian Gulf.

At this point, other theaters all over the globe come into play. U.S. and Western European leaders take a number of precautionary moves against lateral escalation: NATO forces are put on a higher state of alert; mobile theater weapons like Pershing IIs and ground-launched cruise missiles (GLCMs) are deployed out of their cantonment areas; ballistic missile submarines (SSBNs), including those of Britain and France, are put to sea. Popular European and Japanese opposition to

U.S. military moves in the Gulf, strong to begin with, bursts into outright violence as groups take to the streets protesting any cooperation with U.S. aggression. Finally, the North Korean regime sees U.S. preoccupation in Southwest Asia as the opportunity it has long awaited. It launches a full-scale ground invasion of the south with the immediate objective of taking Seoul.

The United States is stunned by the attack on its naval forces and by the sudden escalation of the conflict to Asia. The standard plan for the defense of Korea cannot be executed because of combat losses and the disruption of mobilization assets and plans by the conflict in Southwest Asia. The only U.S. forces who can respond to the continuing Soviet advance in Iran are Air Force units in eastern Turkey. The United States persuades the Turkish government to permit it to launch more tactical nuclear strikes against Soviet forces, and against the airbases from which bomber strikes originated in the Soviet Union itself. A homeland has been touched.

At the same time, the war expands at sea. After the loss of two carrier battle groups, remaining U.S. naval commanders in the Indian Ocean, fearing further Soviet preemption, begin "defensive" conventional strikes against the Soviet naval task forces deployed near their own units. Since the Soviets have already attacked U.S. naval forces in the area, this step is taken on the basis of standard operating procedures, without specific authority from Washington. It seems that a general naval war has begun. Fighting between U.S. and Soviet combatants thus erupts and rapidly expands eastward from the Gulf along the major sea lanes all the way back to Northeast Asia. A large part of the Soviet Pacific fleet is destroyed.

The U.S. strike against airbases in the Soviet Union is militarily effective and produces heavy civilian casualties in nearby towns. The Soviets are surprised by the Turks' action and feel that they have to be taught a lesson. Responding in kind to the American attack, the Soviets strike the bases from which the U.S. aircraft originated with small yield nuclear weapons, as well as a few main operating bases in western Turkey for good measure.

Now there has been a direct Soviet nuclear attack on a NATO country. Instead of standing firmly behind Turkey, the major Western European governments, following the lead of their publics, tend to blame the United States for the initial escalation to nuclear weapons.

They reason that they will suffer the same fate as Turkey unless they disassociate themselves from the United States. Britain and France withdraw their independent nuclear deterrents from any semblance of joint NATO planning or control and put them on a higher state of alert in case they have to be used unilaterally. All European military forces move to higher states of alert as a precaution. In the meantime, the massive North Korean invasion of the south has bypassed and cut off the strong defenses surrounding Seoul and is pushing the Republic of Korea Army and the U.S. Eighth Army southward to Pusan in a replay of the late summer of 1950. Since Korea is not receiving its planned augmentation—naval forces have either been destroyed or are committed to Southwest Asia, while ground and air forces based in the continental U.S. are moving to Europe—the U.S. feels it has no alternative and uses tactical nuclear weapons against North Korean forces in the Kaesong and Chorwon corridors.

The Soviet leadership decides that the pattern of American behavior up to this point—first-use of nuclear weapons in Iran, higher alert rates and dispersal of nuclear weapons in Europe in the face of strong European protests, expansion of the war to sea, direct nuclear attacks on the Soviet homeland, and now nuclear use in Korea—are all signs of a reckless U.S. leadership virtually out of control. In addition, they entirely misinterpret British and French efforts to separate their nuclear forces from U.S. operations, seeing them as preparations for joint strikes with the United States. The Soviets do not view American actions as a response to their invasion of Iran and the North Korean invasion of South Korea, but rather as a calculated attempt to inflict damage on the Soviet Union and take advantage of the situation created by the current crisis. Some Soviet leaders have a more sinister interpretation of U.S. behavior, believing that higher U.S. alert rates are a preparation for a massive American nuclear strike. The military argues that the United States cannot be permitted to whittle away at their forces and those of allies like North Korea; that according to doctrine a nuclear war once begun cannot be kept limited; and that any advantages of preemption will be lost if American forces proceed to yet higher alert rates. Hence the Soviets themselves launch a massive countermilitary strike against U.S. overseas bases and several selected important targets in the continental United States. A countermilitary strike, unlike the U.S. concept of a counterforce strike, does not deliberately seek to avoid hitting civilian targets and to minimize collateral damage; hence while some Soviet nuclear weapons hit isolated military installations like Shemya Air Force Base in the Aleutians, others hit population centers like the ports of Bremerton, Washington, and San Diego, California. The United States then feels compelled to respond in kind.

SCENARIO 2: ESCALATION OF AN ARAB-ISRAELI CONFLICT

Case A: Israel Loses. Secret negotiations among Syria, Iraq, and Jordan have produced a Northern Front coalition that launches a massive surprise attack on Israel, with the initially limited goal of seizing and holding Israeli-occupied territory as a means of increasing its bargaining leverage. As in 1973, the Arabs achieve nearly total strategic surprise. There are three important differences from 1973, however. First, the Arabs have acquired equipment and trained manpower to launch a series of conventional strikes into the interior of Israel, including SS-21 and SS-22 missiles. The Israelis fear, but are not certain, that the Syrians and/or Iraqis have covertly acquired some nuclear device, for which they clearly have a delivery vehicle. Second, the Soviet Union has dramatically increased its military involvement in Syria and Iraq. Soviet officers serve in combat units, Soviet troops man ground-based air defenses and interceptors, and other Soviet ground forces perform garrison duties in rear areas. In addition, a large Soviet naval task force deploys to the eastern Mediterranean at the outset of the war. Finally, the United States and Israel are at a low point in their relationship. U.S. economic and military assistance to Israel is temporarily suspended pending U.S. efforts to reverse the recent Israeli decision to annex the West Bank.

Through support from Soviet forces and qualitative improvements in the Arab militaries, the Northern Front allies do much better than expected, inflicting heavy casualties on Israeli forces on the Golan Heights. Successful attacks on reserve mobilization centers and heavy casualties from the conventional bombing of major Israeli cities have created hysteria in Israel. An apocalyptic sense arises that this may be the final showdown with the state's opponents. There is also considerable anger at the Soviets for playing so direct a role, and an increasing resentment of the United States for not doing enough.

There is, in fact, a growing feeling in the Israeli leadership that the war was brought on by the American aid freeze, and that Israel may have to go it alone on this occasion.

Suddenly, Jordanian and Iraqi forces break through into pre-1967 Israel and advance rapidly into the narrow interior of the country. The Arabs, encouraged by their unexpected success, expand their political objectives to the reconquest of as much of Palestine as possible. There is a sudden sense of panic in Israel; Israeli ground forces become demoralized and begin collapsing suddenly. As an impending Arab victory becomes clear, other Arab states like Egypt and Saudi Arabia, which had been sitting on the fence, begin to join in the battle with their sophisticated American weapons.

The government in Jerusalem, despairing of American help, decides to take matters into its own hands. After appealing for a cease-fire and warning of possible nuclear use, the Israeli air force drops several medium-yield nuclear bombs on secondary cities of the main Arab belligerents, as well as on major targets of military value, including power facilities, ports, and airfields. Jerusalem announces that its nuclear stockpile is an order of magnitude larger than current intelligence estimates and that it has ballistic missile delivery vehicles capable of striking the most distant target. It warns the Arabs, in the meantime, to withdraw or face further retribution.

The Arabs are stunned by this development, which has caused more than 100,000 deaths. They believe that Israel has exhausted its stockpile of nuclear weapons, however. Instead of withdrawing, they appeal to the Soviet Union either to provide them with nuclear weapons or to retaliate against Israel directly.

The Israeli strike has caused thousands of casualties among Soviet forces; to preserve its own prestige and credibility Moscow feels it must take some action against Israel in response. The United States, moreover, has been deeply shocked by the Israeli use of nuclear weapons and the large numbers of civilian casualties it caused, and the Soviets believe they can take advantage of this wedge between the United States and Israel to avoid direct confrontation with Washington. Now that Israeli ground forces have been seriously weakened, the Soviets send several divisions of airborne troops to shore up Arab forces in Israel and administer the final coup de grace. In addition, there is evidence of Soviet efforts to transfer nuclear weapons to Syria.

The Israeli government, believing that this may be Israel's last act as a state, orders another even larger nuclear strike against the principal population centers of the Arab belligerents, Soviet ground forces deploying into the area, Soviet naval units in the Mediterranean and Persian Gulf, and certain population targets in the southern Ukraine itself. This last act serves no clearcut military or political purpose. It is undertaken as an act of pure revenge for Soviet support for the Arabs.

The final Israeli nuclear strike coincides with a belated U.S. effort to intervene militarily on Israel's behalf, involving higher alert levels for U.S. forces worldwide, including strategic nuclear forces, deployment of airborne units from the continental United States to the eastern Mediterranean, increased resupply and intelligence activities, and a quarantining of the Syrian and Israeli coastlines by the U.S. Sixth Fleet. The Soviet military from the beginning has suspected that Israel was acting as a U.S. proxy in its attacks on Soviet forces. It now believes that the United States and not Israel was responsible for the last series of attacks; in particular, Soviet intelligence does not believe Israel's delivery system capable of reaching the Ukraine. The Soviet Union has by now suffered hundreds of thousands of casualties from the nuclear strikes and feels that it has no choice but to retaliate against the ultimate source of the aggression. Selective nuclear strikes with SS-20 missiles are ordered against U.S. overseas bases, facilities, and naval forces, including the Sixth Fleet carrier battle groups.

Thereafter, events follow the course outlined in scenario 1, with both the United States and Soviet Union escalating their use of nuclear weapons up to the point of homeland strikes.

Case B: Israel Wins. As a result of the resumption of cross-border terrorist attacks into northern Israel with the acquiescence of Syria, a hard-line Israeli government decides to "go to the source" once and for all and destroy the radical Arab government in Damascus. As in case A, the Soviets have substantially increased their support for Syria by manning Syrian ground-based air defenses and interceptors and providing other types of ground forces to perform garrison duty. They have, moreover, provided the Syrians with a new generation of tactical missiles minus their nuclear warheads; some in Israel believe that the warheads themselves have been covertly transferred.

The war begins with a major Israeli air force attack on Syrian air defenses, which kills many Soviet soldiers. Israeli armored forces quickly outflank Syrian defenses on the Golan Heights, prompting the Soviet government to issue a warning that it will not stand idly by if Israel does not adhere to the U.N.-mandated ceasefire passed with U.S. approval on the first day of the war. Israel disregards the Soviet warning altogether and within two or three days the Israeli defense forces have surrounded and bypassed Damascus, pursuing the fleeing Syrian government northward. It quickly becomes clear that Israeli aims are much more ambitious than originally believed.

The Israeli government, moreover, seems to be making a deliberate effort to humiliate the Soviets. With the evident desire to teach the Soviets to stay out of the Middle East and to demonstrate Soviet lack of conventional options, the Israeli military sinks Soviet ships in port, shoots down large numbers of Soviet-piloted interceptors, destroys Soviet transport aircraft, and goes so far as to sink a Soviet cruiser near the Syrian coast.

The desperate Syrian government appeals for massive Soviet help, in particular for the transfer of nuclear weapons that can be mounted on its recently acquired SS-21 and SS-22 missiles. The Soviets find that they have no good options for conventional intervention: airborne forces that could be deployed in the theater lack the heavy equipment to go up against Israeli armor; naval forces would be ineffective in altering the emerging status quo on the ground; and air force units deployed into Syria have been destroyed almost as soon as they arrived. The Soviets therefore see no alternative but to transfer several small-yield nuclear warheads to their forces in Syria, which then launches several nuclear-armed SS-21s into Israel.

Israel is in shock. A day earlier it was dominant; now it has sustained civilian casualties representing a significant percentage of its total population. Fearing that the Syrians have not used up their supply of nuclear warheads, Israel launches a retaliatory nuclear strike against major population targets in Syria and Iraq, and against Soviet military forces (primarily naval surface combatants) deployed in the region.

Hereafter, the case B scenario could develop much as in case A, with the Soviets confusing U.S. and Israeli nuclear attacks, worldwide alerts, and so on.

Actions to Reduce the Probability of Nuclear War

The scenarios in the previous section provide a useful point of departure for discussion of actions to lower the risk of nuclear war, since they point to specific ways in which conflicts can escalate, and therefore ways in which the escalation process can be broken. Several initial observations are in order.

First, it is easy to imagine how direct conventional conflict between the superpowers can begin in the region. It is somewhat harder to imagine how nuclear weapons might first be used in a limited way, either against regional actors or against superpower forces deployed in the area. The most implausible elements of both the Iranian and Arab-Israeli scenarios concern how conflict escalates from this level to large-scale strikes on the superpower homelands. In this respect the Middle East is the opposite of Europe, where it is easy to imagine a conventional NATO-Warsaw Pact conflict turning into a nuclear war, but very difficult to understand how that conventional conflict would get started in the first place.

Second, to account for these implausible escalation thresholds, both scenarios require a serious misunderstanding or miscalculation on the part of one or both superpowers. In the Iranian scenario, for example, a Soviet decision to preempt is based on the belief that a large-scale U.S. nuclear attack is imminent.

Third, alerts or higher states of force readiness, used either in a precautionary way or as signals, are one important way in which the crisis can escalate laterally out of the Middle East/Persian Gulf region.

Fourth, naval forces play a similarly important role in globalizing regional conflicts. This is because: (1) naval forces are the easiest to deploy in regional conflicts, where they either become instruments of intervention or targets; (2) to have naval combatants in close proximity with one another is destabilizing in a crisis because the general rule in naval warfare is that whoever shoots first wins; and (3) war at sea, once begun, is very difficult to contain geographically.

Fifth, escalation to homeland strikes is relatively more plausible in the context of multiple simultaneous conflicts in different geographical theaters—for example, a Persian Gulf crisis plus a Korean conflict plus mobilization in Europe plus war at sea, and so on.

It is important to note that preventing nuclear war is not the sole objective of U.S. foreign policy; rather the problem is to lower the risks of U.S.-Soviet war while preserving U.S. interests in the Middle East/Persian Gulf region. Although the nuclear war scenarios described above are possible, they are highly unlikely and cannot be the basis of day-to-day policy. Excessive fear of nuclear war or too great a policy emphasis on avoiding the risk of war can lead to disastrous consequences for American interests and allies in the short run; in the long run overemphasis on war-avoidance may lead to miscalculations on the part of adversaries that would have the ironic result of making war more likely. To take an extreme example, one could lower the risk of nuclear war with the Soviets over the Persian Gulf to practically zero by deciding ahead of time that no developments there, including a Soviet invasion of Iran, merited American military intervention. Such a policy, however, would raise the probability of conventional aggression by removing deterrents to Soviet action. This could in turn lead to further aggression in other theaters where the United States would feel compelled to resort to nuclear weapons; alternatively, since the United States would never be able to renounce its interests in the Gulf altogether, it might undertake panicked and desperate measures to redress the military imbalance at the last moment. It goes without saying that the United States can also increase the chances of nuclear war by defining its interests too expansively as well, such as when U.S. forces provoked Chinese intervention in Korea by driving too close to the Yalu River in 1950. The issue for policy is to find an appropriate definition of interests that is neither too broad nor too narrow.

Bearing these considerations in mind, we will discuss four categories of actions that can be taken to lower the risk of nuclear war in the Middle East/Persian Gulf: (1) doctrine and policy; (2) forces; (3) procedures; and (4) cooperative measures.

DOCTRINE AND POLICY

Because it is so easy to see how local conflicts might lead to conventional superpower intervention and war in the Middle East/ Persian Gulf, the most obvious policy-related actions the United States could undertake are efforts to prevent these conflicts from arising in the first place. The history of peacemaking in the Middle

East is a long and troubled one, with many failures and several important successes. Unfortunately, not all of the region's conflicts are susceptible to negotiated settlement, and in particular to settlement through U.S. mediation. The United States has virtually no influence over developments in the Gulf such as the Iran-Iraq war or an internal power struggle in Iran. Indeed, we should recognize that in suggesting policies to settle conflicts in the Middle East/Persian Gulf, we are talking primarily about the Arab-Israeli conflict, where the United States has in fact played a constructive role in the past. Attempts to inject the United States into situations where it has little leverage can be damaging by undermining U.S. prestige and drawing the nation into unwanted involvements—the most recent example being Lebanon in 1982–84.

Successive U.S. administrations have concluded that the negotiated settlement of the Arab-Israeli dispute is a highly desirable goal, and not simply because of the risk of nuclear war. But while a broad consensus exists on ends, there is considerable disagreement on means (for example, comprehensive versus piecemeal solutions, territorial compromises, inclusion of the Soviet Union, and so on). It is not clear whether a truly comprehensive settlement is possible any longer, given the pace of Israeli West Bank settlement activity and the limitations of Arab leadership arguably evident in their reaction to the 1982 Reagan peace plan. In any event, this approach has several important limitations.

First, many political negotiations can achieve results only in conjunction with threats, or the actual use, of force. Once can argue that peace between Egypt and Israel was possible only as a result of the October War, which gave Egypt the self-confidence needed to proceed with a separate peace and gave Israel a powerful incentive to make territorial concessions. Diplomacy that ignores the underlying realities of power politics is doomed to failure; in particular, such progress as has been made to date on the Arab-Israeli conflict has been underwritten in large measure by America's strong military support for Israel. Needless to say, the acceptance of a certain level of conflict in the short run can get out of hand and work at cross purposes to the long-term goal of peace.

Second, negotiations frequently serve as a means of advancing particular political interests and do not in themselves necessarily lead to greater stability in the long run. The specific content of a negotiated settlement is more important than the fact of negotiations. Many Israelis have argued that "resolution" of the Arab-Israeli dispute through the creation of a West Bank Palestinian state could lead to a situation more unstable than the current one, by creating an irredentist threat to both Israel and Jordan, and might moreover increase Israeli reliance on nuclear weapons. Arab critics have similarly charged that the Egyptian-Israeli peace treaty freed Israel to take military action against Syria and the Palestine Liberation Organization (PLO) in Lebanon.

Third, the inclusion of the Soviet Union in Arab-Israeli negotiations, while superficially attractive, can backfire, because of the fundamental asymmetry of U.S. and Soviet interests noted earlier. To a much greater extent than is true for the United States, Soviet influence in the Middle East depends on the existence of a certain level of conflict; while Moscow has clearly wanted to mitigate the dangers of conflict in the past, a thoroughgoing political settlement would not serve its long-term interests. Granting the Soviets a coequal role, as in the abortive 1974 Geneva Conference, is likely to be a formula for deadlock and rules out other less ambitious but more practicable solutions.

The United States can of course engage in efforts to achieve local political settlements as one means of reducing the risk of nuclear war. The Arab-Israeli peace process will inevitably depend very much on tactical considerations like the character of the Israeli government, internal politics in the PLO, inter-Arab relations, and so on. The most fruitful approach is likely to be an incremental one, like the Camp David process, which has significantly lowered, at least for the intermediate future, the probability of another Arab-Israeli war on the scale of 1973, with all its attendant risks of superpower confrontation. In the absence of striking new developments such as the emergence of another Sadat, the most that one can hope for is probably a regulation of the conflict, rather than its final resolution. Controlling the number of participants, the types of weapons, and the scope and intensity of future Arab-Israeli wars is not an insignificant aim in view of the objective of reducing the risks of nuclear war.

A second important type of policy the United States can undertake is the clear communication of its interests in the region. Although the Soviet Union has generally recognized and respected the strength of U.S. and Western interests in both the Persian Gulf and Arab-Israeli theaters, one cannot take such forebearance for granted. Stakes are built on objective political and economic interests and are communicated in the long run by clear statements of purpose. If the United States is indeed prepared to fight for oil, then authoritative pronouncements like the Carter Doctrine or formal defense commitments spelling this out are all to the good. Moreover, rhetorical positions must be backed by concrete measures such as military capabilities to defend them and the demonstration of national will to use those capabilities when necessary. In the short run, it is important that U.S. political leaders reinforce these long-term commitments during a crisis with clear-cut statements of what they will and will not tolerate.

The real difficulty lies in laying down red lines while avoiding overcommitment, a problem that has plagued U.S. postwar foreign policy. The Middle East/Persian Gulf differs from Europe in that U.S. interests and stakes have changed over time and are much less well defined: most Americans will better understand the need to defend West Germany, which will want our support, than Iran, which may not. The American public and Congress have swung from support of Dulles-era pactomania to an extreme reluctance to use force in support of overseas interests. In the present post-Vietnam and post-Lebanon mood, it is not clear that a national consensus exists for even as clear-cut a strategic interest as the defense of oil, much less for related objectives like the defense of the territorial integrity of Israel or Pakistan. (A formal commitment to the state of Israel will also involve significant costs to the United States in terms of its relations with other Arab states and may affect its ability to defend its interests in the Gulf.) Attempts to communicate fundamental interests are frequently indistinguishable from threats, which tend to scare people, as in the case of the nuclear alert at the end of the October 1973 War, for which Kissinger and Nixon were severely criticized in some circles. Ultimately, there is no simple solution to these problems: leaders must be prudent in defining national interests and must take the time to explain the reasons for that definition to the American people.

FORCES

With respect to the Persian Gulf theater, the first and most important policy to reduce the risk of nuclear war is the creation of a conventional deterrent to Soviet intervention. As we have seen, the logistical problems in projecting forces to the Gulf create powerful incentives for rapid U.S. escalatory decisions and may push Washington to a decision to use nuclear weapons. A stronger conventional deterrent will make Soviet action less likely, if deterrence breaks down, buy time to permit a defusing of the crisis through diplomatic means.

It can be argued that a weak deterrent is worse than no deterrent at all, since it will be insufficient to deter a Soviet intervention in the first place but large enough to involve the United States automatically in a war it cannot win. One can argue further that since geographical realities make *any* U.S. effort to defend Iran against Soviet invasion inadequate, the existence of CENTCOM is itself an invitation to disaster.

Even under the most optimistic assumptions about U.S. ability to build adequate forces and deploy them to the Gulf in a crisis, it is highly unlikely that the United States would be able to defend Iran against a fully determined Soviet invasion. Successful deterrence does not, however, necessarily rest on the ability to prevail should deterrence fail, but rather on the ability to impose costs on one's adversary that are enough to outweigh any potential gains.[14] As we have seen, the Soviets have behaved cautiously in this region in the past. The risk of direct combat with U.S. forces, even if ultimately successful, is not something Moscow would undertake lightly, particularly in a secondary theater. It is not unreasonable to expect that the sort of rapid deployment force that can be built under existing budgetary and political constraints will succeed in deterring Soviet intervention.

Several steps can be taken to improve the Persian Gulf deterrent. The first is the procurement of additional support and mobility forces to move and sustain CENTCOM in the Gulf, including increased strategic and theater airlift, kits to allow aircraft to operate out of unimproved airfields, ammunition and spare parts stocks, and the like. These forces are traditionally shortchanged in military procurement and are more critical in the short run than additional units.

The second step is the improvement of U.S. basing structure in the Gulf. An overt U.S. presence obviously runs the risk of provoking nationalist resentment and leading to the sorts of instability to which CENTCOM was supposed to respond; but there are many much less visible steps that can be taken short of this, such as joint strategic planning, prestocking of logistics, and so on.[15]

A third step is the creation of lighter army divisions that can be moved to the Gulf more rapidly than a standard mechanized division. Some have questioned whether the army, which currently plans to create two new light divisions, is trading off too much firepower for increased mobility, given that these forces would have to face Soviet motorized rifle divisions in a conflict in Iran. The concept is nonetheless a sound one: speed will be critical if the United States is to create a defensive line in southern Iran and present the Soviets with a choice of whether or not to attack; heavy mechanized or armored forces are in any event not appropriate to the terrain in the Zagros.

A fourth and more expensive step would be the simple expansion of the number of units available for intervention in the Gulf. Currently, CENTCOM has no forces of its own; in a crisis, units must be stripped from other theaters, weakening the deterrent in Europe and the Far East. This is acceptable as long as the United States faces an isolated Persian Gulf contingency, but would require sequencing of operations in the event of simultaneous conflicts in multiple theaters, or an abandonment of the Persian Gulf altogether. U.S. plans for the reinforcement of Europe would become hopelessly snarled if the Soviets preceded an offensive against NATO with a diversionary attack in the Persian Gulf.

A final step that could be taken is heavier U.S. reliance on the threat of theater nuclear weapons to deter Soviet intervention in the Gulf. In many respects the considerations regarding this tradeoff are no different from those that apply in Europe: on the one hand, one could argue that the best means of deterring nuclear war is to deter war itself, to which the threat (though not necessarily the actual use) of nuclear weapons would contribute; on the other hand, given Soviet conventional advantages in the theater, nuclear weapons may prove to be the only means of deterring them and actually stopping a Soviet advance if deterrence fails. U.S. stakes in the Persian Gulf are lower overall than in Europe, however, and there is some question whether the United States would want to initiate nuclear use in a peripheral theater. In either case, it is important that nuclear weapons not become a substitute for serious conventional options.

PROCEDURES

Since it will not be possible to avoid superpower crises over local conflicts in the Middle East/Persian Gulf altogether, it is important to be able to manage crises and prevent escalation once they have begun. Obviously, many general crisis-management measures—such as improved technical means of communication between the United States and Soviet Union or the introduction of pauses—are not specific to any one geographical region and will contribute to escalation-control in the Middle East/Persian Gulf as well as elsewhere. There are, however, some measures that are of particular relevance to this region.

As noted earlier, it is particularly difficult to imagine how one might cross the threshold that divides regional conflict from global nuclear war. Alerts and naval forces are two important avenues by which regional crises can become globalized, with misinterpretation playing a major role in each case. This suggests that greater attention must be paid to both these issues.

Alerts have been used both as a precaution against unforeseen developments and as a deliberate signal of determination, as in the October War. In the latter case, U.S. strategic forces were placed at a higher state of readiness worldwide precisely to convey seriousness of purpose. While the message was correctly interpreted in this case, a similar step in a future crisis might be misread as indicating an intent to widen the conflict. Different types of alerts can change standard operating procedures and rules of engagement in ways that could have unexpected results in areas quite remote from the regional conflict that sparked them. It would appear that U.S. national leaders, particularly those outside the military, have a very imprecise notion of what different alert levels entail, much less how they might be interpreted by the other side. For example, by former Secretary of State Haig's account, Secretary of Defense Weinberger raised the alert status of U.S. forces on the day President Reagan was shot without knowing whether this move affected U.S. strategic forces. One simple measure that might be taken is simply to brief national leaders thoroughly on the effects of alerts and, perhaps, historical precedents for their use. Moreover, since different alert levels can be set for each of the individual unified and specified commands, it may be desirable to alert only those forces in the region itself.

Naval forces present special problems because they are likely to be deployed early into a Middle East/Persian Gulf crisis, and they constitute vulnerable, high-value targets in the event of war. Naval warfare introduces a destabilizing element into regional conflicts by putting a premium on preemption, a situation aggravated by the U.S. and Soviet navies' practice of staging realistic maneuvers and exercises which might be taken for the real thing in a crisis. Standard naval operating procedures, which in some cases permit individual commanders to initiate conflict on their own authority in self-defense, could be a source of accidental escalation. While national political authorities should not unduly restrict a unified theater commander's ability to protect his forces, standard operating procedures need to be reviewed and put under strict control, particularly in the early phases of a crisis. It might be desirable to consider ways in which naval forces could be disengaged in a crisis so as to separate them from enemy forces, or to employ them in such a manner that naval engagements, once begun, do not automatically spread to other parts of the world.

Planning for the possibility of multiple simultaneous conflicts in geographically remote theaters and improvements in the worldwide command and control of U.S. forces will be important if the United States becomes involved in a major regional crisis, which can have unexpected lateral spillover effects. For example, allocating forces from the western Pacific to the Persian Gulf would have a major impact on the Korean balance and might encourage instability there to which U.S. forces would have difficulty responding (indeed, the two phenomena are related). Multiple crises are perhaps more probable than isolated ones, since the temptation will exist to take advantage of superpower preoccupation in one particular area (witness Suez and Hungary in 1956). Moreover, a series of crises may make direct superpower homeland attacks more likely, as in one scenario described earlier. While the solution to this problem may lie more in force structure than procedures (that is, larger, more mobile, and more flexible forces), it is important for the United States to think through ahead of time how it would interpret and react to simultaneous regional crises.

In the end, however, procedures are likely to be much less important for crisis management than simple political judgment and the exercise of statesmanship. Though technical and institutional approaches to political decision-making are currently fashionable, careful study of past crises in the Middle East (indeed crises anywhere) reveals that the single most important factor influencing their outcomes is political prudence on the part of national leaders. In previous Middle Eastern crises, Soviet intervention has been deterred by the timely communication, through both political and military means, of U.S. willingness to defend certain interests, balanced by a healthy respect for certain core Soviet interests. The Soviets have engaged in a policy of deliberate bluff in past crises, backing down, in the face of strong U.S. pressure, out of a respect for the strength of Western power and interests relative to its own. The lack of Soviet military options, particularly vis-à-vis Israel, suggests that the United States could probably have pushed Moscow even further than it did at several points in the past. Yet U.S. leaders have not sought further marginal advantages that might drive the Soviets to extreme actions. Indeed, in many situations the best way of preventing war is to know when to back down, even at the expense of an ally's or one's own short-term interests.

Statesmanship is the art of knowing how to be moderate without seeming weak, distinguishing between bluff and serious threat, and correctly interpreting motives behind an enemy's behavior. Such judgments are highly dependent on context and are not arrived at by a mechanical process; they are instead the product of experience, intuition, and a certain kind of political wisdom that can be learned but not taught. While institutional mechanisms can assist in the collection of information and in improving communications, the content of what is communicated remains the province of the statesman and is by far the dominant factor determining a crisis outcome.

A nation obviously cannot produce statesmen on demand as a matter of national policy. It would be a mistake, however, to see the problem simply in terms of policy mechanisms rather than as one of education. Universities and other institutions of higher learning are frequently tempted to play a prominent role as counselors to princes, but they should not lose sight of their traditional role as educators of princes as well. My own view is that traditional curricula, such as the thorough study of history, are better suited to producing statesmen than are trendier approaches such as psychologically based theories of political behavior. Needless to say, in an area like the Middle East/Persian Gulf, one needs people who are well versed in its politics and history.

COOPERATIVE MEASURES

Various cooperative measures between the United States and the Soviet Union have been proposed for the Middle East/Persian Gulf, including understandings on spheres of interest, Indian Ocean arms control, conventional arms transfer talks, and inclusion of the Soviet Union in the Arab-Israeli peace process. Unfortunately, none of these approaches is likely to be very fruitful.

Informal understandings between the United States and the Soviet Union on spheres of influence—or perhaps spheres of restraint, in which only more threatening types of involvement would be ruled out —are not in themselves bad ideas and have been practiced to some extent in Europe. Several practical obstacles, however, prevent the resurrection of anything like the 1907 Anglo-Russian entente, which divided Iran into Russian, British, and neutral zones. The first is that the countries of the region are no longer the passive prizes of Great Power diplomacy that they were during the period of European colonial dominance; rather they can exercise considerable leverage to prevent the superpowers from making deals affecting their interests behind their backs. (For example, Egypt, fearing that the United States and Soviet Union had agreed to freeze the territorial status quo in the Middle East at the May 1972 summit, succeeded in dragging Moscow into support for the October War.) On the American side, moreover, there would be considerable resistance on principle to the moral cynicism implied by bargaining over spheres of influence. Such understandings, to be workable, would have to be arrived at informally and very quietly by statesmen on both sides.

The primary problem with Indian Ocean arms control is that it imposes disproportionate constraints on American military options in the Persian Gulf, given that the United States must rely heavily on seapower to balance Soviet ground forces in the Caucasus and Central Asia. Such an agreement would be of greatest benefit to India, which would emerge as the hegemonial power in the region; this explains New Delhi's consistent support for the idea. A broader Southwest Asian security agreement that would limit internal Soviet deployments along its southern borders would be somewhat more equitable, but highly impracticable under almost any foreseeable circumstances. Not only are Great Powers reluctant to limit forces on their own territory, but those forces would be reintroduced rapidly in a crisis.

Conventional arms transfer limitations present numerous technical difficulties of measurement and comparability; many states in the Middle East/Persian Gulf, like Jordan and Iraq, are involved not in bilateral but tri- or quadrilateral arms races that would require multilateral controls on a host of recipient and supplier states. The more important problem is that conventional arms transfer talks address symptoms rather than causes. The United States and the Soviet Union can engage in long-term negotiations over strategic arms or conventional forces in Europe because they are not preoccupied with a host of immediate territorial, ethnic, and religious disputes; in the Middle East, these more fundamental issues would quickly overwhelm attempts to regulate arms supply. A more sensible approach would be to address these underlying political differences directly—a hard enough task—after which technical agreements limiting military arsenals would become much more feasible.

Cooperative measures might prove quite useful in regulating the interaction of naval forces. In recognition of the destabilizing potential of peacetime navies, the United States and Soviet Union signed an Incidents-at-Sea agreement as part of their broader détente in the early 1970s. These measures could be updated and extended to include such things as prohibition of the locking-on of fire control radars, forcing submarines to surface during a crisis, and separation of naval forces.

Finally, there is the question of the overall atmosphere of U.S.-Soviet relations. It is important to recognize that friendly talk between Washington and Moscow will make regional crises substantially less dangerous. The most serious Middle Eastern crisis in recent times, involving threats of intervention and nuclear war, occurred in the fall of 1973 at the height of détente. The first three years of the Reagan administration, by contrast, saw a steady deterioration in the tone of U.S.-Soviet relations but the absence of significant Soviet adventurism. The difference between the two was due almost entirely to the presence or absence of local opportunities for superpower involvement, of course, rather than atmospherics. If one's expectations are kept suitably modest, however, good overall U.S.-Soviet relations may facilitate superpower control over regional crises. Henry Kissinger has argued that the existence of détente made the 1973 crisis less severe than it might otherwise have been by creating certain channels of communication. If the U.S. and Soviet Union are to avoid nuclear war, even marginally improved communication is bound to be a good thing.

6 CATALYTIC NUCLEAR WAR

by Henry S. Rowen

THE FORMULATORS of the concept of catalytic war posit an analogy between a chemical reaction between two substances accelerated by a catalyst and a conflict between two nations caused by a third party. In the narrow case of catalytic nuclear war, some other nation or a terrorist group deliberately seeks to catalyze the superpowers or other nuclear powers. In a broader case, a third party's actions, especially the use of nuclear weapons for some other purpose, or accidentally, triggers a sequence of events that leads to nuclear war. In the broadest version, third-party actions draw the Great Powers into a conflict that in the end results in nuclear war.

The deep causes of these imaginable phenomena are the spread of nuclear explosive materials, and of the knowledge to make bombs with them, together with persistent international conflicts. For the foreseeable future, all of these factors will persist.

Fluctuating Perceptions of the Problem

In 1963, President John F. Kennedy predicted that by 1970 there would be fifteen to twenty-five nuclear nations.[1] Kennedy's prediction reflected the widespread view that nuclear weapons would spread essentially as fast as nations acquired the means to make them. Most prognosticators also held that as this process unfolded, the likelihood of nuclear weapons use would grow exponentially.

The record has been quite different. Many states possess a civilian nuclear technological base, and the technological ability to have a bomb has spread as forecast. But states with nuclear weapons number only six or seven. One measure of the rate of spread—the interval between states' first nuclear explosive tests—is encouraging. Since the United States started the series in 1945, the intervals between first tests have been four, three, six, six, and ten years. Since India's 1974 detonation, no other nation is known to have had a first explosive test. The underlying process producing this series is not a law of physics. It is primarily political—and subject to change in unpredictable ways.

Until well into the 1960s, much attention was given to the possibility that Germany and Japan, technically advanced and economically strong, would acquire nuclear weapons. The prospect that part of a divided Germany might get these weapons, following on British and French acquisition, was especially troublesome and led to efforts, such as the NATO Multilateral Force, to forestall this outcome. In time, it became apparent that within both Germany and Japan there was strong resistance to possessing these weapons. Although such resistance should not be regarded as necessarily permanent, it was and is quite powerful.

Attention then shifted to developing countries that would inevitably gain nuclear technology. These often unstable countries are frequently caught up in international rivalries and conflicts. This prospect was especially worrisome as regards what might be called "crazy" states, those ruled by extremist politics and erratic leaders. The prospect of a nuclear Qaddafi or Khomeini is a recurring nightmare. Another worry has been that nuclear weapons might become the object of contest among vying internal factions in unstable states or worse, might even slip from governmental control into terrorist hands. (Possible terrorist attempts to seize U.S. weapons have been the subject of much attention and protective activity.) Moreover, many of these weak states might have vulnerable forces, and one of their neighbors might be tempted to preempt against their emerging nuclear force. Last, and worst, what if states with nuclear weapons might deliberately or inadvertently use them so as to trigger a wider nuclear exchange?

Not even such "responsible" and cooperative nations as the United States, France, and Great Britain are above suspicion. The problems of coordinating nuclear operations pose serious difficulties. The immensity of the stakes involved and the possibility of diverging interests, or at least perceptions of interests, could drive any government to acts that others—and in the end perhaps everyone—would regard as disastrous. The Soviets may attach extra significance to British and French nuclear forces because they believe their use might bring in train the launching of U.S. nuclear weapons. This thought, rarely voiced, and never by European political leaders, is not acceptable to American leaders.

Lately, such concerns have receded, in good part because nuclear weapons are spreading slowly. Even so, the likely future contains enough hazards to warrant our careful consideration of the possibility of a "triggered" or "catalytic" nuclear war.

Conditions in Which Nuclear War Between the Superpowers Might Be Deliberately Triggered by a Third Party

If the Ayatollah Khomeini had nuclear weapons and delivery systems that he believed could catalyze a nuclear war between "the two great Satans," as he refers to the United States and the USSR, might he try to do it? In the 1970s, during confidential SALT discussions, the Soviet government expressed concern that China would seek to catalyze a nuclear war between the Soviet Union and United States (Russia even explored, cautiously, the likely U.S. reaction if the Soviet Union should strike against the emerging Chinese nuclear capability).[2] As discussed in chapter 5, there are reports that in 1973 Israel considered the possibility of dropping a nuclear bomb on Moscow.

The conditions required for a deliberate nuclear attack that would catalyze nuclear war between the United States and the Soviet Union are essentially three:

1. The third party must have nuclear weapons and a delivery capacity;
2. The third party must have a motive or causes; and
3. The superpowers' forces, intelligence, and mindsets must be susceptible to being triggered by such an attack.

In today's world, few nations meet the first or second conditions, though one can be less sure about that as one looks further into the future. The highest hurdle, however, is the third. Even if the United States or Soviet Union were attacked by a third party, special conditions would have to be met to catalyze a general war:

- a high state of political tension between the United States and the USSR;
- forces at a high state of alert;
- intelligence and warning systems unable to discriminate attacks by the third party;
- at least one of the "target" countries having a "hair-trigger" nuclear launch policy (that is, with inadequate procedures for determining the source and size of nuclear attack, especially under time pressure).

Taken together, this is a stringent set of conditions. Motivation to cause such destruction is fortunately rare among governmental leaders, though not wholly unprecedented. Even so motivated, a leader, or others involved in executing such a plan, could be deterred by the prospect of retribution if the plan misfired. And even with the will and the capacity, it is necessary for the other conditions to be met.

Some of them might be, unfortunately. The nuclear powers that were the intended targets of manipulation might have vulnerable national command authorities or nuclear forces, together with a policy of rapid response to signals of attack—even a policy of launch on tactical warning of oncoming missiles. This is a classically unstable posture. If it exists in extreme form, a third party might trigger a disastrous sequence of actions ending in a nuclear exchange.

Are the Great Powers susceptible to such a maneuver? They should not be. The nuclear forces of the United States and the Soviet Union are so large and their major elements are so well protected (for example, under the seas) that a hair-trigger response policy is not justified. Some American officials even so have not excluded the possibility of launch-on-warning. (Since a large nuclear force at sea can survive an initial attack, there is no reasonable justification for such a policy.)

Warning systems provide another check. To detect a small number of nuclear weapons carried, say, into a nation's ports on merchant ships or commercial aircraft, or a bomb smuggled into an embassy, is very difficult. But it is much harder to simulate the main delivery system of a Great Power. Attacks of a size manageable by malicious third parties should be well below the threshold of any rational response policy by the Great Powers. But it is important that their command and control systems be capable of surviving such an attack and attentive to such a possibility. Survivable control together with strong security devices on weapons are the best ways to prevent the twin dangers of weapons being launched without considered central control or not being launched when so ordered by responsible authority.

The conditions for triggering a catalytic nuclear exchange between the Great Powers do not seem to exist today. Britain, France, China, India (which has tested but is not believed to have nuclear weapons), and Israel (which seems not to have tested but is widely believed to have them) do not show the necessary combination of motivation and means. Nor does this conclusion seem likely to change as one considers countries that might acquire nuclear weapons in the next decade, such as Pakistan. Beyond the next decade confidence ebbs. In any case, the main protection will be a well-defended posture and rules of response that allow for crazy acts.

An Exchange Triggered among Other Parties

This leaves the question of an exchange triggered among other pairs of nuclear powers. For instance, if China and the United States were to confront one another, might the Soviet leadership try to play a nuclear catalytic role? Moscow could simulate an attack by either the United States or China. Its leadership might wish destruction on its two principal adversaries. This possibility, however, would hardly escape the attention of the United States and China. Given the stakes involved, each would be exceptionally careful in discriminating among sources of attack. Moscow's recognition of the risk of the plan's misfiring might be sufficient reason to eliminate this possibility.

Other combinations are also unlikely to produce deliberate triggering. Britain, France, and the United States can be ruled out as potential instigators. Among the others—which by 1990 might include the Soviet Union, China, India, Israel, and Pakistan—two pairs of states—Pakistan and India, and the Soviet Union and China—have the greatest potential for entering into crises. The Pakistan-India balance might become especially delicate if one or both have vulnerable forces. No country seems likely to play the triggering role, although remote possibilities might include an Israel sufficiently worried about a Pakistani transfer of weapons to the Arabs or a China sufficiently agitated about India. The difficulty with these cases is that the desired end is so terrible, and the prospect for things going wrong so large, that surely no rational regime would do such a thing. None of these states looks crazy enough.

Beyond 1990 the number of nuclear-weapon-equipped states could grow substantially. The number of combinations of nuclear-armed rivals would grow too. New entrants might include South Africa, Argentina, Brazil, Taiwan, South Korea, and Iran. Some of these states might have leaders willing to use nuclear weapons. Some may come under strong incentives to preempt. But the primary problems posed by such a development flow from the direct impact of the use of nuclear weapons, rather than their setting off a wider exchange.

Nuclear Terrorism

A favorite among novelists is an act of nuclear terrorism. That nuclear weapons might be acquired by non-governmental groups has long been of concern. Although it is unlikely that an individual or even a small group could build a bomb from scratch, the loss of weapons from governmental control seems a less remote possibility. The United States and other nuclear powers not only keep weapons under heavy guard but also design them so that they will be disabled if tampered with by unauthorized people. Probably the greatest longer-run danger under this heading is loss of control over nuclear weapons in politically unstable states. In a recent best-selling novel, *The Fifth Horseman,* the President of the United States receives a message from Qaddafi claiming that a nuclear weapon has been placed somewhere in Manhattan. The weapon will be exploded unless the United States forces Israel to withdraw to its 1967 borders.[3]

Gatherings of leaders for major national ceremonies are times of particular vulnerability: Inauguration Day, or the occasion of the State of the Union Message in Washington, or the May Day parade in Moscow. The "openness" of the United States makes us especially vulnerable. Most of the U.S. government could disappear in an instant. This may seem incredibly remote, but we *are* vulnerable.

Nonetheless, assuming that the precautions noted above have been taken and that the Great Powers have learned to look before leaping with nuclear weapons, the most dangerous aspect of such nuclear terrorism would be its direct impact: the horror and panic from a credible nuclear terrorist threat, and the damage caused if an explosive were detonated. Such action would not likely trigger a nuclear war, given today's conditions. As for stolen nuclear weapons, they would hardly disappear without being missed. In such a case, governments would have even stronger reasons not to launch nuclear forces on the basis of a few nuclear explosions.

In sum, catalytic war may be a long-term danger, but it will be diminished as governments adopt nuclear postures not dependent on warning and rapid response for the survival of their nuclear forces. Moreover, these steps should be taken anyway.

Conditions in Which General Nuclear War Might Be Inadvertently Triggered by a Third Party

A troubling third-party scenario is highlighted earlier in this book. After a general European crisis has led to conventional warfare between NATO and Warsaw Pact forces, first use of nuclear weapons occurs when one of the NATO partners makes a dramatic demonstration attack on four bridges. The purpose of the attack is to force the Soviet Union to believe that continuing the march west will risk general nuclear war. A nuclear exchange between the superpowers follows from a massive Soviet preemptive attack against all theater nuclear forces (French, British, NATO, and even Chinese). The main motivation behind this attack is Soviet fear that as the national nuclear forces move to alert, the probability of accidental or unauthorized launch becomes very large. Since nuclear war thus appears inevitable, the Soviet leadership decides to lead rather than follow.

The key point here is that many players multiply complexity. Wars are marked by confusion and time compression. Although the stakes warrant great care, any crisis involving nuclear powers is not likely to be a model of clarity and deliberateness. If several powers, some nuclear-armed, were caught up in an intense confrontation, a relatively minor event might lead to larger ones. (Meteorologists say that a butterfly's flight may initiate a major weather system.) Such an act might be functionally equivalent to the assassination of the Archduke Ferdinand in 1914.

The focus here is not on technical errors, nor on false reports of attack or unauthorized launching of nuclear-armed missiles or an intent to create a general nuclear conflagration. In contrast to the first situation considered, we no longer need a leader who deliberately tries to set off a nuclear exchange among other states. Rather, for example, a move by North Korea against South Korea might be motivated by the hope that the Soviet Union and/or China would be drawn into the conflict to the North's net benefit. (Something like this may have been behind the 1950 North Korean attack—which probably makes repetition unlikely.) Or a beleaguered Taiwan or Israel might take such action hoping to involve the United States against China or the Soviet Union. History offers various examples of large powers swept along by actions taken in support of small ones. U.S.-China confrontation over the Taiwan Straits occurred before China had nuclear weapons, but in 1973 the U.S.-Soviet set-to over the Arab-Israeli conflict had elements of a nuclear confrontation. A smaller conflict that draws in the Great Powers could escalate into nuclear war. Despite strong incentives to avoid such an end position, step-by-step actions might increase the violence and ultimately lead to the use of nuclear weapons, perhaps on both sides, on a large scale.

The potential danger of such situations is increased if the small powers also have nuclear weapons. Any Arab-Israeli crisis that draws in the United States and the Soviet Union holds the threat, however remote, of Soviet nuclear weapons use against Israel or Israeli use against Soviet forces or—even more remotely—the Soviet homeland.

Fortunately we lack a large data set for analyzing how nuclear weapons might be used in the future. The constraints against their use have held the line for forty years since their first use against Japan. It may be that the least unlikely future use would be (as in 1945) against a neighbor unable to reply in kind—Israel against invading Arabs or, someday, Iraq against a non-nuclear Iran or vice versa. An analogous instance is the use of poison gas by Iraq, Egypt, Vietnam, and the Soviet Union against those unable to retaliate in kind.

This case includes the use by a Great Power against a non-nuclear adversary. Such a possibility received some attention within the U.S. government during the Korean War, the Quemoy-Matsu crisis, and the defense of Dien Bien Phu. There may be Soviet parallels. Inhibitions against such use by the Great Powers are strong, because of the wide distribution of their interests and the heavy political consequences sure to follow. If the stakes are large enough, however, such a step could be given serious consideration and might actually be taken. At some point in the future, moreover, the Soviet leadership might see advantages rather than disadvantages in the use of nuclear weapons: it might reinforce an already formidable reputation for ruthless effectiveness.

Use of nuclear weapons against another nuclear power is obviously a much more problematic matter. Here an important case is preemptive use. Small nuclear powers such as Israel, Pakistan, and India are likely to be in an especially delicate balance of terror. Israel, which struck a putative nuclear explosive material facility in Iraq, would be even more motivated to preempt against a nuclear force. Nor is it farfetched to imagine a first-strike instability between Pakistan and India.

A nuclear response to an attack (possibly non-nuclear) by a much stronger power is the declared policy of France, Britain, and China. The powerful incentives not to carry out such threats, of course, undermine their credibility. Still, if a non-nuclear conflict were to break out in Europe, four powers involved there have the capacity to escalate to the nuclear level. Nuclear use by any one of them could involve all, and escalation to a major exchange would be possible. For instance, an (unlikely) decision by France to use tactical nuclear weapons against advancing Soviet forces in a non-nuclear conflict might induce a preemptive Soviet nuclear strike against not only France but other forces in Europe and even elsewhere. (The stated policy of France is to use these weapons *only* in the defense of French territory, a policy unlikely to evoke such a suicidal Soviet response.) Such small-power-versus-big-power cases have a more worrisome cast if the leadership of the small nuclear power appears "crazy." The threatened use of nuclear weapons by an Ayatollah Khomeini could not simply be brushed aside, even though it probably would be a bluff.

Occasions for a Dangerous State of Great Power Tension

A stipulated condition for catalytic war between the Great Powers is the existence of high tension between them. One can hardly imagine such tension in the abstract—a confrontation has to focus on something, some country or region.

The Arab-Israeli war in 1973 occasioned the most recent serious U.S.-Soviet confrontation. Moscow threatened to send combat troops in support of the trapped Egyptian Third Army; reportedly, it also moved nuclear weapons to the area. The United States apparently put its nuclear forces on a higher state of alert, but in the end, after a hurried trip by Secretary of State Kissinger to Moscow, the Israelis loosened the noose on the Egyptians and the war ended.

This episode illustrates one class of possible triggering events: a regional conflict which sucks in the Great Powers. In this sense small powers are most likely to catalyze a large-power conflict. The Middle East may present the greatest danger of such a conflict, in the form of an Israeli-Syrian conflict or a general conflagration involving several Arab states against Israel. As described in chapter 6, Israel might threaten use of nuclear weapons against the Arabs or actually use them. If the Soviet Union were supporting the Arabs, its forces could become involved as targets or Moscow might be drawn in on behalf of the Arabs to deter the Israeli threat or in response to actual use. Declaratory threats against Israel are, however, more likely than actual engagement against an Israel equipped with nuclear weapons. In any such sequence, there would be great pressure on the United States above all to stop the conflict and also to help Israel. In short, the United States could find itself trying to save Israel, deter Soviet involvement, and limit escalation.

Other conflicts have similar potential to engage the United States and the Soviet Union on opposite sides. The Iran-Iraq war might have done so by now but for Iranian hostility to both Great Powers and the evolution of a Soviet-Iraqi arms relationship.

Perhaps the most worrisome longer-term danger of a Great Power confrontation is an attempted Soviet takeover of a region that the West regards as important but in which its strategic position is weak. The Persian Gulf area is the most likely case in point. The Soviets prefer to extend their influence within divided and weakened countries, rather than to invade. But central authority in Iran might weaken, and a direct Soviet move might occur at some stage. It is more likely to happen if the Soviets continue to have a superior position in the area—that is, with large forces capable of moving into Iran both from the Soviet Union and Afghanistan while the United States has no significant countering presence in or near the area. (There might be similar perceived opportunities in Pakistan.) In this case, the Soviets would have little incentive to use nuclear weapons. Doing so would incur costs without compensating benefits. From its disadvantaged position however, the United States might find posing the threat of nuclear escalation less unattractive.

In some respects the situation would resemble that of Cuba in 1962, but in reverse: the Soviets this time would have local superiority at the non-nuclear level. There would be other differences; today they have a much more powerful nuclear force, both in the Middle East and worldwide, than they did in 1962. Therefore, they might expect us to "blink first" this time; that is, they could expect us to back off in a crisis. But Persian Gulf oil is more important to the United States than Cuba was to the Soviets. So we might not stay out and might not blink. Here are the ingredients for a direct, and conceivably nuclear, crisis. How it would be to our benefit actually to use nuclear weapons in this case, however, given our vulnerabilities in the area, is difficult to see.

Other regions are less volatile. In Europe, the lines are clearly drawn. Although Eastern Europe is politically unstable and experiences periodic upheavals, the Western powers have a clear policy of noninvolvement. Progressive escalation such as led to World War I is unlikely. Perhaps the least unlikely place in Europe for such a process to begin today would be in Yugoslavia, which occupies a gray area.

It should also be noted that Britain and France have been reducing the vulnerability of their nuclear forces by increasing their submarine-based missile forces. Although these forces are not guaranteed to be invulnerable, this step should diminish a potential source of preemptive instability.

East Asia also seems unlikely to produce a catalytic war, broadly defined. Although tension remains high on the Korean peninsula, the demarcation line is clearly drawn there, and none of the supporting outside powers—China, the Soviet Union, or the United States—shows any desire to upset the balance.

Neither in the Caribbean/Latin America nor in Africa is there much likelihood of a serious confrontation. In the first case the stakes are high to the United States (or are so perceived) and low to the Soviets (although some analysts might demur on Cuba). In Africa, they are relatively low for both.

In short, few areas give rise to a Great Power confrontation. Even one candidate is worrisome, however, and the Persian Gulf area is a potential flashpoint.

Could Conditions Change?

Concern about the spread of nuclear weapons goes through cycles. Immediately after 1945 there was a widely shared belief that nuclear technology was so difficult that diffusion would be slow. After the Soviet Union, Britain, and France became nuclear powers, opinion swung to the opposite view. This view overlooked the powerful political inhibitions to other industrial states making bombs. A low-concern phase of the cycle followed, until India tested its nuclear explosive device in 1974 (in the process breaching an agreement with Canada and the spirit of one with the United States). Now attention shifted to developing countries that might be both motivated to acquire nuclear weapons and in time able to make them. Several of these states were so called "pariahs" (Israel, South Africa, Taiwan); others were of dubious political stability (Argentina, South Korea, Iraq, Libya); and many were caught up in conflicts (Israel, the Arab countries, South Korea, Taiwan, South Africa). More recently, concern about this class of states has receded as it has become evident that most of them were not moving vigorously to get nuclear weapons.

This cyclical pattern suggests that we will enter into a new phase of concern in a few years. Several events might trigger new anxiety. One is the Pakistani weapons program, which appears to be moving ahead slowly although it is by no means certain that Pakistan will actually test and/or field weapons. This program was largely a response to the 1974 Indian test and, in turn, it may prompt the Indian government to resume its weapons program.

The prospect of a Pakistan-India nuclear competition is bad enough; even worse is the possibility that Pakistan's weapons technology will be transferred to some Arab states, a worry heightened by the rise of Islamic fundamentalism in Pakistan. Whatever the objective probability of such transfer, Israel showed how sensitive it is to any such threat by its 1981 attack on the Iraqi research reactor. And Israel is not alone in its concern. The wide diffusion of nuclear explosives among Arab states is a development that could radically change estimates of risk in that region and beyond. Despite delays and distractions caused by domestic turbulence, Argentina is moving ahead with efforts to make readily fissionable material. So apparently is South Africa.

Why Was JFK's Prediction Proved Wrong?

The widening gap between the number of states with the technical capability to build nuclear weapons, on the one hand, and the number of nuclear weapon states, on the other, has resulted from a number of factors.

Security guarantees are arguably the most effective nonproliferation policy instruments. The fact that the United States has extended its nuclear umbrella over allies like Germany, Japan, and Korea has greatly reduced their incentive to develop nuclear weapons. While such guarantees are not feasible or credible in all cases—witness South Africa—they have been important in critical cases already mentioned. The Soviet Union, too, has its alliance systems—but with a difference. Coercion rules out non-Soviet nuclear weapons developments within the Soviet empire.

A second strand of policy has been diplomatic leverage—based on U.S. military support—in specific cases. Efforts to persuade countries not to develop nuclear weapons have worked in cases like South Korea and Taiwan. This has often involved both "carrots" of conventional military assistance and "sticks" of threatened withdrawal of support. Yet another strand is the restraint on the supply of sensitive nuclear technologies that could produce weapons-usable materials (highly enriched uranium or plutonium) and thus erode the distance between nuclear energy and nuclear weapons capabilities. The establishment of a Nuclear Suppliers Group that issued a set of guidelines for nuclear commerce in 1978 is an example of U.S. and Soviet cooperation in this area of common interest.

A fourth strand of policy has been the development of an international nonproliferation regime—a set of rules, norms, and institutions under which states have agreed to forgo nuclear weaponry. The presumption has been placed against potential proliferators. That regime includes the Nonproliferation Treaty (signed in 1968) and the International Atomic Energy Agency, a United Nations agency located in Vienna that sends inspectors to civilian nuclear facilities to ascertain that there has been no diversion to military uses.

Another method that should be noted is the Israeli "self-help" form of proliferation control. It is unlikely to be the last instance of governments taking action to avert being faced with nuclear weapons.

Policy actions aside, many governments have come to appreciate that having nuclear weapons incurs risks that are not worth the hoped-for benefits. That is the most encouraging development in an otherwise depressing trend.

At some point, however, it may be necessary to strengthen nonproliferation efforts through actions that include further cooperation among the United States, the Soviet Union, and others. In short, looking beyond 1990, or perhaps beyond 2000, we need to consider a much wider set of possibilities. We have heard this alarm before. We have enjoyed some policy successes. But sometimes the wolf does really appear at the door.

The Scope for Greater U.S.-Soviet Cooperation

There are two kinds of crises in which the governments of the United States and the Soviet Union might seek to avert unwanted consequences: those in which the two parties are directly competing and those in which they are not.

Most of the time we are competing. Examples are the 1962 Cuban crisis and the 1973 Arab-Israeli episode. In the former, the threat of nuclear escalation was explicit, in the latter implicit. In each case, the two parties were in direct communication with each other, maneuvering for advantage in terms of the local stakes. These examples illustrate an important defect in much of the recent discussion about crisis management. There is a tendency to assume that the overriding interest of the parties is to defuse the crisis. Their objectives are usually more complex. Considerations may include the immediate outcome (for example, the removal—or not—of Soviet missiles in Cuba or the survival of the trapped Egyptian army); the longer-term regional stakes (for example, the preservation of Castro's power and his ties to the Soviet Union); the possibility of Great Power conflict and escalation to nuclear war; and the impact on the overall balance of power, what the Soviets call the "correlation of forces." The balancing of these factors continually shifts during a crisis. "Crisis management" means more than avoiding nuclear weapons use. But that goal would certainly be given progressively more weight as a crisis intensified.

Some have suggested that joint crisis centers might help defuse such threatening situations. Such centers might be created by various combinations of countries, not only the United States and Soviet Union. Hopes should be modest. One should not expect such centers to be more than communications centers, with governments' assessments and decisions taking place elsewhere. That said, there may be value in designating places into which information can be fed to facilitate substantive negotiations. That judgment seems applicable to the joint U.S.-Soviet crisis center proposed by Senators Nunn and Warner.

The problems of competing interests are less serious in crises in which the two Great Powers are not centrally involved—although there is an element of competition between them practically everywhere in the world. In such situations a crisis center might be able to accomplish more than if the two superpowers were direct adversaries. It is doubtful that general guidelines or mechanisms for handling third-party contingencies can be drawn up in advance. If the spread of nuclear weapons continues, however, the United States and the Soviet Union will have a substantial common interest in keeping third-party crises and exchanges from spilling over, involving both superpowers, and escalating to nuclear war.

Steps to Reduce the Dangers

Experience shows that states with nuclear weapons behave cautiously toward one another. This record supports a prediction that as more states acquire nuclear weapons, the probability of their getting involved in conflicts will go down. However, this factor is not decisive, as the Cuban missile crisis, Sino-Soviet border clashes, and the 1973 U.S.-Soviet confrontation in the Middle East illustrate.

Beyond exercising greater caution in international involvements, the following steps should be pursued by the United States and others:

- Have well-protected nuclear forces minimally dependent on warning for survival, and strong command and control and intelligence systems. This entails mobile nuclear forces and multiple, protected command centers with a well-defined, constitutional system for the devolution of authority if top leaders are lost.
- Rely as much as possible on non-nuclear forces so as to avoid the direct use of nuclear threats at all.
- Reduce incentives for non-nuclear states to get nuclear explosives and make it technically and politically more difficult for them to do so. This means both trying to help with their perceived security needs, so that nuclear weapons will seem less necessary, and adopting measures that make it harder and politically more costly for them to acquire these weapons.
- Strengthen crisis consultation mechanisms, such as the Hot Line, and create joint crisis centers to make it easier to reduce errors if third parties cause or intervene in a crisis.
- Encourage the use of locks and disabling devices on nuclear weapons and incorporate in governmental standard operating procedures explicit provision for considering deceptive nuclear attacks by third parties, including terrorists. This entails having rules of response keyed to such possibilities.
- Do more to assess the means by which countries might acquire nuclear explosive materials, the incentives for doing so, and how to influence them.

Most of these actions make sense for many reasons; among others, they will help to make catalytic war an even more remote possibility than it is today.

III. Conclusions

7 SOVIET PERSPECTIVES ON THE PATHS TO NUCLEAR WAR

by Stephen M. Meyer

THE PROBLEM of avoiding nuclear war—specifically a U.S.-Soviet nuclear war—has been a principal concern of all American administrations since the beginning of the nuclear age. Soviet leaders have been similarly preoccupied, and for good reason. From 1945 to 1965, only the Soviet Union faced virtual annihilation in the wake of a U.S.-Soviet nuclear conflict. Not until the mid-1960s did Soviet nuclear forces pose a significant and reliable threat to the U.S. homeland.

Unfortunately, though both countries recognize that they must avoid nuclear war, they are far from agreeing on the nature of the problem, or its solution. Each side has other competing priorities. In the Cuban missile crisis, for example, the U.S. leadership saw the only likely avenue for avoiding nuclear war as a (forced) Soviet withdrawal of its missiles from Cuba. Fortunately, the Soviet leaders saw it the same way. Next time, it need not be so.

After confrontation, participants may retain different images of what occurred and may draw different lessons to guide future behavior. In the 1967 Middle East war, diplomatic communication from Moscow to Washington hinted at Soviet military intervention unless the United States restrained the Israelis. The United States put some of its military forces on alert. The Soviets did not intervene; Israeli advances halted as a cease-fire went into effect. In the 1973 Middle East war an identical sequence of events occurred: a Soviet threat to intervene militarily, followed by an American military alert, followed by an end to Israeli advances. What are the lessons to be drawn? The United States may conclude that placing U.S. military forces on alert in response to Soviet threats to intervene in regional conflicts deters Soviet military actions. The Soviet Union may conclude that threatening to employ its military forces in support of allies produces both the standard ("canned") U.S. military alert and, more significantly, coerces the United States into favorable political action. Whose interpretation is correct? The answer depends on one's perspective.

This chapter explores some aspects of the Soviet perspective on the paths to U.S.-Soviet nuclear war. Which paths are perceived as most likely to lead to nuclear war? What are the Soviet leadership's proclivities toward escalation or limitation in conflicts? How have Soviet military forces been structured in relation to these paths, and what responses have been planned?

SOURCES AND METHODS

Students of American decision-making—working with archives, memoirs, government hearings, insider leaks, a continuous circulation of people in and out of the government, and a myriad of interview opportunities—are cursed with conflicting sources. How does one extract signal from the noise? Students of contemporary Soviet decision-making suffer the reverse curse: no documents, almost no relevant memoir materials, no transcripts of government hearings, no leaks, no rotation of officials into accessible private careers, and few interviews. The problem here is first to detect noise, then hope for signal.

The difficulties in studying "Soviet views" on the paths to nuclear war are particularly acute. Who are the relevant Soviets? Who speaks authoritatively? That is, who is involved in high-level governmental decision-making or has access to it? Obviously, we are interested in the members of the Politburo, clusters within the Secretariat of the Central Committee of the Communist Party, the leadership within the Ministry of Defense and the KGB, and the Foreign Ministry. Unfortunately, while many people from these institutions articulate their views in articles, interviews, and speeches, the lack of alternative access makes it close to impossible to separate perspective from propaganda.

Let me begin, then, by noting some sources *not* used in this chapter. First in this category are official Soviet pronouncements on military doctrine and policy. Soviet military doctrine has both sociopolitical and military-technical aspects.[1] Most official statements by party and government leaders address the socio-political aspect of military doctrine, which serves simultaneously as an ideological guide and a justification for state policy. Playing an internal and external propaganda role, it offers us little insight into the concrete aspects of likely Soviet crisis behavior. Brezhnev's pledge that the Soviet Union will not be the first to use nuclear weapons does not rule out Soviet preemptive nuclear attacks against American or NATO nuclear forces. Nor does the fact that Soviet military doctrine is "purely defensive in its orientation" preclude unprovoked Soviet invasions of other countries: Czechoslovakia and Afghanistan, for example. It is a matter of political concept.

A second source not used is the work of Soviet academics. In the areas under analysis here, these writers have little information beyond that published daily in Western newspapers, journals, and books (which are the "classified" sources to which they have access). Moreover, as academics of the state, it is explicitly their job to justify state policy, to place it in the proper—that is, best—political and ideological light.

This chapter's sources include Soviet military planning literature (including work on the military-technical aspect of doctrine), Soviet military historical analyses, Soviet diplomatic behavior, Soviet military force structure and deployment data, and memoir material. While few of these sources speak directly to the issue of paths to nuclear war, all are affected by implicit and explicit assumptions about such paths. For example, the operational aspects of Soviet military doctrine are reflected in military-technical discussions, and more concretely in the Soviet force posture. Changes over time in the military-technical aspect of Soviet military doctrine and in force posture provide even better clues to leadership perspectives. Thus, the method of this chapter assumes that we can learn more about Soviet perspectives on the paths to nuclear war by studying implicit traces and effects than by trying to decipher "statements of policy."

Surprise Strategic Attack: The Bolt from the Blue

No other path to nuclear war has received as much open attention in the Soviet media as the threat of a surprise strategic nuclear attack by the United States. Such discussions are intended primarily to serve as propaganda, but they are built also on a genuine underlying concern. To be sure, Soviet concern over an American "bolt from the blue" is rooted in Soviet postwar military policy.[2] The devastating surprise attack by Nazi Germany on the Soviet Union in 1941 deeply affected Soviet psychology. Stalin's seeming equanimity toward the American nuclear monopoly at the end of the war masked his true concern, which was more accurately reflected in the priority he gave to developing fission and fusion weapons and long-range missiles.[3] The fundamental problem for the Soviet Union during the first two decades of the nuclear age was to develop a significant intercontinental nuclear-strike capability, one that could neutralize the political and military potential of America's strategic nuclear forces.

THE CONCEPT

Soviet military doctrine of the 1950s and early 1960s held that war between the superpowers was expected to begin with devasting nuclear blows against the two homelands, delivered by intercontinental and regional systems. Simultaneously, or in quick succession, theater nuclear forces would rain down on targets in contested regions. The most obvious theaters were Europe and the Far East (when the Soviet Union and China were still allies). Finally, as nuclear stocks were exhausted, conventional forces would move in to seize territory and secure any economic-industrial booty that might have survived. The most likely way that such a war might start would be the U.S. bolt-from-the-blue strategic attack.

To the Soviet leadership the bolt-from-the-blue strategic attack is the pure form of strategic surprise *(strategicheskaya vnezapnost')*. As explained in the authoritative *Sovetskaya Voyennaya Entsiklopedia (Soviet Military Encyclopedia)*:

. . . Strategic surprise may be achieved at the beginning of war (utilizing the unpreparedness of the opponent for war, preempting him at the beginning of military activities).[4]

Little or no political or military warning can be expected. The attacker employs surprise in the hope of catching the target country totally unprepared, thus being able to inflict the greatest possible damage to its military forces and economic-industrial capabilities. Again, the Nazi attack of 1941 serves as the model.[5]

Throughout the 1950s Soviet leaders watched as tens, then hundreds, of American "strategic" delivery systems were deployed around the Soviet periphery. First bombers, then ground-launched cruise missiles, then ballistic missiles were poised in Europe, North Africa, the Near East (Turkey), Japan, and the Pacific. While the Soviets may not have known the precise details of U.S. strategic targeting, their intelligence networks in the United States and in NATO Europe gave them a clear picture of SAC emphasis on preemption in targeting priorities and execution plans. Soviet interpretation of SAC planning held that the first aim was to catch Soviet military forces in a low state of readiness and thus carry out an effective disarming first strike (*vide* the Nazis in 1941). Once this was accomplished, American nuclear forces were expected to turn to attacks on the Soviet economic-industrial base.[6]

This path to nuclear war served as the central doctrinal planning contingency for the Soviet military during the 1950s and through the mid-1960s. The bolt from the blue remains an important contingency. Today, however, the Soviets no longer see it as the most probable path to nuclear war. The paths that took its place, and the reasons for the change, are examined later in this chapter.

CAUSES

What, in the Soviet view, would cause an American bolt from the blue? Here one must turn to the intersection where Soviet interpretation of Marxist-Leninist theory meets Soviet military doctrine.[7] Soviet military historians distinguish deep causes from immediate causes.[8] Deep causes are always socio-political and economic—such as enduring financial crises, asymmetric rates of economic development, and revolutionary tendencies among the masses. From this perspective,

Marxist-Leninist interpretations of history point to an irreversible decline of the American or West German economies, the impending breakup of NATO, or American fear of an "irreversible" shift in the correlation of forces (political, military, and/or economic) as examples of deep causes of an American bolt from the blue. The United States would be forced to take military action against the socialist states before the correlation of economic, political, and military forces shifted beyond reversal. Thus, America would choose to start the decisive conflict between the world's two opposing social systems— the socialist community and the capitalist community.[9]

Immediate causes may be spontaneous and unforeseen events. The triggering event might be anything—a conflict in the Third World, a Dutch decision to withdraw from NATO, or the ideological and nationalist fervor of an American "Hitler."

Once should not place too much emphasis on ideological inputs into Soviet policy. But when one talks about *views* of ways in which nuclear war might begin through rational politico-military decision-making, political and social ideology have a strong influence. In this respect, Soviet leaders have always assumed that the United States was intent upon containing Russia, if not ultimately destroying it. The evidence goes back to the landing of Americans in the Soviet Far East in 1918 and continues to the present. Those schooled throughout their lives in Marxist-Leninist political and historical analysis would find their suspicions chillingly confirmed by such incidents as Mr. Reagan's joke about outlawing the Soviet Union, "with bombing to commence in five minutes."

ESCALATION, LIMITATION, TERMINATION, AND RESPONSE

Soviet leaders have been reluctant to acknowledge the possibility of observing limits in nuclear war if the Soviet homeland is attacked. To a large degree, this stance is part of the Soviet deterrent posture. Given the minimal Soviet intercontinental nuclear capability of the 1950s and early 1960s, they had to threaten unlimited attacks on the U.S. homeland in response to any kind of U.S. attack on the Soviet Union. They had no other options for a credible deterrent posture. (The French have adopted a similar nuclear strategy vis-à-vis the Soviet Union.)

But long after acquiring the technical means for measured nuclear response, Soviet political and military leaders continue to reject the idea of limitation in strategic nuclear war—i.e., war involving the Soviet homeland. They expect that a bolt from the blue would begin with strikes against military targets, followed immediately by attacks on economic-industrial facilities (so-called war-making potential). Therefore, *what might be intended as an American (or NATO) limited nuclear counterforce attack* against the Soviet homeland *would look exactly like the Soviet model of the first phase of an unlimited strategic attack.* If a bolt from the blue fell, one large enough to rule out the possibility of an unintentional launch, Soviet leaders would have every reason not to wait to determine the true scope and magnitude of the attack.

Two technical factors reinforce this Soviet reluctance. First, most Soviet strategic military bases and forces (for example, ICBM and bomber bases) are located in the most populous areas of the USSR. Extensive collateral damage to cities and industry—direct and indirect—is considered inevitable. Second, the Soviet leadership would not have information to enable it quickly to differentiate a "limited" surprise attack from an unlimited one. Even a limited attack would involve thousands of warheads. Many of these would destroy Soviet regional command, control, and communications. And if the attack were a true bolt from the blue, then a good fraction of the Soviet command and control system would probably never become operational. Furthermore, because of the geographic spread of Soviet ICBM fields, it would be impossible to distinguish the trajectories of U.S. warheads targeted only on Soviet ICBMs from those targeted more broadly against economic-industrial centers.[10] Thus, unless the Soviet leadership is willing to wait hours or days to determine the true characteristics of the attack before deciding how to respond, then they must assume that any such attack is an "unlimited" one.

The Soviet military prescription for response to an American bolt-from-the-blue attack is full strategic retaliation with day-to-day alert forces against the U.S. homeland.[11] To accomplish this mission, it appears that by the mid-1960s the Soviet military put into effect a strategy of launch-on-tactical-warning/launch-under-attack (LOTW/ LUA) for some of its day-to-day alert forces—that is, its ICBMs.[12] LOTW/LUA was not intended to be the core of the Soviet approach to nuclear force posture planning, but rather a special case that demanded individual attention.

A deterrent strategy, LOTW/LUA guaranteed retaliation against the United States when no Soviet nuclear forces could dependably survive an American bolt from the blue. If Soviet strategic weapons were not fired before American nuclear weapons exploded, very few if any would have been left for a retaliatory strike. Beginning in the 1970s, however, improvements in the Soviets' strategic posture ensured that a very large portion of their nuclear force would ride out any American attack. The Soviets could thus count on retaliating with a second strike. In retaliatory second strike, Soviet military writings call for attacks on America's military-economic facilities, political-administrative centers, and economic-industrial infrastructure (including electrical power and transportation), as well as military targets. Soviet strategists believe their ability to destroy 45 to 50 percent of the U.S. population and 65 to 75 percent of the U.S. industrial base is an adequate retaliatory capability.[13] Even so, LOTW/LUA remains an active option in Soviet worst-case nuclear planning.

Soviet military writings and exercises suggest that the only way war can be ended is by the decisive defeat of the enemy following multiple salvos of thousands of nuclear warheads. The total defeat of Nazi Germany is the example.

ASPECTS OF THE SOVIET STRATEGIC POSTURE

Given professed Soviet fears of a U.S. bolt from the blue, the 1950s must have seemed a particularly grim time. The American strategic nuclear force grew rapidly along all dimensions: warheads, delivery vehicles, and megatonnage. Although the Soviet Union's strategic force grew as well, there was one critical difference: it did not have a reliable delivery capability against the U.S. homeland that would survive a U.S. surprise attack.[14] Instead, Soviet nuclear deployment programs concentrated on blunting U.S. nuclear delivery capabilities based in theaters around the Soviet periphery— which, in fact, constituted the bulk of U.S. strategic forces.[15] A fundamental asymmetry remained: the U.S. could threaten annihilation of Soviet armed forces and Soviet society, while the Soviet Union could only try to limit damage by striking regionally based American forces, threatening to destroy most of Western Europe in the process.

Curiously, although surprise attack played such a crucial role in Soviet military doctrine during this period, the Soviet strategic force posture did not reflect that concern. No Soviet bombers were ever placed on ready alert—either in the air or on the ground.[16] Their nuclear bombs were stored in depots guarded by KGB troops. The nuclear warheads for Soviet ICBMs, medium-range ballistic missiles (MRBMs), and other missiles were kept in special storage facilities (also guarded by the KGB). Some were even located as far as fifty miles from missile launch areas.[17] In many cases U.S. bombers based in Europe and North Africa could have reached Soviet territory before Soviet warheads were moved to missile sites and readied for launch.

This was hardly a posture consistent with fear of a bolt-from-the-blue strategic attack. A few partial explanations for this peculiar inconsistency can be offered. First: the Soviet leadership, may have felt that the probability of such an attack was quite low. After all, the United States failed to use nuclear weapons against China during the Korean War, despite its doctrine of massive retaliation. Second: Soviet leaders may have felt that the Soviet conventional and nuclear threat to Europe also served as a surrogate hostage deterrent against an American attack. Third: the Soviet political leadership may have been more afraid of nuclear weapons in the hands of its own military than in the hands of the American military. Historically Soviet civil-military relations have been very uneven. The Soviet political leadership has always feared "Bonapartism"—military leaders usurping political power. Fourth: the state of Soviet weapons technology may have been such that the potential for accidents or other mishaps made it dangerous to mate nuclear warheads and bombs with delivery vehicles unless war was imminent. The limited hard evidence available suggests that all of these help to explain the discrepancy between Soviet military doctrine and Soviet nuclear force posture during this period.[18]

The Soviets did make one immediate response to the surprise-attack contingency. They adopted a policy of strategic deception.[19] The bomber gap of the 1950s and the missile gap of the early 1960s are familiar American intelligence "failures." In the former case, intelligence estimates suggested that the Soviet Union could field a strategic bomber force quantitatively superior to that of the United States by the late 1950s. In the latter case, intelligence estimates projected a quantitatively superior Soviet ICBM force by the mid-1960s. Both estimates turned out to be grossly in error: the United States held clear nuclear superiority into the late 1960s. Not generally recognized, however, were deliberate Soviet efforts to magnify those false impressions. The Soviet air force knew that it was creating the illusion of a massive Soviet strategic bomber delivery capability when, at a 1955 air show, it repeatedly circled the same strategic bomber squadron over crowds seeded with Western military observers. Likewise, Khrushchev wanted the West to believe that the Soviet Union was mass-producing ICBMs in the late 1950s, when the actual rate was closer to a half dozen per year. He deliberately set about creating that impression in his speeches and interviews. These strategic Potemkin villages were designed to convince the United States that it could no longer threaten the Soviet homeland with virtual impunity.

Meanwhile, Khrushchev had begun laying the groundwork for a credible Soviet strategic nuclear force posture. Nuclear armed missiles were to become the bulwark of the Soviet armed forces. He tried to impose significant resource cuts in procurement, operations, and maintenance for the conventional ground forces, tactical air forces, and navy. In most instances he succeeded.

The task of coping with the surprise strategic attack contingency was assigned to the ICBM force of the newly created (December 1959) Strategic Rocket Forces.[20] The Soviet bluff was to be replaced by the Soviet land-based intercontinental missile. Soviet interest in a LOTW/LUA strategy was reflected in the decision to procure missiles produced by the Yangel design bureau rather than those produced by the Korolyov design bureau. The critical difference between the two competing designs was that the former could be launched on very short notice, while the latter could not.[21] Within several years after the Cuban missile crisis, nuclear warheads were placed on day-to-day alert strategic missiles. Owing to limitations of Soviet technology and the particular shortcomings of their second- and third-generation liquid-fueled missiles, only a small fraction of ICBMs could be kept on day-to-day alert. But these were sufficient to fulfill the LOTW/LUA mission of assured retaliation.[22] The low reliability, poor accuracy and comparatively small quantity of these "ready" ICBMs imply that Soviet launch-on-tactical-warning systems would have been most usefully targeted against American urban-industrial areas.

By the late 1960s these investments paid off. As Marshal Krylov, Chief of the Strategic Rocket Forces, observed in an article in the restricted journal *Military Thought:*

... With the presence in the armament of troops of launchers and missiles which are completely ready for operation, as well as systems for detecting enemy missile launches and other types of reconnaissance, an aggressor is no longer able to suddenly destroy missiles before they leave their launchers in the territory of the country against which the aggression is committed. They will have time during the flight of the missiles of the aggressor to leave their launchers and inflict a retaliatory strike against the enemy. Even in the most unfavorable circumstances, if a portion of the missiles is unable to be launched before the strike of missiles of the aggressor, as a result of the high degree of protection of the launchers from nuclear explosions, these missiles will carry out combat missions entrusted to them . . .[23]

The combination of long-range radar and silo-based ICBMs enabled the Soviets to mount a credible *retaliatory threat* to the U.S. homeland in the event of a U.S. surprise first strike.[24]

The 1970s saw further development of the Soviet ICBM force, especially in terms of its reliability, technical characteristics, and survivability (through hardening of silos and canisterizing). The percentage of ICBMs on day-to-day alert grew rapidly as fourth-generation missiles were deployed. Soviet missions and targeting options grew in parallel with the evolving capabilities of the ICBM force.[25] Today, the Strategic Rocket Forces continue to bear the burden of coping with the threat of surprise strategic attack, guaranteeing Soviet retaliation with the option of LOTW/LUA or a second strike.

In contrast, other elements of the Soviet strategic posture do not reflect states of readiness consistent with a perceived threat of surprise strategic attack. No Soviet strategic bombers are on alert. Soviet ballistic missile submarines (SSBNs) have maintained low on-station rates (in comparison to the U.S. norm). Thus, only a comparatively small fraction of Soviet SLBMs are available at any given time for second-strike retaliation under surprise attack conditions.[26] The Soviet civil defense system requires at least a week's preliminary effort to protect Soviet industrial assets effectively.[27] Mobilizing the bulk of Soviet non-nuclear forces requires weeks of preparation. Despite popular impressions, most of the Soviet military machine is not geared up to go to war at a moment's notice. This is where other possible paths to nuclear war are reflected in Soviet military doctrine.

Anticipated Strategic Attack and Preemption

By the late 1960s the threat of an American bolt-from-the-blue attack had ceased to be the driving force behind Soviet doctrinal guidance. While still an important and ever-present element in Soviet military planning, it was no longer the yardstick against which overall Soviet force posture was evaluated. This change was largely the result of successful Soviet military-technical developments implemented to cope with the bolt from the blue. Today, it appears that the broad sweep of Soviet force planning is guided by the belief that a nuclear war between the United States and the Soviet Union would most likely occur in the context of some crisis or conflict rather than arise spontaneously. That is to say, the Soviet leadership could expect strategic warning of an impending American nuclear attack. Here we are really talking about two paths. The first path, with nuclear war arising directly from crises and confrontations, is termed the "anticipated" strategic attack. The second, involving escalation from conventional conflict, is considered separately in the next section.

The Berlin crises and the Cuban missile crisis, for example, offered strategic warning of the possibility of nuclear war. Political, diplomatic, and military activities provided early signals of a possible clash. The value of strategic warning is that it allows one to move military forces from a day-to-day alert posture to a generated alert posture, substantially increasing strategic nuclear capabilities (especially with respect to strategic defenses). The Soviet force posture and deterrent posture—active defense and civil defense in particular—are far more formidable under generated alert conditions.

Today, the anticipated strategic attack is one of the primary doctrinal contingencies in Soviet force posture planning.

THE CONCEPT

The view of the Soviet political leadership, as articulated by the late Leonid Brezhnev, is that the social, economic, and political struggle between the two social systems—communism and capitalism—must continue even when diplomatic relations are good. Political confrontations are inevitable as the global correlation of forces shifts in favor of progressive movements supported by the socialist community. Often political confrontations can be resolved through diplomacy, but there is always a possibility that the capitalist countries will lash out militarily in a desperate effort to halt the further shifting of the political correlation of forces. Hence the potential for military confrontation and war—including nuclear war—always exists.

In the context of an anticipated strategic attack, the Soviet military envisions an American nuclear attack targeted against the full array of objectives: Soviet strategic and theater nuclear forces, command and control, general purpose forces, economic-industrial capabilities, and political-administrative centers. To launch so comprehensive an attack, some mobilization and alert actions are expected to be necessary. Indeed, such actions on the part of the adversary are probably among the major indicators of strategic warning for the Soviet leaders.[28]

The Soviet political leadership is responsible for interpreting strategic warning indicators, subsequently alerting the Soviet military establishment to the possibility of impending nuclear war, and making the decision to move the armed forces to higher levels of readiness.[29] Should the political leadership fail—as it did in 1941—then this kind of attack might be more devastating than the bolt from the blue, for the attacker would have used the crisis period to mobilize its forces (including command and control, reconnaissance, and targeting means).[30] But assuming vigilant political leaders, the most an enemy could hope to accomplish would be a first-strike attack against Soviet military forces on generated alert.

ESCALATION, LIMITATION, RESPONSE, AND TERMINATION

Notions about escalation and limitation are precisely the same as those pertaining to the bolt from the blue. Quite different, however, is the issue of response.

The whole purpose of anticipating the strategic attack is to be able to blunt its effects by combining preemptive strikes with active and passive defense measures.[31] *Preemption and defense together represent the Soviet military's preferred strategy under the anticipated strategic attack scenario.* It is a strategy of damage limitation. Anticipation is central to Soviet abilities to limit damage to the homeland in a nuclear war. The initial Soviet preemptive strike, using generated alert forces, would try to destroy enemy nuclear capabilities before they could be used against the Soviet Union. Weapons installations, military bases, command and control facilities, and relevant military-industrial areas would all be part of the primary target array. From the perspective of the socio-political aspect of Soviet military doctrine, a Soviet anticipatory preemptive strike is not considered the launching of a preventive first strike, or even first use of nuclear weapons. The enemy's assumed decision to launch its nuclear forces, and the detected activities that would prompt Soviet anticipation of that decision, are tantamount to the first use of nuclear weapons.[32] Telltale preparatory actions by the enemy might include communication of release authority, dispersal of mobile nuclear forces, full strategic force generated alert, and so on.

Following a Soviet preemptive strike, Soviet strategic defenses—active and passive—would attempt to limit damage further by reducing the effectiveness of surviving enemy nuclear attack forces. Air defense and ballistic missile defense systems would be used against surviving enemy nuclear forces as they attacked Soviet territory. The civil defense system would then be expected to absorb whatever shock was produced by enemy nuclear warheads and bombs that penetrated the active defense shield.

The Soviet military may plan for preemption under this contingency, but their planning does not depend on it. Consider a major crisis where both sides put their nuclear forces on generated alert. If Soviet decision-makers felt preemption would not produce results significantly greater than launching on tactical warning, other considerations might weigh in against it.[33] This would be especially true if strategic warning was ambiguous. Preemption and LOTW strategies converge here largely because both American and Soviet forces would be on generated alert, with enhanced offensive and defensive capabilities.

RELATIONSHIP TO FORCE STRUCTURE

The evidence for a central role for anticipation and preemption in Soviet strategic planning can be found in the evolution of their nuclear force posture over the past twenty-five years. If one examines the changes in the actual mix of Soviet strategic forces that have been bought and compares those mixes with alternative "equal cost" force mixes, the results point consistently to decisions to purchase a force mix that maximizes preemptive capabilities, within the limits of economic and technical constraints and strategic arms accords. The most visible Soviet effort to create a preemption option is concentrated in their ICBM force, where targeting of American ICBM silos, strategic bomber bases, and command and control are emphasized. Theoretically, the Soviet Union could destroy about 90 per cent of the U.S. ICBM force if the United States did not launch on warning. Soviet preemptive capabilities against U.S. SSBNs, however, are negligible.[34] Ironically, these same Soviet force mixes tend also to maximize American preemptive capabilities. Thus, the Soviet military must assume that, all else being equal, it will be able to anticipate an American nuclear attack and beat the Americans in the draw.

As noted, the peacetime readiness of major elements of the Soviet nuclear force posture is tied explicitly to the doctrinal assumption of anticipation (strategic warning). Today, with the notable exception of the ICBM force, Soviet strategic offensive nuclear forces, theater nuclear forces, strategic defense forces, civil defense, and command, control, and communications (C^3) networks are kept in peacetime readiness states significantly below their full (wartime) potential. Indeed, the relentless calls in the Soviet military press for increasing the combat readiness of the armed forces refer to shortening the time required to move from peacetime readiness states to full wartime potential.

With the current generation of Soviet ICBMs the difference between day-to-day and generated-alert levels is likely to be minimal. However, the number of ready submarine-launched ballistic missiles (SLBMs) could be increased by a factor of three or more with strategic warning.[35] Some one hundred intercontinental bombers could be loaded with nuclear weapons and dispersed to Arctic bases or put on air alert. Theater nuclear forces, including SS-20 IRBMs, require special preparation before they are battle ready. Air defense radars, missile batteries, and command posts could be brought up to full working status. Interceptor crews could be put on alert, increasing air interception capabilities significantly. For example, two of three Soviet air defense tracking radars in the Kamchatka Peninsula region were not operating during the Korean airliner incident of 1983. The vast Soviet C^3 structure could be brought up to full readiness, including alternate strategic command posts. Finally, the civil defense system could be mobilized.

Some of these activities would take hours (for example, SS-20 dispersion and launch readiness, intercontinental bomber dispersion, C^3 mobilization, and air defense mobilization); others require days (for example, surging SLBM forces to full readiness). And some, such as civil defense, would need a week or more to be effective. Without exception, that is, all these strategic force mobilization activities— moving from day-to-day readiness states to generated alert—require more time than the tactical warning assumed in the bolt-from-the-blue contingency. They require strategic warning. In short, *the Soviet strategic capability for damage limitation—to preempt, defend, and "survive"—depends on strategic warning if it is ever to be marginally effective.*

Escalation from Conventional War

Escalation from conventional war is the second fundamental contingency considered in Soviet force posture planning today. Evidence of this contingency appeared first in Soviet military writings of the early 1960s. Corroborating evidence soon appeared in Soviet military exercises.[36] Escalation from conventional war has been the most intensely exercised contingency in Soviet and Warsaw Pact exercises since the late 1960s.

THE CONCEPT

Soviet military doctrine of the 1950s and early 1960s posited that any war between the two superpowers would begin with intercontinental nuclear warfare. Slowly, changes in military technology, Soviet military thinking, and NATO military planning produced changes in Soviet military doctrine.[37] During the 1960s a new contingency was cautiously presented: war between the two opposing social systems might begin with conventional operations and then escalate to nuclear strikes.

Initially, the Soviets claimed that escalation to global nuclear war was inevitable. Conventional conflict between the two superpowers and their allies was seen as merely an initial phase of what was to be nuclear war. However, "inevitable" soon gave way to "most likely," and then "probable." By the mid-1970s Soviet military doctrine held out the possibility that wars might even be fought with conventional weapons only. Yet the odds were still great that conventional war would escalate to nuclear war.

In many ways this escalation contingency is a subcase of the anticipated strategic attack contingency. The assumption is that a crisis of some sort leads to an East-West military confrontation, which leads to large-scale conventional warfare in Europe. This conventional war might last for a brief period before nuclear attacks begin, or it might last for quite a while (on the order of months). In either case the conventional phase would provide critical strategic warning time.

Massed conventional air operations and conventionally armed missile strikes would begin the war, as the two sides attempted to destroy each other's military forces, bases, logistics and supply facilities, and command and control capabilities. These conventional air and missile strikes would reach deep into the territories of the warring sides in the theater. Meanwhile, massive artillery barrages would open the ground campaign, in which tens of thousands of tanks and armored vehicles would be engaged. Soviet military planning stresses that the most important mission for all Soviet general purpose forces (and possibly chemical forces) during this conventional phase would be to destroy NATO nuclear forces in the theater. Presumably, this includes conventional air strikes, chemical attacks, and special operations missions against British and French forces.

The Soviet military pictures escalation to nuclear use beginning either with theater forces first (as NATO doctrine prefers to envision it), or with simultaneous theater and intercontinental nuclear strikes.

Though the scenarios vary, the sequence of steps is essentially the same: someone decides to "go nuclear" after a fierce conventional conflict has begun.

ESCALATION, LIMITATION, AND TERMINATION

Although Soviet military thinking has gradually moved away from the notion that a conventional war must inevitably escalate to global nuclear war, *all Soviet general purpose forces are admonished to be prepared to fight in a nuclear environment at any time.* Escalation could occur at any point in the conflict. One of the more obvious turning points would be the disintegration of NATO's conventional defense. As a point of reference, Soviet military historians note that Hitler turned to his new weapons (the V-1 and the V-2 rockets) when German forces began to lose the conventional campaign.[38]

The escalation pattern that most dominates contemporary Soviet military planning pictures conventional war escalating directly to full-scale "strategic" theater nuclear conflict.[39] That is, the first Soviet theater nuclear forces employed are likely to be the SS-20 IRBMs and the BACKFIRE bombers. SS-N-6 SLBMs might also be used. Operational-tactical weapons (SS-22 and SS-23 missiles and Su-24 fighter-bombers) and tactical nuclear systems (SS-21 missiles, nuclear artillery, and MIG-23/27 aircraft) would be used nearly simultaneously. Thus, in the theater Soviet escalation jumps up to strategic theater nuclear warfare, then down to tactical (battlefield) nuclear use.[40] At this point, the war could escalate to intercontinental nuclear use. Alternatively, depending on the circumstances, intercontinental nuclear strikes might commence simultaneously with strategic nuclear warfare in the theater.

Anticipation of an enemy's intention to use nuclear weapons is a fundamental aspect of Soviet thinking about escalation from conventional war. Nuclear preemption of NATO's theater nuclear forces would be the Soviet response. NATO and American command and control activities related to transmitting release authority to nuclear forces in the theater, and the physical dispersion of those forces, are likely to figure prominently in strategic warning assessments. Given their emphasis on timely preemption, it is unlikely that the Soviet military would wait to determine whether NATO's initial nuclear strikes were intended to be demonstrative in nature, or merely were phased for greater effectiveness. Any form of NATO nuclear use is likely to unleash a full Soviet strategic theater nuclear strike, since current Soviet military thinking is to meet NATO's first nuclear use with a Soviet first *decisive* nuclear use.

Do the Soviets believe in limited theater nuclear warfare? Perhaps no other question is asked so frequently. If by limited theater nuclear warfare one means *differentiation among targets within a theater,* the answer is clearly yes. In particular, Soviet military writings talk about the desirability of sparing enemy economic-industrial facilities in the theater that might contribute to rebuilding the Soviet economy.[41]

If by limited theater nuclear war one means *homeland sanctuaries,* the answer is again yes. That is to say, Soviet military doctrine does recognize the possibility that nuclear weapons could be used in theater warfare without escalating to global nuclear war if the Soviet homeland is not attacked. Soviet ICBM and intermediate-range ballistic missile (IRBM) forces are organized into separate batteries and regiments. Similarly, Soviet strategic and theater bombers are organized into separate squadrons. Thus Soviet theater nuclear systems can be fired without launching intercontinental systems, so that the military leadership can observe a homeland sanctuary limit if it is instructed to do so. But is there any evidence that the Soviet political leaders are so inclined? Former Secretary of State Henry Kissinger reports in his memoirs that during the spring of 1972 Soviet General Secretary Leonid Brezhnev proposed a treaty in which the two sides would pledge not to use nuclear weapons against each other's homelands even if their forces were engaged in war elsewhere in the world, and even if they were using nuclear weapons against each other's allies. Kissinger reports querying Anatoly Dobrynin, Soviet ambassador to the United States, about the precise nature of the sanctuary limits proposed. Kissinger reports:

. . . To my amazement, a written Soviet reply was received on September 7, 1972, articulating their purposes unabashedly. The answer to my three questions was as follows: The proposed agreement did not preclude the use of nuclear weapons in a war involving NATO and the Warsaw Pact; however, their use would have to be confined to the territory of allies; employment against the territory of the United States and the Soviet Union was proscribed . . .[42]

This recognition of homeland sanctuary limits in nuclear war is not inconsistent with Soviet rejection of limited nuclear war in Europe, nor is it inconsistent with Soviet military planning since the 1970s. The key distinction is in the definition of Europe. Soviet military analysts interpret the American discussions of limited nuclear war in Europe to include the European part of the Soviet Union. And indeed, many U.S. discussions do read this way. And certainly, the deployment of American Pershing IIs and ground-launched cruise missiles (GLCMs) in Western Europe reinforces this impression. Thus, Soviet protestations that no limited nuclear war could be fought in Europe are intended to put the United States on notice that any American or NATO nuclear weapons hitting Soviet territory from anywhere will be considered a strategic attack by the United States on the Soviet Union, requiring a full strategic response. (Recall President Kennedy's warning to the Soviet Union during the Cuban missile crisis.) In other words, the Soviet Union could use SS-20s against targets in West Germany, Belgium, Italy, and the Netherlands under the homeland sanctuary limit. But any use of U.S. cruise missiles or Pershing IIs based in those countries against targets in the Soviet Union would violate the homeland sanctuary limit and lead to global nuclear war.

RELATIONSHIP TO FORCE STRUCTURE

The relationship between this escalation contingency and the Soviet force structure is very strong, particularly with respect to the general purpose forces.[43] First, the combination of a crisis period and a conventional war period (however brief) provides enough "strategic warning" time to move all Soviet nuclear forces from day-to-day alert to generated-alert status. Thus, capabilities relevant to both the Soviet preemption/damage limitation strategy and the LOTW/LUA strategy increase relative to peacetime capabilities. Likewise, all levels of political and military command and control are improved, and the potential contribution of the national air defense system and civil defense system to protecting homeland assets grows.

Second, since the 1970s Soviet general purpose forces—the ground forces, the air forces, and the navy—have been specifically configured to fight in either an all-conventional or a nuclear war environment.

Soviet military procurement emphasized the option to wage war with conventional means only. Massive new investments were made in tactical aircraft, self-propelled artillery, conventional munitions, attack and support helicopters, and surface naval forces.[44]

Third, the Soviet general purpose force mobilization concept assumes a homeland situation that is not complicated by showers of incoming American nuclear warheads. In fact, since the late 1970s Soviet strategic planning has placed increasing significance on military-economic mobilization of domestic resources during the course of a crisis and into the conventional war phase.[45] More than half of existing Soviet ground-force divisions require from 60 to 120 days to mobilize from peacetime status to full wartime readiness levels. The Soviet strategic transportation system—mostly railroads—would need weeks to move the men and matériel demanded by deployment plans and military tables of organization and equipment. The utility of Soviet general purpose force capability is only notable in a context in which large-scale nuclear warfare has not taken place.

Accidental Nuclear War

While the Soviets have said much about their attitudes toward the deliberate paths to nuclear war, they have been much more reticent about the nondeliberate paths. One of the few revealing statements about the accidental path to nuclear war appeared in the 1965 edition of the authoritative *Marksizm-Leninism o voyne i armii (Marxism-Leninism on War and the Army):*

Deliberate premeditation to prepare and unleash war does not exclude the well-known role of numerous accidents, which can serve as the casus belli for war. Although fulfilling a secondary function, the role of accidents may change depending on concrete historical conditions.

Two circumstances sharply increase the role of accidents in the outbreak of war.

First, there is the tension of international relations . . . The climate of the "cold war," the atmosphere of military psychosis, and the fear of the fabricated "red danger" . . . all which make accidents capable of bringing about nuclear war.

Second, there are the existing rocket-nuclear weapons in the hands of aggressive forces. The growing stocks of these weapons means that an increasing number of people service them. And in this situation the probability of the unexpected grows. As is well known, there have been several accidents in the U.S.A. where active bombers with nuclear weapons have crashed. Analogous events have occurred with rockets equipped with nuclear warheads.

Accidents involving crashing bombs and rockets and nuclear explosions on the territories of one or another country could be interpreted as an attack by an enemy and serve as the signal for the beginning of war.

A fateful role is played by bomber pilots. As a result of mistakes or evil intentions, nuclear bombs might fall. It is entirely possible for there to be errors in the command and control of American strategic bombers and rockets or, for example, errors of interpretation made by radar operators.

In such circumstances, accidents can play tragic roles, serving as signals for global military catastrophe.[46]

The evolution of the Soviet nuclear force posture also provides clear evidence of standing concern over the possibility of unintended or unauthorized use of Soviet nuclear weapons. In this context, it is worth reviewing some of the points made earlier in this chapter.

The Soviet nuclear weapons program began in 1943 and was managed and controlled by the KGB—not the military. KGB control did not end until Stalin's death in 1953.[47] Soviet military sources report that nuclear weapons did not actually become available to the armed forces until 1954.[48] Throughout the 1950s and early 1960s, nuclear warheads and bombs were kept separate from delivery systems. Soviet strategic bombers were never held on day-to-day ground or air alert armed with nuclear weapons. The bombs were guarded by KGB forces. Nuclear warheads for Soviet ICBMs, MRBMs, and other missiles were held at separate storage locations and were guarded by the KGB. Not until the mid-1960s were nuclear warheads placed on Soviet strategic missiles on day-to-day alert.[49] While thousands of Soviet tactical and operational-tactical theater nuclear delivery systems were deployed in Eastern Europe after the late 1950s, the warheads and bombs for these systems were traditionally retained in the Soviet Union—not held in theater depots.[50]

Two separate command and control lines link Soviet nuclear forces with the political leadership in Moscow; one is military and the other is KGB.[51] KGB forces continue to guard Soviet nuclear depots. There is some evidence that each Soviet ICBM launch control center has a crew of four: two officers from the Strategic Rocket Forces and two officers from the KGB.[52] Correspondingly, one might speculate that KGB officers serve aboard Soviet SSBNs as a critical junction in the command and control over SLBM forces.

Each of these force posture measures suggests that the political leaders of several successive Soviet regimes have been strongly concerned about maintaining tight day-to-day political control over Soviet nuclear systems. Evidently they perceive some threat of unauthorized operation or accidental use.

High-level concern about preventing unauthorized use of Soviet nuclear weapons was explicitly revealed in an unusually frank statement by the late Defense Minister Dimitri Ustinov in a *Pravda* article in July 1982. The article was a policy statement, directed to an internal audience, that many specialists have interpreted as a defense of the Brezhnev declaration of no first use of nuclear weapons. Ustinov observed that one of the most urgent tasks requiring attention was:

... setting up a still more strict framework in the training of troops and staff, the determination of the composition of arms, the organization of still more strict control [*kontrol*] for the assured exclusion of the unsanctioned launch [*pusk*] of nuclear weapons from tactical to strategic.[53]

Western interest in Soviet views on accidental nuclear war has centered on three issues: (1) How does the Soviet nuclear command and control system employ positive and negative release? (2) What form of authority do military commanders have to use nuclear weapons? (3) Do Soviet nuclear weapons have mechanical or electronic locks that prevent unauthorized or unintended launch?

SOVIET NUCLEAR RELEASE

While we cannot be certain how Soviet nuclear release authority would work in a crisis or war environment, available evidence consistently points to positive release as the dominant form of nuclear control. That is, Soviet nuclear weapons cannot be used without explicit release from higher authorities. Ultimate authority to use nuclear weapons rests with the Soviet political leadership. This has been emphasized in a text written for officers and generals in the Soviet armed forces:

The decision to use such dangerous weapons as nuclear weapons became the exclusive prerogative of the political leadership. It, first and foremost, and not the military command, determines the need to use the means of mass destruction, selects the basic objectives and the moments for inflicting strikes with them.[54]

The General Staff would act as implementing agent when orders came down from the political leadership to release nuclear weapons to the operational commands. (The KGB would presumably act as an independent line of authentication in the positive release process.) The General Staff would also be the direct controlling agent for all Soviet strategic nuclear forces. These forces—ICBMs, SLBMs, IRBMs, long-range bombers—are distributed among the Strategic Rocket Forces, the air forces, and the navy for peacetime administration alone. In a crisis or war situation, the General Staff would take direct control over the deployment and operation of Soviet strategic nuclear forces.

In the case of theater nuclear weapons, release authority would be transmitted from the General Staff to the theater command (if it existed) or directly to the FRONT command.[55] Since it is believed that Soviet tactical and operational-tactical nuclear warheads and bombs would be held initially at FRONT depot locations, and since all nuclear transport capabilities are part of FRONT logistics support, no doubt the FRONT command would act as controlling agent for dispersing nuclear warheads to lower commands. Consistent with all other Soviet troop control procedures, no lower command (that is, army or division) could use its nuclear systems without authorization from above. Here again, it is believed that independent KGB authentication of release would be required.

Once nuclear weapons have been released to lower commands, however, a considerable amount of freedom of action may be permitted. Writing in the restricted General Staff journal *Voyennaya Mysl (Military Thought)*, General Lieutenant I. Zav'yalov observed:

> Transfer of nuclear weapons to the disposal of strategic, operational, and tactical command echelons gives each great independence and enables them to choose for themselves the means and methods of military operations within the zones of their responsibility and within the bounds of their authority.[56]

If Zav'yalov's description is accurate, it means that political control over the use of Soviet nuclear forces would dwindle rapidly once nuclear release was authorized. It also suggests that Soviet political leadership would withhold nuclear release authority until prepared to see the military actually use the weapons.

It is worth noting that the September 1983 incident in which a Soviet regional commander ordered the destruction of a Korean airliner over the Sakhalin Islands offers no insights into Soviet nuclear command and control procedures. Soviet air defense commands are under standing orders to shoot down any intruder aircraft refusing to land unless explicitly instructed not to do so.[57] That is, the release procedure for air defense systems over Soviet territory is a fully negative control system; positive release, in contrast, would be required for use of nuclear weapons.

HARDWARE CONTROLS

What kind of hardware controls do the Soviets have? During the 1960s the United States installed permissive action links (PALs) on its theater nuclear weapons and analogous mechanical and coded locks on strategic systems to prevent unauthorized use. (These were later updated to more dependable and effective electronic locks). In December 1962, the U.S. government gave the Soviets some details about the American nuclear safeguard system in the hope that the Soviets might pursue similar measures with their own forces. A year later, General-Colonel V.F. Tolubko, Deputy Chief of the Strategic Rocket Forces, acknowledged:

Recently, I happened to have been introduced to publications from the foreign press with information about "precautionary measures used in the USA against the accidental initiation of nuclear war." These measures are entirely permeated with distrust towards the people of the rocket units. They refer to, as affirmed in the American press, the possibility of "human error in command situations," likely "psychological disorders by some individuals, occupying strategic posts." For the Americans there really are these dangers—due to "the lone madman," as communicated in the press—of perhaps rather easily beginning a general nuclear war.

Among the Soviet people one will not find even the thought of such a thing. Our rocket troops have strong nerves, fine consciousness, and they are filled with a sense of deepest responsibility for the security of the Motherland.[58]

In other words, hardware controls are unnecessary when nuclear weapons are commanded by the politically disciplined soldier of

Marxist-Leninist heritage. Of course, Tolubko neglected to mention the separation of Soviet nuclear weapons from delivery systems that existed at the time and the insertion of the KGB in the command and control loop. To be sure, the Soviet approach was less sophisticated than the American approach, but it was also safer.

But twenty-one years later, Marshal Tolubko, now Commander-in-Chief of the Strategic Rocket Forces, revealed that there had been some slackening in his confidence in socialist man:

[Our] modern missile weapons are highly automated systems, with modern electronic-computing technology, for remote control and monitoring. Built-in diagnostic systems permit continuous monitoring of all essential parameters, provide for the most reliable functioning of equipment, safe utilization, and *fully exclude unsanctioned operation* [emphasis added].[59]

Soviet strategic missiles were in fact given electronic locks to prevent unauthorized use. As noted above, Ustinov's professed concern about the unsanctioned launch of Soviet nuclear weapons—"from tactical to strategic"—suggests that such controls will be extended to all nuclear systems, if they have not been already.

HARDWARE FAILURES

Hardware failures could conceivably precipitate an accidental nuclear war. The Soviet military has kept its officers informed about the problem with well-documented and detailed discussions of U.S. nuclear weapons accidents and breakdowns of U.S. strategic command, control, and early warning systems.[60]

Of course the Soviet military has much more direct experience with hardware failures. Crashes of Soviet strategic bombers were not uncommon in the 1950s. The Mya-4—the Soviet version of the B-52 —had so many problems that, allegedly, Soviet pilots feared to fly in it.[61] (At least one Soviet source claimed that nuclear bombs were sometimes on board training flights during the 1950s, though this would have been inconsistent with Soviet control procedures at the time.[62]) First- and second-generation Soviet missiles often went astray during test launches, crashing into populated areas. Many blew up on launch pads.[63] Soviet missile-carrying submarines are known to have experienced many problems at sea. Recent examples include a Soviet ballistic missile submarine that got into trouble in the Pacific Ocean when fires inside the vessel could not be put out; (smoke was seen venting from a missile launch tube) and an errant Soviet cruise missile that strayed over Norwegian territory and crashed in Finland.[64]

Catalytic Nuclear War

The possibility of a catalytic path to nuclear war is not addressed directly by Soviet leaders in public. Yet Soviet diplomatic and military behavior reflects some concern that the United States and the Soviet Union might be drawn into war by the actions of third parties.

The catalytic nuclear war path has several variant forms. The first posits that the Soviet Union is involved in a politico-military conflict with some third country. The United States then weighs in, and the two superpowers end up in a military face-off. There is evidence that Soviet leaders have considered this possibility in past crises. In preparation for the invasion of Czechoslovakia in 1968, for example, Soviet commanders and staff (down to the battalion level) were briefed about the possibility of encountering NATO forces inside Czechoslovakia. They were instructed to hold their positions but not to fire.[65]

An equally revealing episode occurred one year later during the Sino-Soviet conflict along the Ussuri River. The Soviet leadership is reported to have begun informing its Warsaw Pact allies that it was considering a surgical nuclear strike against Chinese military facilities (including nuclear installations).[66] This may well have been a disinformation campaign in support of Soviet coercive diplomacy. However, several Nixon administration officials claim that the Soviets actually sounded out the U.S. government about its attitude toward a Soviet preemptive strike against Chinese nuclear facilities.[67]

The second variant involves the catalytic effects of conflict among Soviet and American allies. A major source of friction between the Soviets and the Chinese during the 1950s was Soviet failure to provide concrete assistance to the Chinese in their effort to retake Taiwan. While the Soviets were good at propaganda support, they did not offer the military muscle that the Chinese needed to stand up to the United States. In fact, the Soviets continually restrained the Chinese out of fear that a war between Taiwan and the People's Republic of China (PRC) would trigger an American attack on the Soviet Union.[68] Thus the Soviets allowed alliance relations with the Chinese to suffer rather than risk the possibility of catalytic nuclear war with the United States.

Soviet concern about catalytic nuclear war during the 1950s and 1960s was undoubtedly conditioned by Moscow's perception of an extremely unfavorable strategic balance. Today such concerns might be tempered by the belief that the United States would not risk such an action in a era of U.S.-Soviet strategic parity.

The third variant of the catalytic path recognizes that the use of nuclear weapons by a third power could set off a U.S.-Soviet conflict. Indeed, Soviet nonproliferation policy may be partly motivated by a sense that nuclear weapons in the hands of third powers might be used in regional wars around the periphery of the Soviet Union. Most prospective nuclear powers are allies or clients of one of the superpowers, and many are engaged in long-term hostilities with one another. The Middle East is the most obvious example. The use of nuclear weapons by a state in this region against any ally or client of either the United States or the Soviet Union could draw in one superpower, thereby bringing in the other. Certainly, the Soviets must worry about nuclear proliferation in its own right, given that most of the likely new nuclear powers are located on or near its borders. But the Soviets could easily eliminate this threat (as the Israelis demonstrated vis-à-vis Iraq) if they did not have to contend with a possible American counter-intervention. Thus it is likely that the catalytic path to U.S.-Soviet nuclear war figures somewhere in Soviet nonproliferation policy.

Here the case of China comes up again. Initial Soviet willingness to aid China to develop nuclear weapons soured as the Chinese attitude toward an East-West nuclear war became more apparent to the Soviet leaders. It seems that the Chinese leadership accepted Soviet propaganda at face value: in the aftermath of a global nuclear war, the socialist states would emerge victorious and prosper. This view was reinforced in Chinese minds by Soviet claims that they would soon achieve nuclear offensive and defensive superiority over the United States. This claim was widely accepted in the United States. The Chinese did not know it was a bluff and thus could not understand why their Soviet ally would not threaten nuclear war in support of China's claim over Taiwan during the 1958 crisis. Despite their initial support, the Soviet leaders then decided that a Chinese nuclear weapons program was too dangerous; the Chinese might start a cata- lytic nuclear war that would engulf the Soviet Union and the United States.

There is yet another dimension to this path: one that is peculiar to Soviet military thinking. This is the view that an enemy might take advantage of an ongoing local war or other third-party military crisis as a springboard for launching a generated-alert surprise attack against the Soviet Union.[69] In the most sinister form of this variant, the adversary actually creates a local crisis as a guise for preparations to attack the USSR. Such a local war is not a true catalyst, but merely a form of deception that enables the enemy to mobilize its military forces in the hope of achieving strategic surprise.

Observations and Implications

This chapter has tried to gather fragments of evidence that might illuminate the Soviet perspective on the five major paths to nuclear war. At best, however, such an approach yields a partial picture. Therefore, in examining the implications of this material, it is useful to consider also those things that we do not know or cannot know with certainty.

It is clear that *there is no single Soviet strategy for waging nuclear war.* Instead, there is a complex progression of strategic options: preemption, launch on tactical warning, launch under attack, and second strike. The choice of which to implement will depend heavily on the particular circumstances of the time. Because Soviet military thinking is strongly predisposed towards preemption, it is worth con- sidering some of the special problems associated with a Soviet decision to preempt.

STRATEGIC WARNING AND THE SOVIET STRATEGY OF PREEMPTION

A Soviet decision to preempt is closely tied to strategic warning of impending nuclear war. But what constitutes strategic warning? We simply do not know what aspects of U.S. and NATO politico- military activity the Soviets actually monitor for strategic warning, or how they weight the various indicators in their assessment process. Yet these indicators, and their relative significance in Soviet perceptions of threat, will greatly influence Soviet actions in a crisis.

One possible indicator is the alert status of U.S. nuclear forces. The stages of the U.S. DEFCON alert system have been described repeatedly in the open press. And the alert system has been exercised frequently enough for the Soviets to develop a clear picture of its various operational implications. Indeed, the United States has most often used its military alert process with the explicit intention of signaling the Soviet Union of American politico-military concerns. The alert of U.S. nuclear forces during the 1973 Middle East war is perhaps the best example. But this practice in itself makes the alert status of U.S. nuclear forces an unreliable strategic warning indicator. Had the Cuban missile crisis taken place in 1982, with 1982 Soviet military forces and strategic concepts, the results could have been disastrous, since the U.S. move to DEFCON 2 (perhaps only to signal resolve) might well have precipitated a Soviet anticipatory preemptive strike.

A second and related indicator might be the dispersal and redeployment of U.S. and NATO nuclear forces. Consider the path of escalation from conventional war. As the war begins, the threat of Soviet air and conventionally armed SS-21 and SS-23 missile strikes reaching deep into West German territory causes SACEUR to order U.S./NATO nuclear systems to disperse. NATO's intent is to decrease the vulnerability of its Theater Nuclear Force—especially Pershing IIs and GLCMs—to Soviet conventional attacks. Yet the Soviet leadership might interpret the dispersion of NATO's long-range theater nuclear forces as a primary indicator of an impending decision to launch. The result: a military recommendation to the Soviet political leadership to authorize theaterwide nuclear preemption.

A third possible indicator is information obtained from electronic intercepts. The Soviet KGB and GRU (military intelligence) routinely monitor domestic communications in both the United States and Europe. U.S. and NATO military communications are closely monitored from Soviet ground-, sea-, air-, and space-based platforms. For example, Soviet trawlers outfitted with intercept equipment listen in on transmissions to and from U.S. naval forces and SSBNs at sea.

Soviet listening posts in the United States and in space attempt to monitor communications traffic between Minuteman launch-control centers and SAC command posts, and between U.S. strategic bomber squadrons and SAC. Intercept of U.S. nuclear release, authentication, or other forms of command, control, and readiness communications could serve as a Soviet strategic warning indicator under any of the paths described.

Even without regard to its content, the very quantity of communications traffic is likely to be seen as significant. In the conventional war scenario introduced above, there would be a large surge in transmissions between the various NATO capitals, SHAPE, NATO command centers, and the nuclear support bases just before NATO theater nuclear forces were dispersed. Even if the Soviets were unable to decipher the messages, the quantitative surge in traffic might serve as strategic warning of a NATO decision to employ its nuclear forces. But similar surges in communications could occur for reasons other than nuclear release. In the context of an ongoing conventional war in Europe, the Soviet Union's inability to determine the content of that traffic could lead it to preempt.

The Soviets regularly monitor other forms of electronic intercept data that could be used for strategic warning purposes. Signal intelligence is generated by the operation of almost all modern military equipment. Radio emissions occur across a wide band of frequencies but are often specific enough to provide generic identification of the source (especially in combination with radio direction findings). An obvious example is the characteristic signals emitted by U.S. aircraft carrier battle groups. The Soviets have deployed a satellite specifically dedicated to land, air, and naval electronic monitoring. Radar intelligence data are produced by the testing and operation of air defense radars, early warning radars, spacetrack radars, and so on. Changes in the operating status of any modern military force will be reflected in electronic emissions. The Soviets will detect these changes and try to interpret their operational significance.

The Soviets most certainly rely on a host of indicators, political and military, to provide strategic warning. The problem is that the associated activities are likely to be indicative of many things other than U.S. or NATO preparations to use nuclear weapons. Activities undertaken by the United States and its allies for crisis control or conflict management may feed into the Soviet strategic warning process and be interpreted in wholly unexpected ways. One must wonder whether military alerts involving nuclear forces can be considered a prudent form of political communication between the United States and the Soviet Union in the contemporary politico-strategic environment. Soviet sources claim that the Politburo laughed at the U.S. nuclear alert of 1973. It was laughable only because it took place in a political environment of warm U.S.-Soviet relations and U.S. military withdrawal from around the world. In the political environment of 1984 a similar alert might not find the Kremlin in such a jolly mood.

SOVIET ALERT PROCEDURES

A second factor influencing the Soviets' preemption decision would be the nature of their nuclear alert system. How many alert stages are there? What actions are encompassed by each level? What branch points exist? What are the return points? How do nuclear control and release procedures vary across the different alert levels?

In the late 1930s the Soviet navy established a staged alert system that enabled the navy command to increase the readiness levels of the fleet in increments appropriate to the situation. Allegedly, the Soviet fleet was at operational readiness level number one (the higher state) at the onset of the Nazi attack in June 1941.[70] Undoubtedly, an analagous staged alert system has been set up for Soviet strategic forces.

In those few contemporary cases where we might have expected to gain some insights into the Soviet alert system—the Berlin crisis of 1961, the Cuban missile crisis of 1962, the invasion of Czechoslovkia in 1968, the Sino-Soviet conflict of 1969—either we did not see much that was relevant, or we failed to recognize what we were seeing. As the U.S. nuclear alert during the 1973 Middle East war amply demonstrates, it could be dangerous to interpret military activity outside the context of standard alert procedures. Intentions could be easily misread.

Nor do we know much about the effects of moving up through the Soviet nuclear alert system on either Soviet politico-military decision-making or Soviet military capabilities. Here the role of military advice to the Soviet political leadership and its influence on crisis decision-making is a very important question. Unlike the United States, the Soviet Union has no other authoritative sources of military advice. As a crisis worsens, does the military have greater access to Soviet decision-makers or less? Where does the KGB enter into the picture? Does it merely supply raw intelligence, or does it provide assessments? Since the Cuban missile crisis there has been significant institutional evolution and organizational change within the Soviet national security decision-making setting. Yet we continue to think of that incident as the archetypical case of Soviet crisis decision-making.

How will Soviet forces fare under sustained alert? Their preparations for a possible invasion of Poland in 1980 revealed the difficulty of maintaining the ground forces in a high state of readiness over an extended period of time. While a nuclear crisis would probably be much shorter, surging Soviet nuclear forces to generated alert might also make it difficult to sustain high readiness—especially if maintenance and logistics support were stressed by bringing the entire strategic force (including air defense forces) to generated alert. If a crisis escalated into a skirmish or an all-out conventional war, Soviet nuclear forces could face the prospect of a relatively lengthy hold on generated alert. Should readiness levels among its strategic forces then begin to decay, the Soviet leadership would be placed in the awkward position of having either to launch a nuclear attack or to settle the conflict on what might be unfavorable terms. At certain stages of the Soviet alert/mobilization process, there may be points of "no safe (graceful) return" that, in the context of an enduring crisis or non-nuclear conflict, would create incentives for nuclear preemption. The Soviet leadership might thus be forced into nuclear escalation when the objective political and military circumstances would not seem to suggest such a move.

THE UTILITY OF PREEMPTION

Still another factor influencing a Soviet preemption decision would be its perceived military utility. Too often, Western discussions consider only the absolute value of preemption: How much of the enemy force would be destroyed by a Soviet preemptive attack? Since, invariably, the answer is "not much," a Soviet preemption decision appears irrational. But the evidence suggests the Soviets calculate military utility differently. They appear to be much more interested in relative utility: How much better off will the Soviet Union be if it preempts, rather than launches on tactical warning or launches a second strike attack? Could strategic defenses better limit damage to the homeland if the Soviet Union preempted? If the Soviet leadership believed there was a strong possibility of war, the issue facing it would be: Given the perceived likelihood of war, does preemption offer a marginal advantage over alternative strategies?

There is a direct tradeoff between Soviet perceptions of the likelihood of war and their calculation of preemption's military value. In fact, it is a tradeoff between perceptions of the possibility of avoiding nuclear war and the possibility of gaining a damage limitation advantage via preemption. In a crisis in which strategic warning was ambiguous, preemption would have to offer substantial damage control benefits to win out over launching on tactical warning. But if Soviet leaders had great confidence in the reliability of their strategic warning and believed nuclear war was unavoidable, then preemption might look attractive quite apart from damage control. If one cannot avoid nuclear war there is no advantage to launching second.

LIMITED NUCLEAR WAR

While it is useful to examine Soviet military concepts of limited nuclear warfare, the fact is *we cannot unerringly predict Soviet behavior with respect to a limited nuclear strike, because even they cannot know how they will behave.* In the context of a faltering NATO defense of Western Europe, for example, a NATO demonstration use of nuclear weapons would most likely result in a Soviet salvo of hundreds of SS-20 warheads against targets in NATO Europe. But it is at least conceivable that it could lead instead to a Soviet withdrawal.

To be sure, Soviet military policy is saturated with standard operating procedures, preplanned execution programs, organizational routines, and other strategic planning constraints that channel responses in specific directions. Embedded psychological, cultural, and political norms may further reinforce certain behavioral patterns. While these factors strongly influence decision-making in Moscow, they do not *determine* it. During gaming exercises Soviet leaders may be certain of their course of action, but neither we nor they can be certain how they would behave if the crisis were no longer a game. Had Khrushchev gamed the Cuban missile crisis in 1961, his game would certainly not have ended with the humiliating defeat Soviet policy actually suffered. Such an outcome would not have been permitted.

But one should not carry this qualification too far. What we know and understand about Soviet decision-making in general, and Soviet national security decision-making in particular, suggests that the decision-making environment may be more constrained than Westerners like to believe. A Soviet decision about nuclear war would take place in a military-dominated environment, with a military doctrine that emphasized preemption. The lack of alternative military-strategic advice implies that Soviet political leaders would be unprepared for policy innovation under stress and susceptible to professional military influence. These signs all point toward greater dependence on prior planning, with less ability or tendency to reach out for creative alternatives.[71] In other words, the evidence examined remains the most reliable indicator of what the Soviets may do in a conflict situation.

Soviet notions of limitation in nuclear warfare seem to differ from those encountered in Western defense literature, especially with respect to assumptions about escalation patterns. The weight of evidence from Soviet military writings, force structure, and exercises suggests that *any NATO use of nuclear weapons is likely to unleash a massive and devastating Soviet theater nuclear strike against all NATO military facilities.* While this is not the only Soviet option, it is by far the most probable. In this light, Western notions of using nuclear weapons for political signaling seem particularly misguided.

CATALYTIC NUCLEAR WAR: BRITISH AND FRENCH NUCLEAR FORCES

The problem of catalytic nuclear war seems very hypothetical until one considers Soviet attitudes toward the independent nuclear forces of Britain and France. As described earlier, the concept of homeland sanctuary seems to be at the core of Soviet thinking about escalation from theater to global nuclear war. How would Soviet political and military leaders respond to a British or French nuclear attack against Soviet territory during a European conflict?

Various Soviet spokesmen have asserted that the Soviet Union considers British and French nuclear forces as NATO nuclear forces. And any nuclear attack by NATO against the Soviet Union would be considered a U.S. attack on the Soviet Union. On the one hand, this position makes perfect sense a priori from a deterrence perspective. And when one considers how British and French nuclear capabilities will grow over the next decade (due to MIRVing), a nuclear strike by either country does have strategic significance. In a conventional war, large-scale Soviet conventional military operations against Britain and France, or even "special operations" against their nuclear forces, could provoke some form of limited (counter-military or demonstrative) nuclear attack against the Soviet homeland. If the Soviet military leadership believed that these were precursor attacks designed to weaken the Soviet generated-alert strategic nuclear posture, then a Soviet strategic preemptive response against the United States might seem warranted. Catalytic nuclear war is plausible as a form of escalation from a conventional war in Europe.

On the other hand, a British or French nuclear strike in the wake of Soviet SS-20 strikes on their territories (as part of a preemptive nuclear attack in the theater) would not be unexpected by the Soviets. Depending on the politico-military context, Soviet leaders might feel that strategic retaliation against the United States would serve no useful political or military purpose. In the end, we cannot know how the Soviets will react to nuclear attacks against Soviet territory by British or French forces, because it is something that the Soviet leaders themselves cannot know.

SOVIET ESCALATION

Since it is commonly assumed that NATO cannot successfully defend against the Warsaw Pact in a conventional war, Western analysts of all political persuasions tend to assume that theater nuclear escalation is largely a Western prerogative. But for those of us who do not see the conventional balance as all that unfavorable to the West, the possibility of Soviet-initiated nuclear escalation in the face of their failure to attain military or *political* objectives is a scenario in need of attention.

Soviet military development during the 1970s was geared specifically to creating the option to wage war in Europe without the necessity of using nuclear firepower. Yet, irrespective of motivation, any Soviet decision to prosecute a conventional war in Europe would mean that someone in the Kremlin had already decided to flirt with nuclear warfare. There are presumably foreseen and unforeseen circumstances under which they would initiate nuclear warfare regardless of NATO nuclear posture or actions. One such circumstance could be failure to maintain expected progress in a conventional war.

Soviet military planning appears to be especially sensitive to time goals. That is, certain military objectives must be achieved within a given period of time for other, more important, military and political goals to be reached.[72] Falling behind schedule could undermine larger conventional operations. A substantial NATO conventional defense (including one eschewing deep strikes into Warsaw Pact territory) that threatened to delay significantly Soviet ground operations goals, for example, could lower the Soviet nuclear threshold and prompt Soviet theater nuclear escalation. Ironically, those wishing to reduce the probability of escalation from conventional war in Europe by advocating NATO no-first-use of nuclear weapons and a simultaneous buildup of Western conventional forces may achieve the opposite effect.

In short, it is presumptuous to assume—as too many in the West are wont to do—that U.S./NATO defense policies are the primary determinants of the risk of escalation to nuclear war in Europe.

THE RISKS OF NUCLEAR WAR

If the general direction of our discussion is correct, then it is possible that the Soviet leaders believe that the risk of nuclear war—in terms of probability and consequences—are increasing. To be sure, certain paths to nuclear war seem less likely than they did two decades ago. After twenty-five years of heavy investments in the Soviet strategic force posture—especially ICBMs, strategic command and control, and early warning systems—a U.S. bolt-from-the-blue attack must seem less probable. Similarly, the possibility of an accidental nuclear war has grown more remote as more technically reliable weapons replace older systems in the Soviet and American arsenals, and improved command and control and safeguards technologies are incorporated into the nuclear forces of both sides.

However, the risks along the remaining three paths may have grown over the past two decades. In particular, the Soviet military's preoccupation with preemption, their now-credible capability to mount preemptive attack, and the uncertainties surrounding their strategic warning assessment suggest that *the risks of nuclear war posed by preemption, escalation, and catalytic events may be greater than commonly assumed.* In contrast to the 1950s and 1960s, when preemption was just so much military theory, under certain circumstances the Soviet military could now make a credible military-technical case for nuclear preemption, especially if political leaders thought Western escalation to strategic nuclear war was imminent. While we cannot know what the Soviet political leaders would choose to do, the fact remains that they now have the necessary mix of doctrine and technical capability to consider the option realistically.

These risks may be compounded further by the ideological and political milieu in which Soviet national security decision-making takes place. The state of East-West relations may significantly affect how Soviet leaders interpret signs of strategic warning. Soviet perceptions of the relative threat posed by the various paths are likely to change over time as a function of their assessment of the "realism" versus "reactionary character" of U.S. foreign policy. Thus, despite military-technical arguments to the contrary, it is possible that the U.S. bolt-from-the-blue scenario has come to seem more plausible to Soviet leaders in recent years. Soviet crisis decision-making may be far more sensitive to the overall East-West political environment than is often acknowledged. In the end, the balance between a Soviet decision to preempt and to launch on tactical warning may be tipped by political images of risk.

Soviet perceptions of the risks of nuclear escalation from conventional war may have grown, ironically, as a result of renewed NATO interest in conventional forces. On the one hand, the massive Soviet effort of the 1970s to equip themselves to wage conventional war in Europe seems to have increased NATO's perceived reliance on the early use of nuclear weapons. Yet the Soviets' desire to raise their own nuclear threshold may have had the effect of lowering NATO's nuclear threshold. On the other hand, recent U.S. and NATO programs to develop conventional deep-strike options (AirLand Battle 2000 and the Rogers Plan), thereby lessening NATO's perceived dependence on nuclear weapons, may drive the Soviets back towards early nuclear preemption in the theater. The curious tradeoff here is that while the probability of conventional war escalating into nuclear war might grow, the probability of war itself might diminish.

Finally, the risks of catalytic nuclear war are likely to be on Moscow's agenda as the British, French, and Chinese continue to make substantial improvements in their national nuclear forces. As the technical characteristics of British and French nuclear forces approach those of the United States, Soviet ability to distinguish a third party nuclear attack from an American attack will diminish (if it now exists). Over the next twenty years, the Chinese nuclear force is likely to pose similar problems of discrimination to the Soviets. Here again, the state of East-West relations can strongly influence Soviet perceptions of threat and risk.

8 ANALYTIC CONCLUSIONS: HAWKS, DOVES, AND OWLS

by Joseph S. Nye, Jr., Graham T. Allison, and Albert Carnesale

THE horror of major nuclear war has encouraged prudence. And prudence has helped Soviet and American leaders to avoid *any* conflict on the scale of the two world wars that took some seventy million lives earlier in this century. So long as nuclear weapons exist, however, there will always be some chance of their use. It is impossible to think clearly about avoiding nuclear war without thinking in terms of probability and risk. Even efforts to abolish nuclear weapons could raise the risks of use under some political conditions.

Few people believe that any objective could justify the loss of half a billion lives or the end of life itself. But many would support actions that might raise the likelihood of major nuclear war from one chance in ten thousand to one chance in a thousand if that were necessary to preserve their way of life, or to avoid a conventional World War III. Some risks are unavoidable if we want to lead certain types of lives. But we should try to reduce unnecessary risks.

This chapter presents the analytic conclusions that emerged from our examination of the question of how to avoid nuclear war. We will show how three distinctive approaches to reducing the risks of nuclear war are motivated by different sets of assumptions. For convenience, we refer to proponents of these three approaches as Hawks, Doves, and Owls. In the concluding chapter, we will present our own agenda of ten principles with specific dos and don'ts for avoiding nuclear war.

The Likelihood of Nuclear War

How likely is a major nuclear war between the United States and the Soviet Union before the end of the century?

   ——— Almost certain   ——— 1 in 1,000

   ——— Approximately even   ——— 1 in 10,000

   ——— 1 in 10   ——— Almost no chance

   ——— 1 in 100

Over the past two years, we have put this question to dozens of groups. In most groups of fifty or more, at least one respondent selected each answer—from "almost certain" to "almost no chance."

Specialists in national security are much more optimistic in their responses than the general public. Nearly half the public says nuclear war is likely before the end of the century.[1] Specialists' answers cluster between 1 in 100 and 1 in 10,000.

Not much is proven by this finding. In this realm there are "specialists" but not "experts." Fortunately, since Hiroshima and Nagasaki, we have had no experience with nuclear war.

This does not mean that one person's estimate is as good as another's. Some are based on more careful and sustained appraisal than others. Choices must be made among actions to reduce risks of war, and such choices necessarily reflect estimates of risk. Two decades ago, the British scientist and novelist C. P. Snow predicted nuclear war within a decade as a "mathematical certainty." Some of his defenders say that if he is right within a century, his prediction will have been justified.[2] But the difference between a century and a decade may make all the difference in the world when it comes to shaping policies to avoid nuclear war.

Is the current situation more or less risky than the previous period of heightened public concern, 1958–62, when Snow made his prediction? Are things worse or are we just more worried? Some observers argue that the chance of nuclear war is lower today than in 1962. They point to technical improvements such as permissive action links; improved command, control, and communication; national technical means of verification; and political factors such as U.S. and Soviet experience in managing crises. They also note that current Soviet leaders seem more cautious than Khrushchev was, though that could change in the future. Others believe that risks are higher now, pointing to the loss of American nuclear superiority; the greater Soviet capability to support forces in Third World areas; the deployment of vulnerable weapons and support systems that place a premium on preemption; doctrinal stress on protracted war-fighting; and the deterioration of U.S.-Soviet political relations.

The previous chapters provide support for both positions. One is struck, however, by how difficult the authors found it to paint plausible scenarios for reaching a major nuclear war along each path. Even when deliberate choices are confounded by accidents, each of the authors strains to reach a major nuclear war. If these specialists are correct, it is not easy to start a major nuclear war. Paul Bracken concludes that the risks of purely accidental nuclear war are much lower today than two decades ago. But he also warns that the continuing development of complex and tightly coupled strategic systems in the United States and the Soviet Union reduces the time for diplomacy to work and increases the potential effects of accidents and misperceptions when both systems are on alert during a crisis. Stephen Meyer points out that despite American concern, the probability of surprise or preemptive attack was actually close to zero in the 1950s and 1960s—because the Soviets did not have the capability we attributed to them. Today they have that capability against land-based missiles, and the dangers of preemptive attack will depend on the conditions (such as the ability to limit damage) that Richard Betts describes in his chapter. Henry Rowen argues that concern about catalytic nuclear war is justifiably lower today than twenty years ago, but those risks may rise in the future if we follow imprudent proliferation policies.

In sum, risks of nuclear war along the different paths change over time. When we allow for combinations of the paths, we see that risks are higher than for any one path alone. Our own assessment of overall risk is closer to the specialists than to the general public. But whether the odds are 1 in 100 or 1 in 1000, they are still too high. Given the consequences of a major nuclear war, a chance of 1 in 1000 must motivate urgent action.

Three Caricatures: Hawks, Doves, and Owls

Thinking about nuclear war quickly leads to the question: what is to be done? In the policy debate of the last decade, answers to this question cluster around two dominant caricatures: the Hawk and the Dove.[3] While neither exactly captures the thought of any individual, these simplifications do highlight central predispositions. They provide starting points for answers to questions about causes of war in general, the likely cause of nuclear war in particular, and the preferred posture for preventing a major nuclear war.

Hawks see the proximate cause of war as one-sided weakness—weakness that tempts an aggressive adversary to exploit advantage. The classic example is Munich. This symbol of unsuccessful appeasement conveys two lessons: (1) Britain and France's unwillingness to resist encouraged Hitler's demands; and (2) early resistance to a more ambiguous threat, during the remilitarization of the Rhineland or even over Czechoslovakia, might well have led to Hitler's ouster at the hands of his generals and might thus have prevented a world war. To avoid war, and nuclear war in particular, Hawks believe we must make our commitments and interests clear and establish a posture of superior military strength (or the closest approximation domestic politics will support). By making it clear to Soviet or other leaders that we cannot be beaten at any level of violence (an escalation ladder), we insure that they will never calculate that war could serve any rational goal. When crises arise, Hawks counsel resolve and steps to make our deterrent threat credible. The motto is "peace through strength."

For Doves, the primary cause of war lies in arms races that become provocative and thus undermine deterrence. Doves worry about arms in themselves and the irresistible momentum of military preparations both because the psychology of arms races prevents conciliation and because threats that are intended to deter may instead provoke. To avoid war, Doves prescribe a policy of conciliation and accommodation.

Doves worry that increasing military strength and threat may not strengthen deterrence but cause it to break down under some circumstances. At some point, greater military strength is transformed from a deterrent threat into a provocative threat. The leaders of the threatened country may feel themselves backed into a corner, their very existence threatened. Rational leaders may then decide to go to war despite horrible consequences if that seems the least bad alternative. They may decide to gamble on a preventive war or a preemptive attack in a severe crisis (along the lines that Betts discusses in his chapter) rather than suffer sure defeat later. The appropriate policy in such circumstances is conciliation and reassurance of the adversary, rather than increasing military strength.

Both Hawk and Dove share a common set of assumptions about the logic of the process by which war might come. In the pure types that we describe in table 1, each sees war as starting deliberately. Both assume that national leaders with accurate information carefully calculate risks, costs, and benefits and control the actions of their governments. In essence, our Hawk and Dove disagree about the right point for an effective deterrent policy along the spectrum that stretches between threat and conciliation. They roost on the same rational branch and argue about the best place to sit on it.

Beyond the frame of reference shared by Hawks and Doves lies a rather different set of concerns, one focused primarily on loss of control and nonrational factors in history. In this view, a major war would not arise from careful calculations but from organizational routines, malfunctions of machines or of minds, misperceptions, misunderstandings, and mistakes. Those who see the problem this way we call Owls.

While our Hawks and Doves focus on deterrence of deliberate choices and often cite World War II, Owls are more impressed by World War I, the assassination at Sarajevo, the leader's misperception of the military situation, and the inadvertent escalation caused by interlocking mobilization plans. Owls believe that crises or conventional war could create an environment for unintended nuclear war.

Loss of control under crisis conditions can take many forms. One danger is misperception of the real situation, such as a false belief that war is inevitable or a false warning that the other side is about to strike. A second danger is mental deterioration under stress. The extreme case would be a leader or key subordinate driven to madness. A more likely situation would be impaired rationality under stress as tired or anxious leaders feel they have no options, become rash or fatalistic, and are bolstered in this reasoning by other members of their inner group. A third danger originates in the difficulty of controlling large complex organizations in time of crisis. During the Cuban missile crisis, President Kennedy found he was unaware of the timing of surveillance flights near the Soviet Union; and in the enforcement of the blockade, the navy followed its standard operating procedures in a manner that was impossible for him to control in detail. A fourth danger emerges when multiple events arise simultaneously. Systems that have been designed with enough slack for one crisis will find themselves stretched taut when crises overlap. Leaders' attention is torn in different directions and stress multiplies. Finally, there is the danger of accident. While Hawks argue that pure accidents are unlikely to lead directly to nuclear war, Owls point out that accidents that happen in the midst of a crisis (or a conventional war) occur when the safety catches have deliberately been released. As Bracken shows, it is when accidents coincide with other factors that they may lead to nuclear war.

The Owl is not an intermediate species between the Hawk and the Dove. The temptation to subsume the Owl's position under the dovish label obscures an important difference. An Owl's emphasis on nonrational factors leads to reliance on a different logic of how war begins. Owls roost on a separate branch.

TABLE I

Three Caricatures: Hawks, Doves, and Owls[4]

Caricature	Primary Cause of War	Dominant Metaphor	Recommended Policy	Potential Error
HAWK	Weakness	Munich	Strength/ Superiority	Provocation
DOVE	Provocation	Pearl Harbor	Conciliation/ Accommodation	Ineffectual Appeasement
OWL	Loss of Control	World War I	Strengthened Controls/ Stability	Unusable Weapons/ Paralysis

In summary, Hawks worry that deterrence may fail if a potential aggressor calculates an opponent's weakness and has an opportunity to take advantage of it. Their policy remedy is to enhance the threat of retaliation by building military strength. Doves worry that deterrence may fail by slipping into provocation. Since additional threats may create a sense of inevitable war, the best remedy is conciliation and reassurance. Owls worry about deterrence because of the nonrational factors that degrade rationality as stress mounts and time is compressed during a crisis. They think the appropriate policy is to avoid crises and increase controls.

Three Potential Errors

Which of these approaches is right? All three are! Each captures an important insight about the potential initiation of nuclear war, and each rests on evidence from the world wars of our century. Yet all three also contain serious potential flaws. Consider the conflict between Hawks and Doves. Hawks generally accuse Doves of ineffectual appeasement; Doves are quick to point out the Hawk's flaw of provocation and inadequate reassurance. Both buttress their arguments by references to the two world wars, that "richest source of parables to help us see where we are going."[5]

Doves often cite the arms race that preceded World War I as a causal factor, but the evidence is ambiguous.[6] The Anglo-German arms race was largely over by 1912. While it had sowed suspicion in both countries, relations between Britain and Germany were actually improving before 1914. A more serious issue was German concern over Russian military and railway improvements, which led some Germans to favor a preventive war in 1914 to avoid a less favorable situation in 1916. But had Germany switched from an offensive preemptive strategy to a more defensive posture, the Russian changes would not have been so important.[7]

A stronger example for the Doves' position comes from Japan's experience in World War II. It is also useful in correcting the Hawk's Europe-centered views of World War II that have characterized recent policy debates. Contrary to popular American mythology, Japan did not attack Pearl Harbor because the United States looked weak or because Japan expected to defeat the United States in the war. On the contrary, Japanese leaders were pessimistic about their ability to defeat the United States. But they were even more pessimistic about their ability to survive if they did not go to war. The United States attempted to deter Japan from further expansion in Asia through policy statements and an oil embargo, but these measures instead convinced the Japanese leaders that their economy and war-making capacity would be strangled within a year in any case. A war now with a high risk of loss was better than certain defeat later. In the minds of Japan's military and expansionist political leaders, the American threat had turned from a deterrent into a provocation, spurring preventive war and surprise attack.[8]

Doves fear a situation in which the Soviet Union is backed into such a corner and Marxist historical optimism turns to a pessimistic view of historical decline: "A bear cornered is even more dangerous than a bear on the prowl." If the Soviet empire in Eastern Europe begins to crumble, and difficulties mount at home, a dramatic new turn in the arms race could tip the American threat from deterrence to provocation in Soviet eyes. Suppose, for example, that the United States seemed on the verge of a breakthrough in strategic defense technology that would disarm the Soviets and allow the Americans to coerce them. The Soviets might then take greater risks in a crisis that might lead to nuclear war, believing that the situation would become intolerable in a few years in any case. The appropriate policy in such circumstances would be conciliation and a bilateral or unilateral dampening of the arms race in strategic defenses.

If provocation is the potential fatal flaw in the Hawk's approach, ineffectual appeasement is the equivalent flaw in the dovish prescription. A clever adversary can deceive the Dove, as Hitler did Neville Chamberlain in 1938. And if defenses are inadequate, as British and French defenses were not in the 1930s, last-minute efforts to switch to deterrence, as the British and French tried over Poland in 1939, will lack credibility.

Owls are not always wise; they too make mistakes. Their dominant concern is with the unintended triggering of war in a crisis, and their preferred solution is increased control and better safety catches to prevent the hair-trigger from ever going off. Their potential policy failure is paralysis and the sticky or frozen safety catch. If controls are so cumbersome that an opponent concludes that nuclear weapons could never be used, the weapons lose their deterrent effect. An aggressor might be tempted to undertake a rash action, such as nuclear decapitation of the enemy's leadership, in the belief that the remaining weapons cannot be unlocked. If the Owl's safety catches appear to be frozen, we are thrown back into the Hawk's concern in which the aggressor is tempted to war because he believes that the victim is unlikely to respond.

Balanced Deterrence

Actual situations are unlikely to conform exactly to the paradigm of the Hawk, the Dove, or the Owl. Pure types rarely exist in the real world. Whatever their value as a source of parables, neither of the two world wars of this century was a pure case. World War I was not purely accidental. Confronted by Slavic nationalism, Austria deliberately chose war rather than face its probable disintegration as an empire. But it wanted a small war, not a world war. When the Kaiser backed Austria, he expected the Russians to back down as they had in a similar crisis over Bosnia five years earlier. What was supposed to be a diplomatic crisis or small war became a world war through a combination of miscalculation and inadvertence. Actions to strengthen deterrence, such as threats of mobilization during the crisis, merely made matters worse. Similarly, while Hawks see World War II as an instance of planned aggression, the scale of the war went far beyond Hitler's plans. But the efforts to appease Hitler in the 1930s and the failure to establish a credible deterrent certainly played a significant role in the onset of the war. And as we have seen, American efforts to deter Japan instead provoked preventive war and surprise attack.

In an actual crisis situation the interaction of rational and nonrational factors will make all three approaches relevant. What starts out as rational is likely to become less so over time. And accidents that would not matter much in normal times or early in a crisis may create "crazy" situations in which choice is so constrained that "rational" decisions about the least bad alternatives lead to outcomes that would appear insane under normal circumstances. As Thomas Schelling has written, "it is not accidents themselves . . . that could cause a war, but their effect on decisions . . . If we think of the decisions as well as the actions we can see that accidental war, like premeditated war, is subject to deterrence."[9] A major nuclear war is less likely to start purely by accident or purely by calculation than by an unfolding combination of the two in a crisis.

In terms of policy for avoiding nuclear war, Hawks, Doves, and Owls each have part of the truth, but not the whole. Hawks are aware that accidents can occur; Doves worry about loss of control; and Owls see the need for both deterrence and conciliation. But the pure types place a different emphasis on different causes, and each camp's prescriptions taken to an extreme could lead to fatal errors. What we seek is *balanced deterrence,* not simply deterrence by increased threats or by greater conciliation, or by shifting the burden of uncertainty about loss of control. As figure 1 suggests schematically, the crucial policy task is one of balance and synthesis—avoiding three polar errors, yet drawing on the strengths of each perspective. We will return to this point when we discuss our agenda of actions for reducing risks of nuclear war.

In practice many people see validity in all three perspectives; thus Hawks, Doves, and Owls may each support a mixture of policies for balanced deterrence (illustrated as the shaded area in figure 2). But

FIGURE 1

Balanced Deterrence Avoids Polar Errors

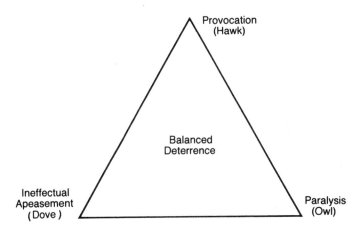

FIGURE 2

Balanced Deterrence and the Overlap of Pure Types

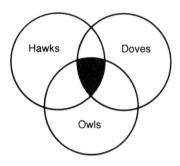

even if the Hawk, the Dove, and the Owl are rarely encountered in pure form, the definition of types helps to illuminate some of the differing assumptions that underlie tensions in current policy debates.

Views of the Soviet Union

To acknowledge that all three approaches are relevant and all three types of error must be avoided still leaves other questions in the policy debate over how to avoid nuclear war. Thoughtful people differ as to which of the three poles is most dangerous in the current world. Different views about the nature of the Soviet Union and its foreign policy complicate such judgments. In recent years, some Hawks have argued that today's situation is analogous to the 1930s; some Doves and Owls see it as similar to 1914.[10]

Both analogies are overdrawn. First, they too easily gloss over the difference between nuclear and non-nuclear war. The unprecedented damage nuclear weapons can do has produced unprecedented prudence—what we have called the crystal ball effect. Any leader can see that major nuclear war will have a horrible outcome. But we also argue that escalation from a conventional war is the most likely path to major nuclear war. In that sense, the failure of deterrence in the two world wars is still of some relevance. Things are neither totally different nor entirely the same.

Second, as we have seen, these analogies oversimplify and distort history. World War I was not purely accidental. Austria deliberately chose war as a means of destroying Serbia, and Germany backed Austria in expectation of a diplomatic victory, not a world war. The early stages involved rational calculation and miscalculation. Only during the crisis did events begin to spiral out of control, and last-minute efforts to draw back from the brink proved futile. As for World War II, not only did events exceed Hitler's planned aggression, but the usual analogies to the 1930s look only at the European dimension, neglecting events in Asia.

If the current Soviet Union is supposed to be like imperial Germany in 1914—an ascendant power seeking a place in the sun—then a militarily enhanced deterrent may be the appropriate response. But is the Soviet Union perhaps more like Austria, a declining empire fearful of disintegration? Then reassurance and conciliation may be more appropriate. In either case, the fear of war, including inadvertent war, is much greater today than it was in 1914, when some leaders welcomed war.

As for the analogy to the 1930s, the current situation differs in at least two important ways. Hitler was a "bellicist," who sought war (though not the one he got) not merely for its fruits, but also for the ideological glorification of his Third Reich. Soviet leaders have not shown such behavior. Moreover, while Soviet foreign policy has had an expansionist thrust, it has been a cautious expansion. Thus far, Soviet leaders have tended to be risk-averse. As one wit put it, the Politburo members may all be hawks, but fortunately they are chicken hawks. Or in our terms, perhaps they include Owls.[11]

Hawks might argue that the Soviet Union has been cautious because deterrence has worked. But it is difficult to know what the Soviet leaders would have intended to do in the absence of American efforts to deter them. (Indeed, one of the dangers of the Hawk's analysis is a tendency to treat deterrence as an almost theological concept. Everything is attributed to deterrence.) Certainly Hawks have some basis for arguing that without deterrence Soviet leaders would have taken greater risks—given the Soviet belief in the vague Marxist notion of a "correlation of forces," as described in Stephen Meyer's chapter, and as evidenced in their relatively adventuresome behavior in the 1970s, when they felt that the correlation had shifted in their favor. But it remains extremely difficult to determine just what creates deterrence in Soviet calculations, and how much is enough.

The secretive nature of the Soviet political and social system is one reason for this difficulty. In many countries, we have sufficient access to elites, the press, and governmental debates to formulate fairly clear impressions of their intentions. But the Soviet Union, for reasons rooted in Russian history as well as communist ideology, restricts our access to people and documentary information. The Soviet system is like a black box to us. We see what comes out, but we have very little notion of what happens inside.[12] Thus, there will always be considerable uncertainty about what deters the Soviet Union.

Two Views of Deterrence

The concept of deterrence itself is slippery. In a sense, there are two quite different yet complementary views of how it works: calculated and existential. Hawks say Soviet actions can be deterred by denying them the prospect of gain and by threat of retaliation. The effectiveness of deterrence depends on Soviet calculations of relative capabilities of the two sides' forces and on the credibility of our commitments. It is difficult to say what is credible. Some say that threats to retaliate to limited Soviet attacks by destroying Soviet cities would not be credible because they would be suicidal—the Soviet response to U.S. retaliation would be the destruction of American cities. We know it, and they know we know it.

Doves, on the other hand, often argue that the knowledge of the possibility of mutual suicide at the end of a process of escalation is sufficient to deter. The mere existence of weapons that could destroy both societies creates a "doomsday machine" and provides the hard core of deterrence. Even a small number of invulnerable weapons is sufficient for deterrence. Owls believe that both types of deterrence play a role. The existence of a capability for mutual destruction deters, but the doomsday machine must be linked to events in a credible way. Otherwise, perceived imbalances of forces could tempt an aggressor to take unwise risks in a crisis. From the Owl's perspective, it is true that uncertainty about loss of control and annihilation deters both sides. But at the same time each side will try to coerce the other by forcing the burden of prudence onto the other, while maintaining freedom of action for itself. If one side believes that its forces are stronger, it may miscalculate how far it can press in this contest.

The credibility of deterrence also depends on what is being deterred. Most analysts believe that it is relatively easy to establish the credibility of threats of retaliation to protect one's homeland. But efforts to extend deterrence to protect other countries may be less credible. Would Americans risk Chicago to protect London or Bonn? Given that the post-1945 balance of power in the world has depended very much on alliance with the great democratic centers of technological and industrial creativity in Europe and Japan, perhaps we would. But would we risk Chicago to force the Soviets to leave Angola or Afghanistan? Almost certainly not.

Extended deterrence is made credible partly by the nature of the stakes. Europe's greater value to the United States makes deterrence there easier than in the Persian Gulf, and the Gulf is easier than many other Third World situations. In some places, extended deterrence is not credible at all. It is a matter of degree.

Extended deterrence can also be made credible by shifting the burden of uncertainty about escalation onto the other side. Even in the Persian Gulf, as Francis Fukuyama argues, strengthening conventional forces and improving their mobility can make it clear that a Soviet offensive would not be a quick and riskless fait accompli. The Soviet Union would have to worry about the likelihood of escalation, with its attendant owlish uncertainties.

One can increase those uncertainties by deploying battlefield weapons that are difficult to control, or by deploying strategic weapons that are vulnerable and therefore likely to be used early in a crisis. By creating a doomsday machine, one poses the threat that nonrational factors will get out of control. This may be an effective deterrent; the risk, of course, is that the threat may not be an idle one.

Finally, it is worth remembering the nonmilitary dimensions of extended deterrence. Extensive cultural, economic, and personal ties reinforce the credibility of American guarantees to Europe. Political disputes (for example, over East-West relations or sharing defense burdens) that damage NATO cohesion may reduce the credibility of extended deterrence far more than would the addition or removal of a few weapons systems.

Foreign Policy Tradeoffs

These problems of extended deterrence raise once again the inescapable issue that sometimes we must trade off our foreign policy goals against our desire to avoid nuclear war. At one extreme, we might avoid nuclear war by surrender; at the other extreme, we could make it more likely by attacking vital Soviet interests. Clearly we wish to avoid both ends of that spectrum. But we should not automatically assume that the more pacific or conciliatory our response, the smaller the chance of nuclear war. In some cases, the contrary might be true. For example, President Kennedy increased the risk of nuclear war, at least temporarily, as a means to get Khrushchev to remove Soviet missiles from Cuba; had he not done so, would the risk of nuclear war in the future have been greater or less? Given Khrushchev's adventuresome behavior, might he not have read conciliation as weakness and gone on to press another crisis over Berlin where the stakes and risks would have been even higher?

To some extent we could avoid nuclear war by reducing our commitments in world politics. A basic problem of foreign policy is to define a proper proportion among goals, available means, and risks. If we had unlimited means at our disposal, the only problem of foreign policy would be determining our list of wishes. We could transform the world in our image. But nuclear weapons are not a magic wand. They are a dangerous means of protecting our interests, and thus it behooves us to define our interests and goals in a prudent fashion. To think that the possession of military strength will deter the Soviet Union where its interests are strong and ours are weak would be a serious error. For example, although the United States has an interest in advancing social change and human rights in Eastern Europe, that interest is far weaker than the Soviet interest in maintaining control over an area it considers vital to its security. Defining our goals in Eastern Europe as long-term change, and avoiding efforts to intervene actively, can help to reduce one of the potential deep causes of nuclear war described in Fen Hampson's chapter. Ironically, given our experience in 1956 and 1968, when we backed away from confrontation during the Hungarian and Czech revolts, it may also be the most humane expression of our interests.

At the same time, we should be careful not to conclude that the more we restrict our foreign policy commitments, the more we reduce the risk of nuclear war. Some people argue, for example, that reducing our commitment to protect Europe would avoid the problem of extended deterrence and the most dangerous path to nuclear war by escalation. But this may not be true. If the Soviet Union gradually established hegemony over Europe (or Japan), and had access to its technological resources, this could have a significant effect on the balance of power in the long run; at some future point we might face even more dangerous threats to our interests. Removing extended deterrence would certainly be costly in terms of our immediate foreign policy interests, and it might not reduce the risks of nuclear war over the long term—perhaps not even in the intermediate term. One effect of removing the American security guarantee might be to frighten Germany or Japan (or Korea) into developing nuclear weapons. The effect of this development on the Soviet Union in particular, and on the rate of nuclear proliferation in the rest of the world, could greatly increase the risks of catalytic nuclear war.

Some risks are unavoidable in the nuclear age, and some efforts to reduce risk are costly in terms of our other foreign policy objectives. However, not all actions to reduce the risk of nuclear war involve foreign policy tradeoffs. In the agenda of actions outlined below, we will try to make clear when items involve significant tradeoffs.

What Is to Be Done?

The agenda for avoiding nuclear war proposed in the next chapter does not simply split the difference between the Hawks and the Doves. It raises a different set of issues to prominence. We think it is important to recognize that nuclear war could result either from calculation or from inadvertence; as the chapters in this book have shown, the most important—and most difficult—task is probably the development of measures to deal with the interplay of rationality and inadvertent events under crisis conditions. As we have argued, a balanced deterrence agenda recognizes that the Hawk, the Dove, and the Owl can all help to avoid nuclear war, and that their perspectives will often be intertwined in real-life situations.

Our agenda may seem to have an owlish cast. If so, that is not a reflection of an underlying bias (we hope), but rather a reflection of our assessment of the *current* situation and where we think the greatest risks lie *at present.* If we believed deterrence were now weak, our list would look more hawkish. Similarly, as we think about the longer term, we would be inclined to stress dovish prescriptions about building common interests between the United States and the Soviet Union. To go back to the triangle in figure 1, an optimal policy for avoiding nuclear war requires balanced deterrence that avoids three types of errors. The agenda in chapter 9 reflects our view that balanced deterrence in the current situation requires more owlish measures. Moreover, as figure 2 suggests, many of these measures may prove to be policies on which moderate Hawks and Doves can agree.

In the current public debate about ways to avoid nuclear war, the left has generally advocated a freeze and formally negotiated cuts in armaments, while the right has favored buildup of strategic forces to regain escalation dominance. Neither of these options is included in our list. In that sense, our agenda reflects our concern with the inadvertent sources of a major nuclear war. It is difficult to imagine rational decisions to start a nuclear war in the absence of nonrational factors that are likely to occur in a crisis. Our list is designed to reduce those factors that would degrade rationality. Our own judgment is that the Owl's approach has been underemphasized in the past decade's debates. Now it is beginning to emerge. While our agenda is far from perfect, we hope it can provide a starting point for a new consensus on a strategy to reduce the risks of nuclear war.

9 AN AGENDA FOR ACTION

by Albert Carnesale, Joseph S. Nye, Jr.,
and Graham T. Allison

BEFORE DISCUSSING our agenda of actions to reduce the risk of nuclear war, we would like to caution any who have turned immediately to the recommendations without reading the book as a whole. Our agenda has deliberately been stated in simple terms, but it rests on the more complex foundation of analytic conclusions presented in the preceding chapter, including in particular our discussion of Hawks, Doves, and Owls. The recommendations presented in this chapter should be considered in that context, so we urge even our most impatient readers to read both chapters.

In recent years there has been no shortage of suggestions for actions to reduce the risk of nuclear war. Hawks, Doves, and Owls each have favored agendas of their own. Some measures on one agenda reinforce items on another; others are inconsistent. Some deal with deep causes of conflict, others with precipitating causes. Some involve changes in plans and procedures; others call for restructuring of military forces. Some could be implemented unilaterally; others would require bilateral or multilateral cooperation. Some would reinforce current American foreign policies; others would undermine them. Some of the suggested actions would have the intended effect of reducing the risk of nuclear war, others would have the opposite effect. In short, the recent debates have produced a collection of suggestions far more disparate than apples and oranges.

The agenda of actions presented here is organized under ten principles that are at roughly the same level of generality. (See table 1.)

The first two principles reflect the Hawks' primary concern for adequate deterrence of aggression (which can influence causation of conflict at all levels). The next six principles address issues more owlish in nature: four deal with precipitating causes of conflict and two deal more with intermediate causes. The last two principles address matters often associated with Doves: the need for progress in arms control and the inadequacy of deterrence for avoiding nuclear war over the long term.

Under each principle can be grouped measures that have been put forward in earlier chapters in this volume or elsewhere. Some we judge to be good ideas (DOs) and some bad (DON'Ts). The choice is not always easy, for uncertainties and subjective elements abound. For example, a given action might both enhance deterrence and increase the chance of accidental or unauthorized use of nuclear weapons, thereby reducing the danger of surprise attack or preemption in a crisis but increasing the risk of "unintended" nuclear war. Whether the action should be taken or avoided depends on one's assessment of the *net* effect on the likelihood of nuclear war. The recommendations that follow reflect our current assessments, including some close calls.

Readers may disagree not only with our judgments, but also with our selection of actions to be considered. This agenda is far from complete; it could easily be expanded with additional measures at the

TABLE 1
Ten Principles for Avoiding Nuclear War

1. Maintain a credible nuclear deterrent
2. Obtain a credible conventional deterrent
3. Enhance crisis stability
4. Reduce the impact of accidents
5. Develop procedures for war termination
6. Prevent and manage crises
7. Invigorate nonproliferation efforts
8. Limit misperceptions
9. Pursue arms control negotiations
10. Reduce reliance on nuclear deterrence over the long term

same level of generality. Greater specificity would lengthen the list still further. And the various actions clearly deserve discussion at far greater length than the brief paragraph each gets in this final chapter. The recommendations offered here are hardly definitive. Our primary objectives are to demonstrate that there are actions that can be taken to reduce the risk of nuclear war and to stimulate thinking by others.

Will some or all of these recommendations be transformed into policies of the United States government? That depends not only on their substantive merits, but also on the extent to which they attract political support or opposition. Citizens play a vital role in this process. Elected officials, especially those approaching reelection campaigns (which at all times includes all members of the House of Representatives), are acutely sensitive to pressures exerted by their constituents. Informed and active citizens can do much to transform potential actions into real ones.

Though we consider all of the actions discussed here to be important, some clearly are more consequential than others. Actions also differ in their feasibility and timeliness, and in the degree to which they will prove controversial. Taking these factors into account, we have highlighted under each of the ten principles the two actions—one to be taken and one to be avoided—that we consider most deserving of attention.

---

1. Maintain a Credible Nuclear Deterrent
- DO modernize the strategic triad.
- DON'T adopt a no-first-use policy.

To avoid war, it is necessary (though not sufficient) to maintain the capability of our military forces and the credibility of our political intentions and resolve. Our nuclear arsenal continues to play an important role in deterring aggression against the territory of the United States, our allies, and other areas of vital interest to us. There currently is rough parity in the U.S.-Soviet nuclear balance; but exactly what deters the Soviets is unknown to Americans, and is likely to remain so. Nevertheless, there seems little doubt that deterrence of deliberate nuclear or conventional attack on the American homeland is effective, robust, and stable. No U.S. or Soviet weapons program in progress or on the horizon will significantly alter the likelihood of such attacks, nor are any new capabilities within reach that would give either side a meaningful strategic advantage. Less hardy is deterrence of Soviet aggression against our allies or other areas of vital interest to us, because the threat to use nuclear weapons in response to attacks outside our homeland is inherently less credible. Our suggestions for actions to be taken and actions to be avoided are designed to ensure that Soviet leaders see no advantage in the balance of nuclear forces and to maximize the credibility of our nuclear deterrent.

Actions to Take

• *DO modernize the strategic triad.* The three legs of the strategic triad (land-based missiles, sea-based missiles, and long-range bombers and air-launched cruise missiles) comprise a diverse and redundant retaliatory force. Each component has unique properties, and their collective ability to survive attack and penetrate defenses is greater than that of each leg in isolation. The triad should be modernized as necessary to ensure that an adequate proportion would survive attack and be able to penetrate Soviet defenses. A modern ICBM force, smaller than the other legs of the triad, should be maintained to contribute to deterrence by the threat of reliable prompt use of small numbers of nuclear weapons against virtually any meaningful military targets and as a hedge against possible Soviet breakthroughs in antisubmarine warfare or air defenses. Such capabilities could be acquired by upgrading current Minuteman ICBMs or by deploying new ICBMs or by some combination of these modernizations. Over the longer term, consideration should be given to missile-carrying submarines smaller than the current versions.

• *DO put alliance politics first.* Deterrence depends not only on military capabilities, but also on perceived readiness to use force. The political cohesion of an alliance is essential to the credibility of its deterrent. In this connection, it is important for NATO to continue implementation of its intermediate-range nuclear force (INF) modernization program, unless an agreement is reached with the Soviets whereby NATO forgoes some of the planned INF deployments in return for similar reductions of Soviet forces. Political disputes that fractionate the alliance and weaken its resolve can be even more destructive than adverse changes in the military balance.

Actions to Avoid

• *DON'T adopt a no-first-use policy.* Rhetorical removal of the threat of intentional escalation to nuclear war in Europe, the Persian Gulf, or Korea would (if believed) psychologically enhance Soviet advantages in general purpose forces and increase the risk that the Soviets might attempt a conventional attack. If the current imbalance in conventional forces were corrected, so that the West could respond effectively to Soviet offensives without any perceived resort to nuclear weapons, then a strategy of no-first-use would be more attractive. There is no indication, however, that the West is likely soon to build up its conventional forces to that level. For the foreseeable future, a no-first-use declaration would be counterproductive militarily and would undermine essential alliance cohesion. Special effort should be made, however, to eliminate any requirements or operating procedures calling for early use of nuclear weapons in response to conventional aggression.

• *DON'T pursue a comprehensive freeze.* Alarm about the risk of nuclear war has increasingly been expressed in calls for a "comprehensive nuclear freeze." Unfortunately, however, a comprehensive freeze is not a good prescription for avoiding nuclear war. For example, because it is difficult to define and verify a freeze on defensive systems, most so-called "comprehensive" freeze proposals deal only with offensive nuclear weapons. But an agreement that froze only offensive forces and not the corresponding defensive ones (including ballistic missile defenses, air defenses, and antisubmarine warfare) could lead to shifts in the offense-defense balance that would weaken the deterrent value of offensive retaliatory forces. In addition, by prohibiting all modernization of nuclear weapons systems, a comprehensive freeze would preclude changes that would reduce the risk of nuclear war, such as modification of long-range bombers to provide faster takeoff (and thus greater survivability) and replacement of large multiple-warhead ICBMs by small single-warhead models. Partial freezes that impose discriminating restraints on weapons technology can be both feasible and beneficial. The merits of such proposals must, of course, be judged on a case-by-case basis.

• *DON'T confuse MAD with a strategy.* Mutual assured destruction (MAD) describes a condition, not an objective. In this condition, each superpower can absorb a first strike and still retaliate massively against its adversary's population and industry. This condition exists today and is likely to persist for the foreseeable future. But MAD is not an objective of American policy. Its "mutuality" is unattractive to most American policymakers (and presumably to Soviets as well). Nor is MAD a military strategy, for it does not serve to guide U.S. targeting (which focuses primarily on Soviet military forces). Public understanding is not advanced by those who pretend that MAD is America's strategy or goal.

• *DON'T assume that cities can be defended.* In announcing his Strategic Defense Initiative (SDI) on March 23, 1983, President Reagan called for a defensive system that "could intercept and destroy strategic ballistic missiles before they reached our own soil or that of our allies" and thereby render nuclear weapons "impotent and obsolete." The long-term goal is understandable and readily shared, but in all likelihood mutual assured destruction will remain the condition of superpowers for decades to come. Because a substantial portion of each nation's population and industry is concentrated in a relatively small number of cities, and each city can be destroyed by a few nuclear weapons, their protection requires a perfect or near-perfect defense against all forms of nuclear delivery, including long- and short-range ballistic missiles and cruise missiles, manned bombers and, for that matter, fishing trawlers, civilian aircraft, and other means for covert delivery. There are sound military reasons favoring continued research on defensive systems, but it should not be assumed that such research will lead to an effective defense of cities.

---

2. Obtain a Credible Conventional Deterrent
• DO strengthen NATO and the RDF.
• DON'T provoke the Soviet Union.

The non-nuclear forces of the United States and its allies are currently inadequate to deter with high confidence or to defend against Soviet conventional attack in Europe, the Persian Gulf region, and other areas of vital interest. Thus the United States finds itself in effect threatening first use of nuclear weapons to counter conventional aggression. By choosing to rely on early nuclear use, the United States and its European and Japanese allies have opted for defense "on the cheap." Current political preferences make an early reversal of this policy unlikely, but it is not unaffordable. The Soviet Union enjoys no economic advantage over the United States. Quite the reverse: the U.S. gross national product (GNP) is roughly twice that of the Soviet Union. Moreover, the United States and its allies enjoy a combined GNP more than four times that of the Soviet Union and its allies. If the Western democracies and Japan rely on a cheaper, more dangerous, more nuclear-weapons-dependent defense, it is because they choose to accept that risk. Insufficient resources are not a plausible excuse.

Actions to Take

• *DO strengthen NATO and the RDF.* Because threats to use conventional force are more credible than threats to use nuclear weapons, improved general purpose forces would enhance deterrence even between the nuclear superpowers. The United States and its allies, each paying its fair share, should continue those conventional force improvements that reduce the chances that the Soviets could achieve rapid victory conventionally in vital areas like Europe and the Persian Gulf. Such improvements include the acquisition of a militarily meaningful Rapid Deployment Force (RDF) and additional airlift and sealift capacities, and upgrading of air defenses in Europe. Our objective should be to escape from the position in which we have to threaten escalation to nuclear use; greater conventional capabilities will strengthen deterrence of Soviet aggression and reduce the dangers of conventional and nuclear war.

• *DO raise the nuclear threshold.* By developing and deploying conventional weapons systems capable of performing some of the functions now assigned to battlefield nuclear weapons, the United States and its allies can raise their threshold of nuclear use. This transition would be complemented by a reversal of the United States' practice of integrating battlefield nuclear weapons with general purpose forces. It must be recognized, however, that conventional forces alone cannot eliminate the risk of nuclear war. After all, the Soviets could choose to use nuclear weapons first.

Actions to Avoid

• *DON'T provoke the Soviet Union.* As the United States and its allies expand and improve their conventional forces, they should be wary of the dangers of threatening vital Soviet interests. Regardless of the peacefulness of the West's intentions, our offensive conventional capabilities should not be strong enough to pose plausible threats to Eastern Europe and the Soviet homeland. NATO should continue to adhere to a military strategy consistent with the fundamentally defensive character of its current forces. An offensive force posture and strategy, whether based on nuclear or advanced conventional technologies, even though intended to enhance deterrence could increase the risk of nuclear war by provoking the Soviets to preempt or by lowering their threshold for nuclear use.

• *DON'T pretend that nuclear weapons deter only nuclear war.* The proposition that the *only* military purpose of nuclear weapons is to deter the adversary's use of nuclear weapons is gaining acceptance as a new conventional wisdom. But we believe it is wrong. So long as nuclear forces are deployed in substantial numbers, they present an inescapable risk that any conventional war might escalate by design or by accident to a nuclear one. How much the United States should rely on the risk of nuclear escalation to deter conventional war is an appropriate topic for debate. That discussion is not advanced, however, by denying that the danger of nuclear escalation affects the calculations of a potential aggressor.

---

3. Enhance Crisis Stability
• DO take decapitation seriously.
• DON'T adopt a launch-on-warning policy.

Though nuclear weapons remain essential for deterrence, our goal is to avoid their use. Nuclear weapons must be a last resort. Our preferred posture is one in which the Soviet Union can gain no advantage in striking first. One current problem is the apparent vulnerability of our fixed land-based ICBMs, which could be destroyed by only a fraction of the Soviets' large force of highly accurate multiple-warhead ICBMs. Our bombers are less vulnerable than our ICBMs, and our missile-bearing submarines at sea are virtually invulnerable.

The weakest and most often overlooked element of our deterrent is the system for coordinating the use of the weapons themselves. It is critical to shape our nuclear forces to minimize incentives for preemption and allow time for diplomacy to work during a crisis.

Actions to Take

• *DO take decapitation seriously.* If there is a chink in our nuclear armor, it is the vulnerability of the command, control, and communications (C^3) structure associated with nuclear weapons. Particularly vulnerable are the people in the political chain of command, almost all of whom usually are located in Washington, D.C. A surprise or preemptive "decapitation" attack against the C^3 structure might be attempted in hopes that surviving weapons could not then be used in retaliation. The Reagan administration's Strategic Modernization Program gives highest priority to upgrading and improving the survivability of the C^3 system. That priority is well deserved.

• *DO send a top leader out of Washington during crises.* Given the danger of decapitation, it is essential that at least one of the seventeen constitutionally designated successors (and an appropriate staff) be outside of Washington in time of crisis. While it is contrary to the instincts of policy makers to be away from the action, at least one top official should be out of harm's way. In a serious crisis, it would be more important to the nation to have the vice president located in an alternative command post than in Washington trying to assist in managing the situation.

• *DO develop a survivable small ICBM.* The ICBM force is the most vulnerable leg of the strategic triad. To reduce the dangers of surprise or preemptive attack against these land-based missiles and to hedge against Soviet breakthroughs in antisubmarine warfare or air defenses, the United States should continue to develop a small ICBM (such as the "Midgetman") and to investigate the most effective modes in which it might be deployed (such as mobile launchers, deceptive basing, and defended silos). Even if ICBMs cannot be made reliably survivable, a modern ICBM force should be retained. The unique ability of ICBMs to perform prompt controlled attacks against a wide variety of targets is an important element of deterrence, and their deployment on land complicates any Soviet first strike against missiles and bombers.

Actions to Avoid

• *DON'T adopt a launch-on-warning policy.* Some have proposed a policy of launch-on-warning or launch-under-attack as a solution to the ICBM vulnerability problem. This cure is worse than the disease, for it would increase unacceptably the dangers of accidental or unauthorized launch. The United States should maintain the capability to launch on warning or under attack, and its declaratory policy should be sufficiently ambiguous that the Soviets could not be confident that it would not do so. But we should not adopt launch-on-warning or launch-under-attack as operational or unambiguous declaratory policy.

• *DON'T seek a first-strike capability.* Neither side could actually achieve a disarming first-strike capability, for the other side has the option of launching its strategic missiles on warning of, or during, an attack. Any attempt by the United States to acquire a disarming first-strike capability would encourage the Soviets to put their forces on a hair-trigger and would increase Soviet incentives to preempt in time of crisis, thereby significantly reducing our own security. Thus, we should not structure our forces to threaten the survival of the full spectrum of Soviet retaliatory forces.

• *DON'T plan for a nuclear demonstration shot in Europe.* Among NATO's contingency plans for responding to Soviet conventional aggression in Europe is a nuclear "shot across the bow" to demonstrate the alliance's resolve. But such a non-military use of nuclear weapons could have an effect quite different from the intended one. On the one hand, it could be seen as evidence of NATO's unwillingness to engage in a "real" nuclear war. On the other hand, if interpreted as a prelude to a substantial nuclear attack, it might induce an all-out preemptive strike by the Soviets. A nuclear demonstration shot in Europe is unlikely to serve NATO's interests.

---

4. Reduce the Impact of Accidents

• DO reduce reliance on short-range theater nuclear weapons.
• DON'T use nuclear alerts for political signaling.

Accidents will happen. Broadly defined as unintended events, accidents are as certain as human fallibility and as Murphy's Law in large complex organizations. We protect against accident by maintaining reserve (not running systems at full capacity), redundancy (having more than one system to rely on), and time (introducing pauses that allow us to correct the effects of accidents). We protect against unauthorized use of nuclear weapons by special procedures and physical barriers such as permissive action links (special electronic combination locks). Given the irrationality of major nuclear war, accidents would be likely to play a significant role in the chain of events leading up to any such conflict. Thus it is important to find ways to introduce reserve, redundancy, and time into organizational procedures for dealing with nuclear crises.

Actions to Take

• *DO reduce reliance on short-range theater nuclear weapons.* Short-range theater nuclear weapons (such as nuclear artillery shells) would prove difficult to control centrally if conflict should arise. Most commanders in the field doubt that release authority would be received in time for their use against an attack. This reduces the deterrent value of these weapons. They do, however, pose a real danger of accidental or unauthorized use in peacetime and especially in the "fog of war." Conventional weapons based on emerging technologies will enable NATO to threaten more credibly to destroy targets, including massed Soviet armored divisions, currently assigned to short-range nuclear forces. Accordingly, we should reduce our reliance on these short-range weapons for deterrence and, to the extent feasible politically, withdraw them gradually from likely regions of conflict.

• *DO add safety devices and procedures.* Current safety devices and procedures such as permissive action links (PALs), weapons designs that prevent accidental nuclear detonation, and rules that require action by two or more people to arm each nuclear weapon should be maintained, improved, and extended. Of particular concern is the absence of PALs on the nuclear warheads on submarine-launched ballistic missiles, enabling launch of these armed weapons even in the absence of an express order from the president or his authorized successor. The United States should consider seriously the possibility of installing PALs on the nuclear weapons on SLBMs. Such PALs would reduce the danger of accidental and authorized use, but at the cost of increasing the potential effectiveness (and therefore the likelihood) of a Soviet decapitation strike. This cost could be reduced in several ways. For example, the PALs need not necessarily be active on all missile submarines or at all times. They might be relaxed on some of the submarines routinely and on most or all of them when ordered by higher authorities.

• *DO upgrade warning systems.* To protect against the danger of false alarms and to enhance confidence in "positive" signals of attack, the United States should maintain redundancy in its intelligence, surveillance, and communications systems. We should also explore with the Soviets the possibility of negotiating an agreement under which each side could place unmanned sensors in the missile fields of the other side.

Actions to Avoid

• *DON'T use nuclear alerts for political signaling.* Nuclear alerts are a dangerous form of communication, especially during crises. When some form of alert appears necessary to ensure the survival of our forces in case of an attack, preference should be given to low-level or partial alerts. Higher alert levels involve a deliberate release of the safety catches that ordinarily protect against accident or unauthorized use of nuclear weapons.

• *DON'T multiply crises.* It has been suggested that if the Soviets initiate a crisis in a region (or of a type) in which they have an advantage, the United States should respond by initiating another crisis in which it has the advantage. (For example, Soviet aggression against U.S. interests in the Persian Gulf region might be countered by U.S. action against Cuba.) Such action is likely to be counterproductive and possibly disastrous. The likelihood of accident goes up with the level of stress on people and systems in crisis, and the time available to correct accidents goes down. As the number of simultaneous crises rises, this danger increases geometrically rather than arithmetically.

---

5. Develop Procedures for War Termination
- DO plan for ending a war if it begins.
- DON'T plan for early use of nuclear weapons.

Planning for terminating a nuclear war is a taboo subject. To the left it implies toleration of limited nuclear war; to the right it smacks of surrender. We wish to avoid all nuclear war, but if war should break out, there still may be a chance to avoid total holocaust. If a nuclear war ever occurs, a top priority will be to stop it. And since escalation of conventional war is the most likely path to nuclear war, war termination procedures should cover the full spectrum of conflict.

Actions to Take

- *DO plan for ending a war if it begins.* The greatest barriers to planning for war termination are emotional and political. Mere discussion of the subject attracts criticism from all quarters. Thinking about it only reinforces the importance of avoiding any war. If, however, despite our best efforts conventional or nuclear war should begin, we should have available plans and procedures to end it. Developing and practicing such plans and procedures is a distasteful but prudent task. It implies neither toleration of limited nuclear war nor belief that nuclear war can be won in any meaningful sense, only a recognition that some nuclear wars could be even more catastrophic than others.

- *DO develop survivable U.S.-Soviet communications.* Communication between the superpowers is clearly an essential component of any system for war termination. Yet the current Hot Line terminals would be destroyed by any attack on national capitals. The two sides jointly should provide the means and establish procedures for reliable, rapid, and effective communication between them not only in peacetime and during political crisis, but also after armed conflict—even nuclear— has begun.

- *DO maintain civilian control over nuclear weapons.* Civilian control over military procedures, especially those associated with nuclear weapons, must be maintained in crises and, to the extent feasible, after war has begun. In particular, delegation of nuclear authority should be limited and conditioned so that it can be readily retrieved, even at the cost of increasing the consequences of decapitation. Negotiations over war termination can have meaning only if cease-fire orders can be issued, transmitted, received, and obeyed.

Actions to Avoid

• *DON'T plan for early use of nuclear weapons.* To provide opportunities for war termination on acceptable terms at the lowest possible levels of damage, preferably before escalation to nuclear war, effort should be made to avoid early use of nuclear weapons. In addition to appropriate plans and procedures, this effort will probably also have to include some strengthening and restructuring of conventional forces.

• *DON'T decapitate.* Deterrence undoubtedly is strengthened by the possibility that a United States retaliatory attack might include among its targets the Soviet political and military leaders and their C^3 network. But if war should start, it is unlikely to be in the United States' interest to respond in a way that produces chaos on the other side. This could make it impossible to conduct the negotiations needed to end a war and could also eliminate Soviet leaders' ability to issue and transmit an order to halt hostilities. Thus, if the United States wishes to preserve the option of a negotiated settlement, it should not rely upon decapitation as part of a response to Soviet aggression.

---

6. Prevent and Manage Crises

• DO prepare decision-makers to deal with nuclear crises.
• DON'T engage American and Soviet forces in direct combat.

Crises greatly increase the prospect of nuclear war. By definition a crisis means an increase in threat and stress and a compression of time. Both constrain rational options and reduce the ability to respond to the effects of accidents. Since World War II the United States and the Soviet Union have developed some de facto rules of prudence to prevent and contain crises. The superpowers have not engaged each other's forces in combat; they have not threatened each other's vital interests; and they have not used nuclear weapons against anyone.

These rules represent a restraint of antagonism that should be recognized, enhanced, and extended. At the same time, it is clear that the U.S.-Soviet relationship is fundamentally competitive, even during crises. Both nations wish to reduce the chances of intended or unintended war, but each also wishes to manipulate the fear of that outcome in order to deter or coerce the other side. The task of crisis prevention and management is thus more complex than it first appears. Nonetheless, initiatives in this realm can reduce risk.

Actions to Take

• *DO prepare decision-makers to deal with nuclear crises.* Nuclear decision-makers often are not experts on the subject. Many new political appointees with responsibilities related to nuclear weapons arrive at their jobs with little knowledge or background in U.S.-Soviet relations, nuclear weapons affairs, or crisis decision-making. They deserve help in preparing to deal with nuclear crises that might occur. We need to find more efficient ways of giving them information on nuclear deployments and practices, the kinds of crisis situations that might arise, and the mechanisms available for dealing with such crises. In addition it would be useful to offer some compilation of lessons learned from the experience of former officials in similar positions of responsibility. Active participation in crisis simulations can also be a valuable experience.

• *DO work with the Soviets to prevent and manage crises.* Discussions of crisis prevention and management with the Soviets could serve several useful functions. For example, such talks could help to sensitize the leaders to the issues involved and to the perspectives of the other side; to clarify perceptions of relative interests in specific geographical areas; and to reinforce and extend specific negotiated agreements like the U.S.-Soviet Incidents-at-Sea Agreement. In particular, the United States and the Soviet Union should seek to create a jointly staffed crisis-monitoring center along the lines proposed by Senators Sam Nunn and John Warner. Among its various virtues, the fact-finding role of such a center could provide a useful mechanism for introducing a pause early in a crisis.

• *DO install bilateral hot lines between all nuclear powers.* Hot lines (or, more formally, direct communications links) offer means for timely exchange of information between heads of government in times of crisis. Such hot lines now exist between Washington-Moscow, London-Moscow, and Paris-Moscow. Similar bilateral direct communications links should be installed between all (or an many as possible) of the remaining pairs of capitals of acknowledged nuclear weapons states (namely Washington, Moscow, London, Paris, and Beijing).

Actions to Avoid

• *DON'T engage American and Soviet forces in direct combat.* The United States and the Soviet Union have not engaged in armed conflict with one another for more than six decades. Keep it that way. Escalation from conventional war to nuclear war, either intentionally or unintentionally, can best be prevented by avoiding conventional war. Special emphasis should be given to ensuring that surface ships and submarines armed with nuclear weapons neither threaten nor are threatened by the navy of the other side. A nuclear war at sea could quickly spread to land.

• *DON'T try to change rapidly the situation in Eastern Europe.* Eastern Europe is viewed by the Soviets as an essential geographical buffer to guard against (another) invasion from the West. At the same time, the United States and its Western allies have strong historical, cultural, and emotional attachments to the people and nations of Eastern Europe and are eager to free them from Soviet domination. Political instability and popular uprisings in the region inevitably will tempt us to take action. But the Soviets will perceive any attempt by the West to bring about rapid change in Eastern Europe as a most serious threat to their vital interests and will respond accordingly. Unfortunately, we must be patient and try to encourage desired changes over the long term.

• *DON'T use nuclear weapons against third parties.* The prohibition on use of nuclear weapons has lasted for forty years. Its value is obvious. Few events are more likely to cause a superpower crisis or to lead to a major nuclear war than the actual use of nuclear weapons.

---

7. Invigorate Nonproliferation Efforts
• DO maintain security guarantees.
• DON'T be fatalistic about proliferation.

President John F. Kennedy's prediction that fifteen to twenty-five nations would have nuclear weapons by the 1970s has proven wrong. Today no more than seven states have nuclear weapons. The fact that thirty or forty other nations could have acquired nuclear weapons, but have chosen not to do so, is a considerable achievement of international relations and good sense, as well as good fortune. The risk of a catalytically induced nuclear war depends very much on how many independent fingers are on nuclear triggers. The spread of nuclear weapons would increase not only the danger that the superpowers would be drawn into local nuclear wars, but also the possibility of decapitation attacks by third parties against the United States or the Soviet Union. In addition, while nuclear terrorism would be unlikely to lead to a major nuclear war, its prospect could have catastrophic effects on an open society like ours, with its permeable borders.

Actions to Take

- *DO maintain security guarantees.* While several factors push countries in the direction of nuclear weapons, concern for national security clearly leads the list. Accordingly, the United States should maintain and reinforce its guarantees of security wherever credible, as in Europe, Japan, and Korea.

- *DO support the nonproliferation regime.* The Nuclear Nonproliferation Treaty and the International Atomic Energy Agency form the core of the international nonproliferation "regime"—an array of agreements, institutions, and practices that has contributed significantly to restraint. The Nuclear Suppliers' Group assists the regime by fostering cooperation among nuclear suppliers in maintaining controls over exports of materials and equipment that might be used to make nuclear weapons. While this regime is not perfect, it symbolizes the presumption against proliferation and provides an inspection system that helps to deter military use of civilian nuclear facilities. The regime should be supported and, whenever possible, strengthened.

- *DO explore sanctions against proliferators.* A nation considering the acquisition of nuclear weapons must take into account the potential adverse responses, including possible punitive measures. The stronger and more likely the international sanctions, the more powerful is the disincentive to proliferate. To this end, the United States should explore with others, including the Soviet Union, a plan for imposing specific agreed-upon political, economic, and security sanctions on countries that violate nonproliferation commitments or otherwise acquire nuclear explosives.

- *DO protect against nuclear terrorism.* The United States should improve its capabilities to gather intelligence on terrorist groups that might acquire nuclear weapons and should prepare to act against such nuclear threats if they emerge. These efforts should be pursued unilaterally as well as in cooperation with other interested countries.

Actions to Avoid

- *DON'T be fatalistic about proliferation.* Even though five, or six, or seven nuclear horses are out of the barn, more than 150 nonnuclear horses remain inside. It is well worth while to close the barn door, even if it cannot be nailed shut. Whether or not further proliferation is inevitable, we should strive to stop it or slow it. The slower the spread of nuclear weapons, the less destabilizing it will be and the better our chances for preventing their use.

---

8. Limit Misperceptions
- DO meet regularly with Soviet leaders.
- DON'T treat nuclear weapons like other weapons.

Facts are not enough. They are filtered through the minds of policymakers. History offers many examples of misperceptions of adversaries' capabilities and threats. To recall an example from World War I, a major factor driving German action in 1914 was the German General Staff's conclusion that by 1916 the Russian military would acquire a capability for offensive action against Germany. In fact, the Russian General Staff had no such intention and could not imagine acquiring such a capability by 1916, or even 1926. Sound strategy must therefore target perceptions as well as reality.

Actions to Take

- *DO meet regularly with Soviet leaders.* Regular discussions between American and Soviet officials at the summit, cabinet, high military, and working levels can contribute greatly to mutual understanding of how each side sees its own interests, the other's, and the risks. If such meetings were held at regular intervals they would become routine, thus reducing political pressure for tangible results from each session. Their purposes might best be served if the parties could agree in advance not to use these sessions for formal intergovernmental negotiations.

- *DO encourage non-governmental contacts with the Soviets.* Contact and exchange between Americans and Soviets other than government officials can play an important, if secondary, role in reducing misperceptions. Since our society is open and theirs closed, the United States is likely to learn more than the Soviets from such exchanges.

- *DO expect the unexpected.* A strategy for avoiding nuclear war must not be based on simple notions of what constitutes an adequate deterrent, on mirror-image models of the adversary, on psychology-free simulations of individual and group decision-making in crises, and on idealized computer calculations of the consequences of nuclear exchanges. Such devices can provide some insights into problems to be addressed and into possible solutions, but they are of little use for predicting the future. The events that might lead to nuclear war are unknown and unknowable: we must expect the unexpected.

Actions to Avoid

- *DON'T treat nuclear weapons like other weapons.* Political rhetoric and military training often suggest that nuclear weapons are no different from other instruments of war-fighting and should be used just as weapons have been used in the past. But nuclear weapons are not "normal," and we know it. They are weapons of terror. The danger that we might come to forget the truth is small, but there is some risk in confusing the Soviets about what we believe.

- *DON'T exaggerate military imbalances.* Exaggerated statements about the existence, nature, extent, and importance of perceived or possible future Soviet military advantages often are made in seeking public and congressional support for defense programs intended to enhance deterrence. Ironically, such statements can themselves weaken deterrence by undermining the credibility of the current threat.

- *DON'T cut off communications as a sanction.* Soviet actions that anger us create domestic pressures for sanctions. Invariably in such situations, American leaders are tempted to reduce or even to cut off contacts with the Soviets. Such temptation should be resisted, for it is in times of worsened relations and heightened tensions that the communications links provided by official and non-governmental contacts are most needed.

---

9. Pursue Arms Control Negotiations.
- DO preserve existing arms control agreements.
- DON'T oversell arms control.

Negotiated arms control has a variety of forms and functions. Some observers believe that comprehensive formal treaties to limit or reduce central force structures may be obsolete. But arms control can be informal as well as formal, and arms control negotiations are a form of communication and reassurance as well as constraint. Even if extensive formal agreements prove difficult to achieve, arms control talks can be used to limit or reduce specific threats, shape future forces, develop confidence-building measures, and increase transparency in the military competition. But arms control is unlikely to produce either miracles or calamities. Kept in that perspective, formal arms control has a modest but useful role to play in an overall strategy for avoiding nuclear war.

Actions to Take

• *DO preserve existing arms control agreements.* While arms control negotiations have been less productive than one might have wished, they have been far from fruitless. For example, the Nonproliferation Treaty, which provides for international inspections of nuclear facilities located in countries that do not have nuclear weapons, clearly serves U.S. interests. Indeed, the United States (as well as the Soviet Union and others) enjoy net benefits from existing arms control agreements, including the formally binding Limited Test Ban Treaty, Outer Space Treaty, Accidents Measures Agreement, and Antiballistic Missile (ABM) Treaty, and the informally observed Threshold Test Ban Treaty, Peaceful Nuclear Explosions Treaty, SALT I Interim Agreement on Offensive Forces, and SALT II Treaty. The survival of these agreements and the preservation of the benefits associated with them require continuous vigilance. Particular care should be exercised to ensure that the activities associated with President Reagan's Strategic Defense Initiative remain in compliance with the ABM Treaty. If strategic defenses are ever to contribute significantly to protecting the territory of the United States and its allies, deep reductions and severe limitations on offensive forces almost certainly would be required. Such constraints are not likely to be accepted, except possibly in a highly cooperative arms control environment.

• *DO pursue crisis stability through arms control.* Explore the possibility of negotiating arms control agreements that enhance crisis stability with the Soviet Union. The following examples appear particularly attractive: a ban or limit on testing of antisatellite (ASAT) systems—especially high-altitude ASAT systems that threaten ballistic missile early warning satellites and communication satellites— could enhance each side's confidence that it would receive adequate warning of attack and be able to communicate with retaliatory forces; quantitative and qualitative constraints on long-range ballistic missiles with hard-target kill capabilities could make ICBMs less vulnerable; a comprehensive ban or gradually tightened limits on nuclear tests would constrain development of newer and potentially more destabilizing weapons; and a ban on forward deployment of short time-of-flight ballistic missiles (such as the Soviet SS-20 and the U.S. Pershing II) and a requirement that missile-carrying submarines "stand off" some specified minimum distance from the adversary's coast would increase the warning time available in case of attack on bomber bases and/or C^3 installations.

• *DO reduce uncertainties through arms control negotiations.* Perhaps the most important potential contribution of arms control negotiations is to reduce uncertainties about the other side's current and likely future forces, practices, and intentions. Ongoing negotiations facilitate communication between responsible and informed representatives of governments and provide forums in which concerns can be expressed, data can be exchanged, ambiguities can be resolved, compliance can be addressed, confidence-building measures can be developed, and agreed-on limitations can be achieved. These factors, separately or in combination, can reduce uncertainties and constrain "worst case" planning on both sides.

Actions to Avoid

- *DON'T oversell arms control.* Public support is essential to progress in arms control. Such support is endangered when exaggerated claims are made about past arms control accomplishments and unrealistic expectations raised for future ones. Overselling arms control can result in dissatisfaction with useful agreements. It also runs the risk of lulling the public and elected officials into complacency, so that they are unwilling to invest adequately in defense.

- *DON'T abuse bargaining chips.* There is merit in the bargaining chip concept. The Soviets are more likely to give up something of value to them if we give up something of value in return. But the concept is distorted and abused when it is invoked to gain domestic support for funding weapons that would not be of value to us (that is, weapons whose costs exceed their benefits) or that we would not be willing to bargain away under any circumstances. Our weapons system development and acquisition programs should make sense in their own terms with or without arms control. Otherwise we may find ourselves without any bargain and stuck with the wrong chips.

- *DON'T restrict arms control to formal agreements.* The traditional objectives of arms control are to reduce the likelihood and consequences of war and the cost of preserving national security. Mutual restraints that serve these objectives can be enshrined in formal treaties, embodied in tacit understandings, or induced by unilateral actions. Each form has strengths and weaknesses relative to the others, and all can and should be used to play useful roles in achieving arms control objectives.

---

10. Reduce Reliance on Nuclear Deterrence over the Long Term

- DON'T assume that nuclear deterrence will last forever.
- DO intensify the search for alternatives to deterrence.

Deterrence based on a threat of nuclear holocaust appeals to no one. Yet for forty years it seems to have worked, preventing not only nuclear war but also global conventional war. We see no reason to believe deterrence will soon fail. It may serve for many more decades, a century, or even longer. On the other hand, we do not believe that the current approach will succeed forever in avoiding major nuclear war. Unless human beings, our institutions, and the complex technological systems on which we now rely achieve perfection, eventual failure of some form appears assured.

Where might an alternative to deterrence be found? Three trails for exploration have been suggested: technology, politics, and social development. Technological advances might lead eventually to devices for countering nuclear weapons delivery systems or for neutralizing the nuclear weapons themselves. (The Strategic Defense Initiative may represent an early segment of this trail.) Politics offers the prospect of gradually transforming the nature of the relationship between the United States and the Soviet Union. (England and France have nuclear weapons, but we do not view them as threats to our survival.) The political trail might even take us beyond the current international system of sovereign states. Finally, the social development trail could lead to a world in which nuclear deterrence plays no role. It may seem utopian, but if we act creatively and deliberately to transform human society over the very long term into one in which nuclear threats no longer seem necessary to preserve peace, our descendants just might be able to eliminate the weapons rather than themselves.

Among these alternatives, we find the political trail the most promising. Despite deep differences in history, culture, values, and ambition, the United States and the Soviet Union share an inescapable common interest. That interest is to avoid a global nuclear war, for they would be the most ravaged victims. Over time, this fundamental interest might well serve as a foundation for cooperative actions that could transform the relationship between the superpowers.

In the near term, the two countries' shared concern provides a powerful incentive to work together in minimizing the prospects for unintended or catalytic nuclear war. Limiting misperceptions, reducing the danger of accidents, preventing and managing crises, and inhibiting the spread of nuclear weapons to additional states or to terrorists—these objectives all serve the common interest and are more likely to be achieved through cooperative action. Wise statesmanship that reduces mutual risks in the short run could eventually bring about changes in the U.S.-Soviet relationship as great as the change in U.S.-China relations over the past two decades. Such change would permit substantially reduced reliance on nuclear deterrence.

These observations offer only a little comfort. We see no certain way to escape some reliance on nuclear deterrence. Indeed, well-intended efforts to escape it before conditions are appropriate could make nuclear war more likely. Nonetheless, the search for less conventional, more imaginative alternatives for the long run must begin. Bold, creative approaches to the subject must be stimulated, nurtured, and rewarded. In particular, the community of defense and foreign policy specialists must resist cynicism toward nontraditional concepts, misplaced confidence that all of the important ideas have been examined, and condescension to newcomers from other fields. We intend to heed this advice as we join with others in exploring the realm of ideas beyond deterrence. In confronting the awesome challenge of avoiding nuclear war, the end as well as the beginning of wisdom is neither fear nor courage; it is humility.

NOTES

1. The Shape of the Problem

1. George Shultz, "U.S.-Soviet Relations in the Context of U.S. Foreign Policy," *Department of State Bulletin* (July 1983): 65.
2. For a more complex discussion see George Quester, *Deterrence Before Hiroshima* (New York: John Wiley & Sons, 1966).
3. For many helpful suggestions on this subject we are grateful to David Hamburg.
4. Alexis de Tocqueville, *Democracy in America* (Garden City, N.Y.: Doubleday Anchor Books, 1969): 412–13.
5. Quoted in Bernard Brodie, *War and Politics* (New York: Macmillan Publishing Co., 1973): 377.
6. Harvard Nuclear Study Group, *Living with Nuclear Weapons* (New York: Bantam Books, 1983), chapter 3.
7. European Security Study Group, *Strengthening Conventional Deterrence in Europe: Proposals for the 1980's* (New York: St. Martin's Press, 1983).
8. National Conference of Catholic Bishops, *Catholics and Nuclear War: A Commentary on the Challenge of Peace* (New York: Crossroads Press, 1983): 336.

2. Accidental Nuclear War

1. See "Missile Alerts Traced to 46 Cent Item," *New York Times,* June 18, 1980, A16.
2. See Charles Perrow, "Normal Accident at Three Mile Island," *Society* 18 (July/August 1981): 17–26.
3. A summary of conventional views of accidental war can be found in Daniel Frei, *Risks of Unintentional Nuclear War* (London: Allanheld, Osmun, 1983).
4. These definitions are drawn from Herman Kahn, *On Escalation* (Baltimore, Md.: Penguin Books, 1965): 284–86.
5. See Barbara Tuchman, *The Guns of August* (New York: Dell Publishing Co., 1962).
6. This account is found in Stanford Research Institute, "World War II German Fire Document Translations," Report MU 5865, Menlo Park, Calif., 1968.

7. See "Report of the DoD Commission on Beirut International Airport Terrorist Act, October 23, 1983," U.S. Department of Defense, December 20, 1983.

8. For a discussion of the competing factors see Paul Bracken, *Command and Control of Nuclear Forces* (New Haven: Yale University Press, 1983), chapter 5.

9. I am indebted to Roger Beaumont for this example.

10. See Graham Allison and Peter Szanton, *Remaking Foreign Policy: The Organizational Approach* (New York: Basic Books, 1976): 36–38.

11. Examples of the problems that arise are described in *Command and Control* . . ., chapter 4.

12. This is a largely overlooked dimension of deterrence. It directly addresses the institutional structure of different deterrent systems. See Paul Bracken, "Deterrence, Gaming, and Game Theory," *Orbis* 27 (Winter 1984): 790–802; "The Political Command and Control of Nuclear Forces," Yale School of Organization and Management Working Paper #31, April 1984; and P. Bracken, M. Haviv, M. Shubik, and U. Tulowitzki, "Nuclear Warfare, C^3 I and First and Second Strike Scenarios," Cowles Foundation Discussion Paper No. 712, Economics, Yale University, August 1984.

13. This is based on conversations with several persons who have worked in these situations.

14. The relationship between SAC's vulnerability and accidental war is well described in Herman Kahn, *On Thermonuclear War* (Princeton, N.J.: Princeton University Press, 1961): 103–7 and 422–26.

15. The following material is drawn from *Command and Control* . . ., chapter 2.

16. See Ralph Lapp, *The Weapons Culture* (New York: W.W. Norton, 1968): 39.

17. I am indebted to Frank Armbruster of the Hudson Institute for this discussion.

18. A discussion of the force generation and alerting problems of bombers is found in Jeremy J. Stone, *Containing the Arms Race* (Cambridge: MIT Press, 1966): 76–89.

19. See for example Donald G. Brennan, *Arms Control, Disarmament, and National Security* (New York: George Braziller, 1961) or Thomas C. Schelling and Morton H. Halperin, *Strategy and Arms Control* (New York: Twentieth Century Fund, 1961).

20. For one example see U.S. Congress, Senate, *Recent False Alerts from the Nation's Missile Attack Warning System,* by Gary Hart and Barry Goldwater, Committee Print (Washington, D.C.: Government Printing Office, 1980).

21. The following description is drawn from Charles Perrow, *Normal Accidents* (New York: Basic Books, 1984): 170–81.

22. *Ibid.*

23. See Paul Bracken, *Command and Control* . . .: 59–68.

24. The estimate indicated by the curve is similar to one often used by the late Herman Kahn, and my own thoughts on this matter were deeply influenced by discussions with him. However, there are important differences in my descriptions, and the conclusions of this paper are my own. See Herman Kahn, "Scenarios vs. Reality," in *The Coming Boom* (New York: Simon and Schuster, 1982): 173–77; and also

Herman Kahn, "Nuclear War: Basic Issues and Concepts," Hudson Institute, January 1969: 1.

25. U.S. Army, *Operations* FM 100-5, July 1976: 10-9.

26. This approach, of course, is the fundamental conclusion advanced in much of modern organization theory; for example, see James G. March and Herbert A. Simon, *Organizations* (New York: John Wiley & Sons, 1958).

3. Surprise Attack and Preemption

1. For elaboration see Richard K. Betts, *Surprise Attack: Lessons for Defense Planning* (Washington, D.C.: Brookings Institution, 1982), chapter 1. Some of the other points in my essay draw on chapter 8 in this book.

2. See John D. Steinbruner, "Launch Under Attack," *Scientific American* 250, no. 1 (January 1984): 37–47; and Bruce G. Blair, *Headless Horseman of the Apocalypse: Command and Control of the U.S. Strategic Forces,* Ph.D. diss., Yale University, March 1984: 310, 321, 337, 432, 469, and *passim.*

3. The term self-deterrence has become popular, but is a misnomer. It really means simple deterrence—that the victim will be deterred from a second strike by the prospect of the third strike (by the original attacker) against cities and other assets that had been largely spared in the initial attack. A belief in the possibility of limited war fed the Japanese risk in 1941 and the decision of the German chancellor to take a "leap in the dark" in 1914. See Konrad H. Jarausch, "The Illusion of Limited War: Chancellor Bethmann Hollweg's Calculated Risk, July 1914," *Central European History* 2 (March 1969): 48, 78.

4. See Irving L. Janis, *Victims of Groupthink* (Boston: Houghton Mifflin, 1972), chapter 6.

5. Schlesinger testimony in U.S. Senate, Committee on Foreign Relations, *Hearing: Briefing on Counterforce Attacks,* 93rd Cong., 2d sess., 1975; Paul H. Nitze, "Assuring Strategic Stability in an Era of Detente," *Foreign Affairs* 54, no. 2 (January 1976).

6. Stephen Van Evera, "The Cult of the Offensive and the Origins of the First World War," *International Security* 9, no. 1 (Summer 1984).

7. Michael I. Handel, *Israel's Political Military Doctrine,* Occasional Paper No. 30 (Cambridge: Harvard University Center for International Affairs, July 1973): 19, 66, and *passim.*

8. See Fred Kaplan, *The Wizards of Armageddon* (New York: Simon and Schuster, 1983): 132–34; David Alan Rosenberg, " 'A Smoking Radiating Ruin at the End of Two Hours,' " *International Security* 6, no. 3 (Winter 1981/1982): 13–15, 27.

9. See Scott D. Sagan, "Nuclear Alerts and Crisis Management," unpublished paper, Avoiding Nuclear War Project, Harvard University, June 1984.

10. Betts, *Surprise Attack:* 247–49.

11. Robert Jervis, *The Logic of Images in International Relations* (Princeton: Princeton University Press, 1970): 18.

12. Stephen Peter Rosen, "Foreign Policy and Nuclear Weapons: The Case for Strategic Defenses," in Samuel P. Huntington, ed., *The Strategic Imperative* (Cam-

bridge: Ballinger, 1982): 142; see also 143–44. Rosen's argument that nuclear weapons have not changed the calculus, however, is unconvincing.

13. Uneven BMD—with one side possessing defenses significantly more effective than the other's—would reduce the danger of preemption because the former would have less to fear and the latter less to gain from it. It would, however, increase the probability that the side with effective defenses might contemplate preventive attack. Limited BMD could be useful to protect national capitals from a few incoming warheads that might have been launched *accidentally* (if only the capital were destroyed, lower-level commanders might respond with retaliation that could produce all-out war that political leaders might otherwise avoid). Moscow already has this protection; Washington does not.

14. Richard K. Betts, "Conventional Deterrence: Predictive Uncertainty and Policy Confidence," *World Politics* 37, no. 2 (January 1985).

15. If deployment of SLBMs (such as the U.S. D-5 now in development) with sufficient accuracy and yield to kill "hard" targets (those protected against destruction by anything but an almost direct hit) were precluded, retention of moderate numbers of MIRVed SLBMs—which currently can threaten only "soft" targets (cities or military facilities not buried in highly reinforced concrete)—might be compatible with this solution.

16. John D. Steinbruner, "Nuclear Decapitation," *Foreign Policy* no. 45 (Winter 1982/83).

17. Plans are already under way on the U.S. side to boost the day-to-day deployment rate of new Ohio-class SSBNs to more than 60 percent.

18. See Richard K. Betts, "A Joint Nuclear Risk Reduction Center," in a forthcoming volume edited by Barry Blechman, *Preventing Nuclear War* (Bloomington: University of Indiana Press, 1985).

19. Soviet military writers have defined preemption in such a way that it is not necessarily incompatible with the official Soviet policy of no first use. If the Americans have irrevocably put preparations for a first strike into motion—however that certainty could theoretically be ascertained—then a Soviet launch to beat them to the punch would not really be a first strike, but only anticipatory retaliation. Soviet writings, however, obscure the issue of whether their preferred option would be preemption, launch-on-warning, launch-under-attack, or a combination (for example, launching part of the force on warning, and part a bit later to forestall the second wave of a U.S. attack).

4. Escalation in Europe

1. These crises are compared in Alexander L. George and Richard Smoke, *Deterrence in American Foreign Policy: Theory and Practice* (New York: Columbia University Press, 1974): 107–39 and 390–446.

2. See Morton H. Halperin, "The Korean War," in Robert J. Art and Kenneth N. Waltz, eds., *The Use of Force: International Politics and Foreign Policy,* 2d ed. (Lanham, Md.: University Press of America, 1983): 292–93; and Robert F. Kennedy, *Thirteen Days: A Memoir of the Cuban Missile Crisis* (New York: W.W. Norton, 1971): 13–14.

3. See A. W. DePorte, *Europe Between the Superpowers: The Enduring Balance* (New Haven: Yale University Press, 1979): 166–96.

4. See Thomas C. Schelling, *Arms and Influence* (New Haven: Yale University Press, 1966): 35–91; and Glenn H. Snyder, *Deterrence and Defense* (Princeton: Princeton University Press, 1961): 5–40. An excellent treatment of the balance of forces in previous failures of deterrence is found in John J. Mearsheimer, *Conventional Deterrence* (Ithaca: Cornell University Press, 1983).

5. A recent discussion of NATO's problems is to be found in the *Washington Quarterly* 7, no. 3 (Summer 1984). For a pessimistic account of what the future bodes for NATO, see Eliot A. Cohen, "The Long-Term Crisis of the Alliance," *Foreign Affairs* 61, no. 2 (Winter 1982/83): 325–43. For discussions of changing European public attitudes towards the alliance see Konrad Kellen, "The New Germans," *New York Times Magazine,* August 5, 1984: 18–20; and Richard C. Eichenberg, "The Myth of Hollanditis," *International Security* 8, no. 2 (Fall 1983): 143–59.

6. J. F. Brown, "The Future of Political Relations within the Warsaw Pact," in David Holloway and Jane M. O. Sharp, eds., *The Warsaw Pact: Alliance in Transition?* (Ithaca: Cornell University Press, 1984): 197–214; and David Binder, "In a Fit of Independence, Eastern Europe Flirts with Bonn," *New York Times,* September 2, 1984.

7. Arch Puddington, "Are Things Getting Better in Eastern Europe?" *Commentary* 76, no. 2 (August 1983): 32–40; and John Van Meer, "Banks, Tanks, and Freedom," *Commentary* 74, no. 6 (December 1982): 17–24.

8. Adam B. Ulam, *Expansion and Coexistence: Soviet Foreign Policy, 1917–73,* 2d ed. (New York: Praeger, 1974): 611–12.

9. George F. Kennan, *Russia, the Atom, and the West* (New York: Harper and Row, 1958): 32–49. A good overview of the politics of the German peace movement is found in Jeffrey Boutwell, "Politics and the Peace Movement in West Germany," *International Security* 7, no. 4 (Spring 1983): 72–92.

10. *New York Times,* August 18 and 19, 1984.

11. See Joshua M. Epstein, "Horizontal Escalation: Sour Notes of a Recurrent Theme," *International Security* 8, no. 3 (Winter 1983/84): 19–31. The best historical treatment of escalation is found in Richard Smoke, *War: Controlling Escalation* (Cambridge, Mass.: Harvard University Press, 1977).

12. For a discussion of how the Soviets might conduct their operations in an invasion of the Persian Gulf, see Joshua M. Epstein, "Soviet Vulnerabilities in Iran and the RDF Deterrent," and Dennis Ross, "Considering the Soviet Threat to the Persian Gulf," *International Security* 6, no. 2 (Fall 1981): 126–58 and 159–80.

13. This debate is reviewed in some detail in Charles Glaser, "The Debate over the Requirements of Deterrence," paper delivered at the Workshop on Explicating the Arms Control Debate sponsored by the Center for Science and International Affairs, Harvard University, Cambridge, Massachusetts, May 1984. I have found the paper an invaluable guide to understanding the different points of view in this debate, and much of the following discussion is drawn from it.

14. The principal spokesman for this viewpoint is Robert Jervis, *The Illogic of American Nuclear Strategy* (Ithaca: Cornell University Press, 1984). Others who have

espoused this viewpoint include McGeorge Bundy, "The Bishops and the Bomb," *New York Review of Books*, June 16, 1983: 3–8; and Spurgeon M. Keeny and Wolfgang K. H. Panofsky, "MAD Versus NUTS: The Mutual Hostage Relationship of the Superpowers . . .," *Foreign Affairs* 60, no. 2 (Winter 1981/82): 287–304.

15. The argument hinges on the belief that the vulnerability of U.S. ICBMs to a Soviet counterforce attack might encourage the Soviets to launch one because the United States would be incapable of conducting a retaliatory response. Remaining Soviet countervalue capabilities after such an attack would also deter a U.S. countervalue response. See Glaser, "The Debate over the Requirements of Deterrence": 10.

16. Colin S. Gray and Keith Payne, "Victory is Possible," *Foreign Policy* 39 (Summer 1980): 14–27; and Paul Nitze, "Assuming Strategic Stability in the Era of Detente," *Foreign Affairs* 54, no. 2 (January 1976): 201–32.

17. Secretary of Defense Harold Brown, Department of Defense, Annual Report, Fiscal Year 1980 (Washington, D.C.: Government Printing Office, 1981): 65–66; and Walter Slocombe, "The Countervailing Strategy," *International Security* 5, no. 4 (Spring 1981): 18–27.

18. A provocative critique of the "bean count" approach to the balance is found in Raymond L. Garthoff, *Perspectives on the Strategic Balance*, Staff Paper (Washington, D.C.: Brookings Institution, 1983). The political significance of the balance is also explored in Richard K. Betts, "Elusive Equivalence: The Political and Military Meaning of the Nuclear Balance," in Samuel P. Huntington, ed., *The Strategic Imperative: New Policies for National Security* (Cambridge, Mass.: Ballinger, 1982): 101–104.

19. The importance of such perceptions is stressed in what Robert Jervis has called the "third wave" of deterrence theory. See "Deterrence Theory Revisited," *World Politics* 31, no. 2 (January 1979): 301.

20. George W. Ball, "The Cosmic Bluff," *New York Review of Books*, July 21, 1983: 37–40; and Robert S. McNamara, "The Military Role of Nuclear Weapons: Perceptions and Misperceptions," *Foreign Affairs* 62, no. 1 (Fall 1983): 59–80.

21. For various perspectives on this debate, see Frank Blackaby, Jozef Goldblat, and Sverre Lodgaard, eds., *No-First-Use* (London: Taylor and Francis, 1984); and John D. Steinbruner and Leon V. Sigal, eds., *Alliance Security: NATO and No-First-Use* (Washington, D.C.: Brookings Institution, 1983).

22. Charles Glaser, "Why Good Defenses May Be Bad," *International Security* 9, no. 2 (Fall 1984): 92–123.

23. Comprehensive discussions of the strategic defense initiative are found in Ashton B. Carter, *Directed Energy Missile Defense in Space*, Background Paper (Washington, D.C.: Office of Technology Assessment, April 1984); Ashton B. Carter and David N. Schwartz, eds., *Ballistic Missile Defense* (Washington, D.C.: Brookings Institution, 1983); and Sidney D. Drell, Philip J. Farley, and David Holloway, *The Reagan Defense Initiative: A Technical, Political, and Arms Control Assessment* (Stanford Center for International Security and Arms Control, 1984).

24. Senator William Proxmire, " 'Star Wars' Protection, But Not For Europeans," *New York Times*, July 23, 1984.

25. This perspective is spelled out in Lawrence Freedman, "New Technology and

Western Security Policy," paper delivered at the Twenty-Sixth Annual Conference of the International Institute for Strategic Studies, Avignon, France, September 13–16, 1984.

26. Fred S. Hoffmann, "New Technologies and Western Security Policy," paper delivered at the Twenty-Sixth Annual Conference of the International Institute for Strategic Studies, Avignon, France, September 13–16, 1984.

27. Stephen Meyer, *Soviet Theatre Nuclear Forces: Part I: Development of Doctrine and Objectives,* Adelphi Paper No. 187 (London: International Institute for Strategic Studies, Winter 1983/84).

28. BDM Corporation, *Soviet Navy Declaratory Doctrine for Theater Nuclear Warfare,* Contract No. DNA 001–76–C–0230 prepared for the Director of the Nuclear Defense Agency, Washington, D.C., September 30, 1977; L.F. Brooks, "Tactical Nuclear Weapons: The Forgotten Facet of Naval Warfare," *U.S. Naval Institute Proceedings,* January 1980: 28–33; Gordon H. McCormick and Mark E. Miller, "American Seapower at Risk: Nuclear Weapons in Soviet Naval Planning," *Orbis* 35, no. 2 (Summer 1981): 351–68; and Steven Miller, "The Northern Seas in Soviet Strategy and U.S. Strategy," in Sverre Lodgaard and Mark Thee, eds., *Nuclear Disengagement in Europe* (London: Taylor and Francis, 1983): 117–38.

29. Harold Brown, *Thinking about National Security Policy: Defense and Foreign Policy in a Dangerous World* (Boulder, Colo.: Westview Press, 1983): 63.

30. Paul Bracken, *The Command and Control of Nuclear Forces* (New Haven: Yale University Press, 1983): 168–69; and Leon V. Sigal, *Nuclear Forces in Europe: Enduring Dilemmas, Present Prospects* (Washington, D.C.: Brookings Institution, 1984).

31. Meyer, *Soviet Theatre Nuclear Forces,* 27.

32. French nuclear policy is reviewed in Lawrence Freedman, *The Evolution of Nuclear Strategy* (New York: St. Martin's Press, 1982): 313–30.

33. See, for example, John J. Mearsheimer, "Why the Soviets Can't Win Quickly in Central Europe," *International Security* 7, no. 1 (Summer, 1982): 3–39; William W. Kaufmann, "Nonnuclear Deterrence," in Steinbruner and Sigal, *Alliance Security,* 43–90; and William P. Mako, *U.S. Ground Forces and the Defense of Central Europe* (Washington, D.C.: Brookings Institution, 1983).

34. See, for example, Congressional Budget Office, *Army Ground Combat Modernization for the 1980s: Potential Cost Effects for NATO* (Washington, D.C.: U.S. Government Printing Office, November 1982): 30; and Philip Karber, "To Lose an Arms Race: The Competition in Conventional Forces Deployed in Central Europe 1965–1980," in Uwe Nerlich, ed., *Soviet Power and Western Negotiating Policies,* Volume 1: *The Soviet Asset: Military Power in the Competition over Europe* (Cambridge, Mass.: Ballinger, 1983): 31–88.

35. Barry R. Posen, "Inadvertent Nuclear War? Escalation and NATO's Northern Flank," *International Security* 7, no. 2 (Fall 1982): 49.

36. A good review of the literature is found in J. P. Kahan and others, *Preventing Nuclear Conflict: What Can the Behavioral Sciences Contribute?* Rand Note N–2070–CC/FP/RC (Santa Monica, Calif.: Rand Corporation, December 1983).

37. See Robert J. C. Butow, *Tojo and the Coming of War* (Stanford: Stanford Univer-

sity Press, 1961); and Gordon W. Prange's masterful historical study, *At Dawn We Slept: The Untold Story of Pearl Harbor* (Middlesex, England: Penguin Books, 1981).

38. C. R. M. F. Cruttwell, *A History of the Great War 1914–1918,* 2d ed. (St. Albans: Granada Press, 1982): 376–89.

39. See Jack Snyder, *The Ideology of the Offensive: Military Decision-Making and the Disasters of 1914* (Ithaca: Cornell University Press, 1984); Snyder, "Civil Military Relations and the Cult of the Offensive, 1914 and 1984"; and Stephen Van Evera, "The Cult of the Offensive and the Origins of the First World War," *International Security* 9, no. 1 (Summer 1984): 58–100 and 108–46.

40. Reported in Alexander L. George, "Crisis Management: Lessons From Past U.S.-Soviet Crises," paper presented at the annual meeting of the American Association for the Advancement of Science, May 24–29, 1984, New York City: 17–18.

41. The opposite tendency, toward excessive group cohesion and patterns of thinking, is the subject of Irving L. Janis's classic study, *Groupthink: Psychological Studies of Policy Decision,* 2d ed. (Boston: Houghton Mifflin, 1982).

42. McGeorge Bundy and others, "Nuclear Weapons and the Atlantic Alliance," *Foreign Affairs* 60, no. 4 (Spring 1982): 753–68.

43. Morton H. Halperin, "The Political Use of Nuclear Weapons," paper delivered at the Avoiding Nuclear War Faculty Seminar, John F. Kennedy School of Government, Harvard University, Cambridge, Massachusetts, December 14, 1983.

44. See Desmond Ball, *Déjà Vu: The Return to Counterforce in the Nixon Administration* (Santa Monica, Calif.: California Seminar on Arms Control and Foreign Policy, December 1974) and "Developments in U.S. Strategic Nuclear Policy under the Carter Administration," ACIS Working Paper No. 21, Center for International and Strategic Affairs, University of California, February 1980.

45. Karl Kaiser and others, "Nuclear Weapons and the Preservation of Peace: A German Response," *Foreign Affairs* 60, no. 5 (Summer 1982): 1157–70.

46. *New York Times,* May 20, 1984.

47. For area defense, see Ben Dankbaar, "Alternative Defence Policies and Modern Weapons," in Mary Kaldor and Dan Smith, eds., *Disarming Europe* (London: Merlin Press, 1982): 163–92; and R. Lewis and others, *A Survey of NATO Defense Concepts,* Rand Note N–871 (Santa Monica, Calif.: June 1982): 45–46, 68–69. The history of this concept is explored in Adam Roberts, *Nation in Arms: The Theory and Practice of Territorial Defense* (New York: Praeger, 1976).

For mobile/maneuver, see John J. Mearsheimer, "Maneuver, Mobile Defense, and the NATO Central Front," *International Security* 6, no. 3 (Winter 1981/82): 104–22.

AirLand battle is perhaps the best known tactical innovation. It is described in the Army Field Manual, *Operations: FM 100-5* (Washington, D.C.: U.S. Army Adjutant General Publications Center, August 20, 1982). Helpful discussions of the evolution of AirLand battle concepts are found in Archer Jones, "FM 100–5: A View from the Ivory Tower" and Stephen W. Richey, "The Philosophical Basis of the AirLand Battle," *Military Review* 64, no. 5 (May 1984): 17–22 and 48–53. For a provocative and novel application of the ideas of offensive tactics to strategy see Samuel P. Huntington, "Conventional Deterrence and Conventional Retaliation in Europe," *International Security* 8, no. 3 (Winter 1983/84): 32–56.

48. Lt. Col. Bloomer D. Sullivan, "Logistical Support for AirLand Battle," *Military Review* 64, no. 2 (February 1984): 2–16.

49. This is all too evident from the recent outpouring of articles in military journals on new doctrine and tactics for fighting a conventional war.

50. The history of this controversy is discussed in David N. Schwartz, *NATO's Nuclear Dilemmas* (Washington, D.C.: Brookings Institution, 1983); and Sigal, *Nuclear Forces in Europe.*

51. See William Kaufmann, "Nonnuclear Deterrence," 83–90; and Barry R. Posen and Stephen Van Evera, "Departure from Containment: Defense Policy and the Reagan Administration," *International Security* 8, no. 1 (Summer 1983): 3–45.

52. Report of the European Security Study, *Strengthening Conventional Deterrence in Europe: Proposals for the 1980s* (New York: St. Martin's Press, 1983); General Bernard W. Rogers, "The Atlantic Alliance: Prescriptions for a Difficult Decade," *Foreign Affairs* 60, no. 5 (Summer 1982): 1145–56; and Senator Sam Nunn, "NATO: Can the Alliance be Saved?" Report to the Senate Armed Services Committee, May 13, 1982 and reprinted in *Survival* 24, no. 5 (September/October 1982): 234–36.

53. Fen Osler Hampson, "Groping for Technical Panaceas: The European Conventional Balance and Nuclear Stability," *International Security* 8, no. 3 (Winter 1983/84): 74–76.

54. See Jonathan Dean, "MBFR: From Apathy to Accord," *International Security* 7, no. 4 (Spring 1984): 116–39; Lothar Ruehl, *MBFR: Lessons and Problems,* Adelphi Paper No. 176 (London: International Institute for Strategic Studies, 1982); and Jane M. O. Sharp, "Security through Détente and Arms Control," in Holloway and Sharp, eds., *The Warsaw Pact,* 161–94.

55. See F. Stephen Larrabee and Dietrich Stobbe, *Confidence Building Measures in Europe,* East-West Monograph No. 1 (New York: Institute for East-West Security, 1983).

56. Colonel Lynn M. Hansen, "Confidence and Security Building at Madrid and Beyond," in East-West Monograph No. 1, 134–64.

57. Report of the Independent Committee on Disarmament and Security, *Common Security: A Program for Disarmament* (London: Pan Books, 1982).

58. Robert S. McNamara, "18 Ways to Reduce the Risks of Nuclear War," *Newsweek,* December 5, 1983: 55.

59. These institutional problems and dilemmas are the subject of Joseph S. Nye, Jr., ed., *The Making of America's Soviet Policy* (New Haven: Yale University Press, 1984).

60. These issues are discussed in Karl Lautenschläger, "Technology and the Evolution of Naval Warfare," *International Security* 8, no. 2 (Fall 1983): 3–51.

61. William Kaufmann gives a 57-division Pact attack a 70 percent chance of defeating

a NATO force of 30⅓ deployed divisions without barriers, and only 40 percent with them. The probabilities would be the same if a 90-division Pact force faced a 36⅓ NATO division force. See "Nonnuclear Deterrence," pp. 63–71.

62. A timely analysis of crisis control measures is found in William Langer Ury and Richard Smoke, *Beyond the Hotline: Controlling Nuclear Crisis*, A Report to the United States Arms Control and Disarmament Agency (Cambridge, Mass.: Harvard Law School, 1984).

5. Escalation in the Middle East and Persian Gulf

1. See my article "Nuclear Shadowboxing: Soviet Intervention Threats in the Middle East," *Orbis* 25, no. 3 (Fall 1981): 579–605.

2. The well-known Brezhnev letter of October 25, 1973, which provoked a U.S. nuclear alert and caused such concern over the prospect of superpower conflict, was in fact a proposal for a joint U.S.-Soviet peacekeeping force that would enforce the ceasefire previously agreed to by both sides and prevent destruction of the Egyptian Third Army.

3. The so-called Carter Doctrine was enunciated in President Carter's State of the Union Message on January 20, 1980.

4. British attempts to contain Russian expansion southward ultimately led to a formal division of Iran into spheres of influence in the Anglo-Russian Entente of 1907.

5. Figures quoted in Albert Wohlstetter, "Half-Wars and Half-Policies," in W. Scott Thompson, ed., *From Weakness to Strength* (San Francisco: Institute for Contemporary Studies, 1980): 134–35.

6. Israel's net strategic value to the United States is a complicated question beyond the scope of this paper. My own view is that the unwillingness of pro-Western Arab states to cooperate with the United States on issues like base access is due to a wide variety of historical, cultural, and political factors, of which the Palestinian issue is just one. Even if Israel were to disappear tomorrow the conservative states in the region would still be very reluctant to collaborate with the United States; indeed, Israel provides a convenient excuse for not doing what most Arab states would not be inclined to do in any case.

7. Gerold Guensberg, tr., *Soviet Command Study of Iran (Moscow 1941): Draft Translation and Brief Analysis* (Arlington, Va.: SRI International, 1980), 1 (hereafter referred to as *Soviet Command Study*). This study, prepared by the Soviet General Staff in early 1941, presents a plan for the invasion of Iran quite similar to the one that was actually carried out in August of that year. It was subsequently captured by the Germans during their invasion of the Caucasus, and then by the Americans when they occupied Berlin in 1945.

8. See *Soviet Command Study*, p. 127.

9. As recently as the Lebanon war of 1982, Moscow failed to take military action on behalf of Syria when its forces in Lebanon were defeated by Israel.

10. Mohammed Haykal, *The Sphinx and the Commissar: The Rise and Fall of Soviet Influence in the Middle East* (New York: Harper and Row, 1978): 98.

11. *Ibid.*, p. 71.

12. While current U.S. plans call for the insertion of a battalion-sized force into the

Gulf within hours of a decision to intervene, it will take upward of thirty days, depending on circumstances, to move a single division to Iran.
13. *Soviet Command Study,* pp. 116, 126, 159, 193, 211.
14. It has never been clear that NATO could mount a successful defense of Western Europe, which does not mean that it lacks deterrent effect.
15. In addition, Israel could prove to be a highly useful ally in the event of a Gulf crisis, given its military capabilities, stability, and commonality of weapons systems with U.S. forces. In peacetime, any hint of U.S.-Israeli strategic cooperation will have negative repercussions for U.S. dealings with the Arab states, but these have perhaps been exaggerated: during the 1970 Jordanian crisis King Hussein was willing to accept Israeli military help when his throne depended on it, and a similar calculation is likely to affect the thinking of the conservative states of the Gulf in a severe crisis.

6. Catalytic Nuclear War

1. Harvard Nuclear Study Group, *Living with Nuclear Weapons* (New York: Bantam Books, 1983): 215.
2. H.R. Haldeman, *The Ends of Power* (New York: Times Books, 1978): 90.
3. Larry Collins and Dominique Lapierre, *The Fifth Horseman* (New York: Simon and Schuster, 1980): 13–19.

7. Soviet Perspectives on the Paths to Nuclear War

The author wishes to thank M.I.T.'s Soviet Security Studies Working Group, Peter Almquist, Ted Warner, and Fen Hampson for their comments and criticisms on earlier drafts of this chapter.

1. N.V. Ogarkov, *Vsegda v gotovnosti k zashchite otechestva* (Moscow: Voyenizdat, 1982), 53–58; V. Zemskov, "On the Ideological and Theoretical Bases of Soviet Military Doctrine," *Military Thought,* no. 1 (1972): 40–53.
2. For a general treatment of Soviet views on nuclear warfare during the 1950s, see Raymond Garthoff, *Soviet Strategy in the Nuclear Age* (New York: Praeger, 1958) and Herbert Dinerstein, *War and the Soviet Union* (New York: Praeger, 1962).
3. David Holloway, *The Soviet Union and the Arms Race* (New Haven: Yale University Press, 1983), chapter 2.
4. M.M. Kir'yan, "Vnezapnost'," *Sovetskaya Voyennaya Entsiklopediya,* vol. 2 (Moscow: Voyenizdat, 1976): 160.
5. I. Bagramyan, "Kharakter i osobennosti nachal'nogo perioda voyny," *Voyenno Istoricheskiy Zhurnal,* no. 10 (1981): 21; V. Matsulenko, "Nekotoryye vyvody iz opyata nachal'nogo perioda Velikoy Otechestvennoy voyny," *Voeyenno Istoricheskiy Zhurnal,* no. 3 (1984): 535–43.
6. Garthoff, *op. cit.,* chapter 6; Dinerstein, *op cit.,* chapter 7; V.D. Sokolovskiy, *Voyennaya Strategiya* (Moscow: Voyenizdat. 1963), chapters 2 and 6. For an analysis of contemporary Soviet views of U.S. nuclear war plans of the 1950s and 1960s, see I. Perov, "Yaderniy shantazh Vashingtona," *Zarubezhnoye Voyennoye Obozreniye,* no. 6: 9–14.
7. See M.P. Skirdo, *Narod, armiya, polkovodets* (Moscow: Voyenizdat, 1970): 8–29; Shushko, N. Ya., and S.A. Tushkevich, *Marksizm-Leninizm o voyne i armii* (Mos-

cow: Voyenizdat, 1965), chapters 1 and 2; and D.A. Volkogonov, *Marksistko-Leniniskoye ucheniye o voyne i armii* (Moscow: Voyenizdat, 1984), part 1.

8. Shushko and Tyushkevich, *op. cit.,* 20.

9. Ogarkov, *op. cit.,* 46; Skirdo, *op. cit.,* 53; M.M. Kir'yan, *Voyenno-tekhnicheskiy progress i vooruzhenyye sily SSSR* (Moscow: Voyenizdat, 1982): 313.

10. See the map in International Institute for Strategic Studies, *The Military Balance: 1984-1985* (London: 1984): 155.

11. Day-to-day alert status (daily peacetime readiness) connotes a readiness condition in which only a portion of the strategic force is prepared for immediate use. Generated-alert status connotes a readiness condition in which the entire strategic force is mobilized to full wartime readiness levels. Day-to-day alert forces are considered here assuming that a successful bolt-out-of-the-blue attack precludes moving to generated alert.

12. B.V. Panov, *Istoriaya Voyennogo Iskusstva: Uchebnik dla voyennlykh academiy sovetskikh vooruzhennikh sil* (Moscow: Voyenizdat, 1984), 460. For an excellent analysis of the doctrinal and technical evidence of a Soviet launch-on-warning strategy, see Vann Van Diepen, *Strategic Force Survivability and the Soviet Union* (S.M. dissertation, Department of Political Science, M.I.T., 1983).

13. These levels are substantially above those commonly considered in Western discussions: 25 per cent of population and 50 per cent of industry. K.V. Tarakanov, *Matematika i vooruzhennaya bor'ba* (Moscow: Voyenizdat, 1974): 185–86.

14. N.S. Khrushchev, *Khrushchev Remembers: The Last Testament* (Boston: Little, Brown & Co., 1974): 39–42.

15. On Soviet theater nuclear forces and targeting see Stephen M. Meyer, "Soviet Theatre Nuclear Forces: Parts I & II," *Adelphi Papers,* nos. 187 and 188 (London: International Institute for Strategic Studies, 1984).

16. United States House of Representatives, *Department of Defense Appropriations for 1980, Part 3.* Hearings before the Subcommittee of the House Appropriations Committee, 96th Congress, 1st Session, 1979, 476–477; Joint Economic Committee, *The Allocation of Resources in the Soviet Union and China 1981,* Part 7, 97th Congress, 1st Session, 1981, 199.

17. Edward Klein and Robert Littell, "Shh! Let's Not Tell the Russians," *Newsweek,* April 27, 1969, 25; Oleg Penkovskiy, *The Penkovskiy Papers* (New York: Doubleday, 1965): 331.

18. On Western Europe as a surrogate hostage, see Thomas Wolfe, *Soviet Power in Europe: 1945–1970* (New York: Praeger, 1970): 152–53; 180: N.S. Khrushchev, *Khrushchev Remembers* (Boston: Little, Brown & Co., 1972): 517. On Soviet civil-military relations see Roman Kolkowicz, *The Soviet Military and the Communist Party* (Princeton: Princeton University Press, 1967) and Michael Deane, *Political Control of the Soviet Armed Forces* (New York: Crane & Russak, 1977). On problems with Soviet weaponry, see Penkovskiy, *op. cit.,* 340 and Khrushchev, *Last Testament,* 39.

19. Arnold Horelick and Myron Rush, *Strategic Power and Soviet Foreign Policy* (Chicago: University of Chicago Press, 1965).

20. Panov, *op. cit.,* 460.

21. Khrushchev, *Last Testament,* 50–51.

22. Harold Brown, *Department of Defense Annual Report FY 1979* (Washington, D.C.: Department of Defense, 1978), 72. Joint Economic Committee Hearings before the Subcommittee on Priorities and Economy in Government of the Joint Economic Committee, *Allocation of Resources in the USSR and China,* Pt. 4, 95th Congress, 2nd Session, June 26 and July 14, 1978, 118. A proportion as low as 30 percent has been cited by authoritative sources. Clarence Robinson, "SALT May Allow 3 New Soviet Missiles," *Aviation Week and Space Technology* 110, no. 26 (1979): 22.

23. N. Krylov, "The Nuclear Missile Shield of the Soviet State," *Military Thought,* no. 11 (1967): 13–21.

24. M. Cherednichenko, "Military Strategy and Military Technology," *Military Thought,* no. 4 (1973): 53. The evidence suggests that long-range radar was the only reliable Soviet early warning system until the late 1970s. The maximum range of these radars was 4800 km, leaving only ten to fifteen minutes warning time. See Mathew Partan, *Soviet Examinations of US Early Warning and Strategic Detection Radars* (Center for International Studies, M.I.T., research memo, 1984) and Stephen Meyer, "Space and Soviet Military Planning," in William Durch, ed., *National Interests and the Military Use of Space* (Cambridge, Mass.: Ballinger Publishing Co., 1984), 61–68.

25. S.A. Tyushkevich, *Sovetskiye vooruzhennyye sily* (Moscow: Voyenizdat, 1978): 466.

26. U.S. House of Representatives, *op. cit.,* 476. Soviet SSBN on-station rates as low as 10 to 15 per cent have been cited in the past, in comparison to 50 per cent on station rates for the U.S. SSBN fleet. Today, the Soviet SSBN alert rate is slowly rising and is probably between 20 and 25 per cent.

27. U.S. Arms Control and Disarmament Agency, *An Analysis of Civil Defense in Nuclear War* (Washington, D.C., December 1978); P.T. Egorov, I.A. Shlyakhov, and N.I. Alabin, *Grazhdanskaya Oborona* (Moscow: Izdat. vysshayashkola).

28. Tarakanov, *op. cit.,* 64–66; Skirdo, *op. cit.,* 145.

29. Skirdo, *op. cit.,* 122–23, 144–46.

30. S.P. Ivanov, *Nachal'nyy period voyny* (Moscow: Voyenizdat, 1974), chapter 5.

31. Active defense connotes efforts to destroy incoming enemy weapons (e.g., air defense, anti-missile defense). Passive defense connotes efforts to lessen vulnerability to the destructive effects of enemy weapons (hardening, dispersion, and sheltering).

32. This is an important qualifier in evaluating the Brezhnev pledge that the Soviet Union would not be the first to use nuclear weapons. First-use has political as well as military content. Nonetheless, the initial Brezhnev statement appears to have bothered some in the military leadership and required a defense by Minister of Defense Ustinov. The pledge has been repeated many times since Brezhnev's death.

33. This is what appears to be implied in D.F. Ustinov, "Otvesti ugrozu yadernoy," *Pravda,* July 12, 1982, 4; N. Tetekin, "Glavniy polazatel' kachesvennogo sostoynia voysk," *Krasnaya Zvezda,* November 10, 1982, 2; and V. Khalipov, "Neobkhodimoye usloviye sotsial'nogo progressa," *Krasnaya Zvezda,* April 14, 1983, 2.

34. The analysis of alternative Soviet strategic force mixes uses a Soviet strategic force planning model taken from the General Staff journal *Military Thought.* See Peter

Almquist and Stephen M. Meyer, *Mathematical Modeling of the Correlation of Nuclear Forces* (Washington, D.C.: Report prepared for the Defense Advanced Research Projects Agency, 1984). On Soviet strategic force capabilities and targeting see Robert Berman and John Baker, *Soviet Strategic Forces* (Washington, D.C.: Brookings Institution, 1982)

35. In response to U.S. deployments of Pershing II and GLCM in Europe, the Soviet Union has placed two additional SSBNs on day-to-day alert status.

36. For a discussion of these changes in doctrine and strategy, see Meyer, *Soviet Theater Nuclear Forces,* and Phillip A. Peterson and John G. Hines, "The Conventional Offensive in Soviet Theater Strategy," *Orbis* 27, no. 3 (1984): 695–739.

37. Kir'yan, *op. cit,* 312–13; Cherednichenko, *op. cit.*

38. On NATO escalation see V. Viktorov, "Boyevaya podgotovka ili boyevoye razverttyvaniye," *Krasnaya Zvezda* April 3, 1984: 3. On German use of V1 cruise missile see K. Franishin and V. Parshin, "Borba S Krylatymi raketami v gody vtoroymirovoy voyna," *Vestnik PVO,* no. 1, January 1984, 77–79.

39. "Strategic" refers to the use of Soviet SS-20s, BACKFIRE bombers, and SLBMs for attacks against all NATO military facilities. See Meyer, *Soviet Theater Nuclear Forces.*

40. This would be especially true if the Soviet decision was in reaction to an unanticipated use of nuclear weapons by NATO. Soviet long-range theater nuclear forces are centrally controlled and therefore would be the most responsive of all Soviet TNF systems. See Meyer, *Soviet Theater Nuclear Forces* and Panov, *op. cit.,* 463.

41. This pertains only to theaters adjacent to Soviet territory. It does not include the United States. See M. Shirokov, "Military Geography at the Present Stage," *Military Thought,* no. 11 (1966): 57–64, and M. Shirokov, "The Question of Influences on the Military and Economic Potential of Warring States," *Military Thought,* no. 4 (1968): 33–39.

42. Henry Kissinger, *Years of Upheaval* (Boston: Little, Brown & Co., 1982), 277.

43. For a full discussion of Soviet general-purpose force capabilities under this contingency, see Meyer, *Soviet Theater Nuclear Forces,* and Hines and Peterson, *op. cit.*

44. Joint Economic Committee, *op. cit.,* 218–29.

45. Ogarkov, *op. cit.,* 58–63.

46. Sushko and Tyushkevich, *op. cit.,* 22–23. In the 1968 edition this section was shortened. It was noted that despite precautionary measures, technical errors could still spark accidental nuclear wars. The discussion of the accidental path to nuclear war was deleted from subsequent editions of the book.

47. Holloway, *op. cit.,* chapter 2.

48. K. Vershinin, "The Influence of Scientific Technical Progress on the Development of the Air Force and its Strategy in the Post War Period," *Military Thought,* no. 5 (1966): 36–44, and also his "The Development of The Operational Art of the Air Force," *Military Thought,* no. 6 (1967): 1–13.

49. Penkovskiy, *op. cit.,* 331; John Barron, *KGB* (New York: Reader's Digest Press, 1974): 10. One can speculate that this security system was part of the original decision to bring nuclear weapons into the operational inventory.

50. Brown, *op. cit.,* 69.

51. These links include a dedicated KGB satellite network. See Meyer, *Soviet Military Planning*.

52. Andrew Cockburn, *The Threat: Inside the Soviet Military Machine* (New York: Random House, 1983), 189. For an interesting description of an alleged visit to a Soviet missile silo, see Aleksandr Prokhanov, "Yadernyy Shchit," *Literaturnaya Gazeta*, no. 46, (November 17, 1982): 10.

53. Ustinov, *op. cit.*

54. Skirdo, *op. cit.*, 121.

55. A FRONT is a formation somewhat similar to an American field army and is nominally composed of twenty divisions. A theater of military operations is a unified geographic area which encompasses many FRONTs. Central Europe may be a separate theater. See Department of Defense, *Soviet Military Power* (Washington D.C.: GPO, 1984), 50.

56. I. Zav'yalov, "The Evolution of the Correlation of Strategy, Operational Art, and Tactics," *Military Thought*, no. 11 (1971): 37.

57. Interview with former Soviet Air Force pilot Victor Belenko in: *Congressional Record, Senate*, September 22, 1983, s12692. Mark Whitaker et al., "Why the Russians Did It," *Newsweek*, September 19, 1983: 24.

58. V.F. Tolubko, "Galvnaya raketnaya sila strany," *Krasnaya Zvezda*, November 19, 1963: 1.

59. V.F. Tolubko, "Novoye perdovoye—v uchebyy protsess," *Krasnaya Zvezda*, January 26, 1984, 2.

60. L. Cherous'ko, "Opasnaya igra s ogram," *Aviatisia i Kosmonavtika*, no. 4, 1984, 14–15.

61. Khrushchev, *Last Testament*, 39.

62. Penkovskiy, *op. cit.*, 343.

63. Penkovskiy, *op. cit.*, 340; Khrushchev, *Last Testament*, 46–53.

64. Kensuke Ebata, "Soviet 'Golf II' Limps Back to Vladivostok," *Jane's Defense Weekly* (October 6, 1984), 566.

65. Victor Suvorov, *The Liberators* (London: Hamish Hamilton, 1981), 158–59.

66. Thomas W. Robinson, "The Sino-Soviet Border Conflict," 280–281 in Steven Kaplan, *Diplomacy of Power* (Washington, D.C.; Brookings Institution, 1981), 265–313.

67. Henry Kissinger, *White House Years* (Boston: Little, Brown & Co., 1979), 183–90; H.R. Haldeman, *The Ends of Power* (New York: Times Books, 1978), 88–93.

68. John Thomas, "Soviet Behavior in the Quemoy Crisis of 1958," *Orbis* 6, no. 1 (1962): 38–64.

69. Ivanov, *op. cit.*, 160–76.

70. V. Chernavin, "Leniniskiy stil' raboty-zalog uspeshnoy deyatel'nosti shtabov," *Morskoy Sbornik*, no. 1 (1984): 7–14.

71. Dennis Ross, *Consensus Decisionmaking in the Politboro* (Los Angeles: Ph.D. dissertation, Department of Political Science, UCLA, 1982; Jiri Valenta and William Potter, *Soviet National Security Decisionmaking* (London: George Allen and Unwin, 1984).

72. In Soviet military exercises time norms are set for different phases of an assigned mission. If the time norms are exceeded, a failure is recorded even if the mission

was accomplished. Soviet combat modeling also focuses heavily on time analysis as part of the overall assessment of military operations. See F. Gayvoronskiy, "Nekotoryye tendentsii v razvitii Sovietskogo voyennogo iskutsstva po opytu Velikoy Otecchestvennoy voyny," *Voyenno Istoricheskiy Zhurnal,* no. 5 (1983): 12–20, and I. Makarenk, "Rastim masterov ornya," *Krasnaya Zvezda,* January 28, 1984, 2.

8. Analytic Conclusions: Hawks, Doves, and Owls

1. The Public Agenda Foundation, *Voter Options on Nuclear Arms Policy* (New York, 1984); *Time,* January 2, 1984, 51.
2. Thomas Powers, *Thinking About the Next War* (New York: Alfred A. Knopf, 1982), 17.
3. Robert Jervis refers to believers in "deterrence and spiral models" in *Perception and Misperception in International Politics* (Princeton: Princeton University Press, 1976). Glenn H. Snyder and Paul Deising refer to "hard and soft liners" in *Conflict Among Nations* (Princeton: Princeton University Press, 1977). Like the terms in the current public debate, these dichotomies are inadequate because they compress two different causal views (Dove and Owl in our parlance) under one label (whether it be "Dove," "spiral," or "soft").
4. These perspectives are defined by views of precipitating causes (calculated versus nonrational) and intermediate causes (too little threat versus too much threat) of failed deterrence. Logically there are four possible positions: calculated onset/too much threat = Dove; calculated onset/too little threat = Hawk; nonrational onset/too much threat = Owl; nonrational onset/too little threat = pure accidental war. Since there seem to be no historical instances of purely accidental war, we have described only three perspectives. Moreover, Owls are likely to include the policy implications of accidental war in their own worries.
5. Freeman Dyson, *Weapons and Hope* (New York: Harper & Row, 1984), 15.
6. Paul Kennedy, "Arms Races and the Causes of War, 1850–1945," in *Strategy and Diplomacy, 1870–1945* (London: George Allen and Unwin, 1983), 163–77.
7. Stephen van Evera, "The Cult of the Offensive and the Origins of the First World War" and Jack Snyder, "Civil-Military Relations and the Cult of the Offensive, 1914 and 1984," *International Security* 9 (Summer 1984).
8. This issue is discussed in detail in Scott Sagan, *The Failure of Deterrence: Pearl Harbor and Nuclear Strategy,* unpublished manuscript, Avoiding Nuclear War Project, Harvard University, 1983.
9. Thomas C. Schelling, *Arms and Influence* (New Haven: Yale University Press, 1966), 227–29.
10. Miles Kahler, "Rumors of War: the 1914 Analogy," *Foreign Affairs* 58 (Winter 1979/80).
11. See Benjamin Lambeth, "Uncertainties for the Soviet War Planner," *International Security* 7 (Winter 1982/1983).
12. The U.S. political process also contributes to the problem. See J.S. Nye, ed., *The Making of America's Soviet Policy* (New Haven: Yale University Press, 1984).

GLOSSARY

ABM Antiballistic Missile. See *Ballistic Missile Defense.*

ABM Treaty See *Strategic Arms Limitation Talks.*

Accidental War Agreement Formally titled "Agreement on Measures to Reduce the Risk of Outbreak of Nuclear War Between the United States of America and the Union of Soviet Socialist Republics," this agreement was signed in 1971. It stipulates that both states will take a number of measures—such as improving safeguards against the accidental or unauthorized use of nuclear weapons—to prevent the unintentional outbreak of nuclear war.

AirLand Battle A recent U.S. Army strategy of extending the depth of the battlefield behind enemy front lines and making greater use of mobile forces and coordinated ground and air attacks.

Air-Launched Cruise Missile (ALCM) A cruise missile carried by and launched from an aircraft. See also *Cruise Missile.*

Antisatellite System (ASAT) Weapons designed to destroy or disrupt the operation of an adversary's satellites in space.

Antisubmarine Warfare (ASW) Measures designed to identify, track, hinder, and destroy an adversary's submarine fleet.

Assured Destruction A situation in which a nation has the theoretical capability to absorb a nuclear attack and still inflict an unacceptable level of damage on the attacker.

Ballistic Missile Any missile designed to propel a payload up and through the atmosphere and then release it to travel to its target under the influence of gravity and (as it reenters the atmosphere) aerodynamic forces.

Ballistic Missile Defense (BMD) Measures for actively defending against reentry vehicles launched by ballistic missiles. It is less difficult to protect small, hard targets such as missile silos than large, soft targets such as cities.

Ballistic Missile Early Warning System (BMEWS) A system of radars located at Clear, Alaska; Thule, Greenland; and Fylingdales Moor, U.K. It provides warning and tracking of Soviet ICBM launches.

Battlefield Nuclear Weapon Short-range tactical nuclear systems—such as the Army's Lance missile or 155mm field guns—that are designed for use against enemy forces in the field. See also *Theater Nuclear Forces.*

Civil Defense Passive measures for defending a population against nuclear attack, such as sheltering and evacuation of populated areas.

C³I Command, Control, Communications, and Intelligence: The complete set of equipment, people, and procedures used by the national leadership and commanders at all levels to monitor and direct the operation of military forces in the conduct of both their day-to-day activities and wartime missions.

Collateral Damage The additional destruction to the surrounding area that results from an attack upon a specific military target.

Comprehensive Test Ban Treaty A treaty which, if achieved, would ban all testing of nuclear weapons.

Confidence-Building Measures/Confidence and Security-Building Measures (CBM/CSBMs) Arms control steps that do not focus directly on the limitation or reduction of military forces but that reduce the risks of war and enhance the stability of an adversarial relationship through other means (for example, the Hot Line). Such measures can be unilateral, bilateral, or multilateral.

Counterforce The employment of strategic forces against the weaponry and command and control centers of an adversary.

Countervalue The employment of strategic forces against enemy population and economic centers (that is, cities).

Crisis Stability This form of stability exists when neither side sees a net benefit in initiating the use of nuclear weapons. It occurs when both sides have secure second-strike forces and neither would gain a decisive advantage by going first.

Cruise Missile (CM) An air-breathing missile that is basically a pilotless airplane. Current cruise missiles fly at subsonic speeds; are difficult to detect by radar; can carry nuclear, conventional, or chemical warheads; and can be launched from a wide variety of platforms.

Damage Limitation The utilization of nuclear weaponry against an adversary to minimize the destruction to one's own nation.

Decapitation The attempt to mitigate a retaliatory response by destroying as much of an adversary's leadership and command structure as possible.

Delivery Vehicle The devices (for example, ballistic missiles and aircraft) used to deposit nuclear weapons on a particular target.

Deterrence The prevention of a given action by a threat of counteraction. Basic deterrence refers to prevention of an attack on one's homeland by threatening nuclear retaliation against the adversary's homeland. Extended deterrence applies the threat of nuclear retaliation in response to attacks on allies and regions of vital interest.

Distant Early Warning Line (DEW Line) A line of 31 conventional radars running along the Arctic shore from western Alaska to Iceland for detection of aircraft and cruise missiles.

Dual Key A political arrangement whereby nuclear weapons belonging to one nation but based in another would be used only if both sides agreed to their use.

Dual Capable The characterization given to systems capable of delivering both conventional and nuclear weapons.

Emerging Technology (ET) Newly available technological improvements in conventional weaponry in areas such as reconnaissance, surveillance, target acquisition, and interdiction.

First-Strike Capability The ability to conduct a *disarming* first strike against one's opponent. (It does *not* mean simply the ability to strike first.)

Flexible Response A strategy of being able to respond to provocation with different levels of force. Flexible response was adopted as a declaratory policy under the Kennedy administration and—although the notion itself is somewhat vague—it has been embedded in American strategic doctrine in some form ever since.

Forward-Based System (FBS) Generally used to describe American forces and weapons that are located around the periphery of the Soviet Union and are capable of striking targets within it.

Generated Alert A situation in which a nation has increased the readiness of its forces beyond their normal peacetime status to full combat capacity in anticipation of their imminent use. It involves actions such as removing submarines from port, dispersing bombers, and releasing nuclear weapons from storage facilities.

Horizontal Escalation The expansion of a conflict, either deliberately or otherwise, to encompass other regions or participants.

Hot Line The colloquial expression for a direct communications link between governments. The Washington-Moscow Hot Line was first installed in the wake of the Cuban missile crisis in 1963 and was upgraded in 1971 and again in 1984.

Incidents-at-Sea Agreement An agreement signed between the U.S. and Soviet Union in 1972 to reduce the risk that naval incidents might lead to a confrontation between the two superpowers.

Intercontinental Ballistic Missile (ICBM) A land-based ballistic missile capable of delivering a warhead to intercontinental range (about 3500 miles). See also *Ballistic Missile.*

Intermediate-Range Nuclear Forces (INF) Substantively identical with *Long-Range Theater Nuclear Forces,* INF was adopted by the United States as the name for the recent negotiations with the Soviet Union over LRTNF in Europe. See also *Theater Nuclear Forces.*

Intermediate-Range Ballistic Missile (IRBM) A ballistic missile with a range of about 1,500 to 3,500 miles. See also *Ballistic Missile.*

Launch Under Attack (LUA) A doctrine in which a nation's strategic forces will be launched during an attack, but only after confirmation that enemy weapons have detonated on its homeland.

Launch on Warning/Launch on Tactical Warning (LOW/LOTW) Generally used to describe a doctrine in which a nation launches its strategic systems after it receives warning from a number of sensors that an adversary has initiated a nuclear attack.

Limited Test Ban Treaty (LTBT) A treaty banning nuclear weapons testing in the atmosphere, under water, and in outer space. It was negotiated among the United States, the United Kingdom, and the Soviet Union in the wake of the Cuban missile crisis in 1963 and has now been signed by over 100 nations.

Long-Range Theater Nuclear Forces (LRTNF) See *Theater Nuclear Forces.*

Massive Retaliation A U.S. declaratory policy of the 1950s that threatened the Soviet Union and China with massive nuclear attack should they encroach upon vital American interests (which were not defined clearly).

Medium-Range Ballistic Missile (MRBM) A ballistic missile with a range of about 500 to 1,500 miles. See also *Ballistic Missile.*

Minimum Deterrence A policy of retaining only enough nuclear weapons to provide an assured destruction capability.

Multiple Independently Targetable Reentry Vehicle (MIRV) Two or more reentry vehicles carried by a ballistic missile, each of which can be individually directed toward a separate target. See also *Reentry Vehicle.*

Mutual and Balanced Force Reductions (MBFR) These negotiations began in 1973 with the goal of reducing the level of conventional forces in Europe.

Mutual Assured Destruction (MAD) A situation in which two or more states could absorb a nuclear first strike and still be capable of causing an unacceptable level of damage to the attacker.

National Command Authority (NCA) The top military and political command of a nation. Specifically, it consists of the head of state and and duly appointed successors.

Nonproliferation Treaty (NPT) A treaty designed to restrict the spread of nuclear weapons. It was originally signed by the United States, the United Kingdom, and Soviet Union in 1968 and has since been joined by approximately 110 nations.

North American Aerospace Defense Command (NORAD) NORAD is a combined U.S./Canadian command responsible for the detection and monitoring of any missile or bomber attack on North America.

North Atlantic Treaty Organization (NATO) A defensive alliance of North American and Western European states that was founded in 1949. NATO's current membership consists of Belgium, Canada, Denmark, the Federal Republic of Germany, Great Britain, Greece, Iceland, Italy, Luxembourg, the Netherlands, Norway, Portugal, Spain, Turkey, and the United States. France withdrew from the integrated military command in 1968 but remains a member of NATO.

Nuclear Suppliers Group A group of nations formed in the late 1970s with the goal of preventing the proliferation of nuclear weapons by restricting the export of sensitive technologies. The group includes Belgium, Canada, Czechoslovakia, France, the Democratic Republic of Germany, the Federal Republic of Germany, Italy, Japan, the Netherlands, Poland, Sweden, Switzerland, the United Kingdom, the United States, and the Soviet Union.

Payload The total weight of the reentry vehicles carried by a missile.

Permissive Action Link (PAL) A mechanical or electronic locking device that is placed upon a nuclear weapon to prevent its unauthorized use.

Precision Guided Munition (PGM) An accurate conventional weapon that can be directed toward its target after firing.

Rapid Deployment Force (RDF) Developed after the Carter administration's 1980 commitment to defend oil supplies in the Persian Gulf "by any means necessary, including military force," the RDF is a quick-reaction conventional force designed to be transported rapidly to remote locations.

Reentry Vehicle (RV) The shell around each warhead on a ballistic missile. It protects the warhead during its reentry through the atmosphere.

Sea-Launched Cruise Missile (SLCM) A cruise missile launched from a surface ship or submarine. See also *Cruise Missile.*

Sea Lines of Communication (SLOC) The maritime paths over which personnel and material are transported, especially in time of war.

Short-Range Ballistic Missile (SRBM) A ballistic missile with a range of less than about 500 miles. See also *Ballistic Missile.*

Single Integrated Operational Plan (SIOP) The highly classified plan for employment of U.S. nuclear weapons in the event of war.

Stealth A combination of new technologies and design principles to be incorporated in advanced aircraft and cruise missiles to render them virtually invisible to enemy radar.

Strategic Arms Limitation Talks (SALT) A series of negotiations between the United States and the Soviet Union that dealt with offensive and defensive strategic arms. The first round, SALT I (1969–1972), resulted in two formal agreements: the ABM Treaty, which is of unlimited duration and imposes strict constraints on antiballistic missile systems; and the Interim Agreement, which was a five-year pact freezing ICBM and SLBM launchers. The second round, SALT II (1972–1979), was designed to replace the Interim Agreement with a long-term comprehensive treaty providing for broad limits on strategic offensive weapons systems. The treaty was negotiated and signed during the Carter administration, but it was withdrawn from the ratification process after the Soviet invasion of Afghanistan and thus has never been legally binding. Both the United States and the Soviet Union, however, have stated that they will not undercut the SALT II treaty.

Strategic Arms Reduction Talks (START) Negotiations between the United States and the Soviet Union over reductions in strategic offensive weapons. The talks began in 1982 and were suspended in late 1983 when the Soviet Union protested the deployment of Pershing II and cruise missiles in Europe.

Strategic Defense Initiative (SDI) A research program announced in 1983 by President Reagan with the goal of defending the United States and its allies against nuclear attack.

Strategic Warning Detection of actions that indicate that a nuclear attack could be forthcoming within a matter of days or hours, such as removing submarines from port, dispersing aircraft, or releasing nuclear weapons from storage facilities.

Submarine-Launched Ballistic Missile (SLBM) A ballistic missile launched from a nuclear submarine. See also *Ballistic Missile.*

Tactical Warning Detection of a nuclear attack in progress—that is, after enemy weapons have been launched.

Theater Nuclear Forces (TNF) A term used to refer to weapons systems based in a region in which they would be used. The term is most often applied to weapons based in Europe (including the European portion of the Soviet Union) and intended for use there.

Threshold Test Ban Treaty (TTBT) A treaty signed in 1974 (but not yet ratified) between the United States and the Soviet Union that limits the yield of underground nuclear weapons tests to a maximum of 150 kilotons.

Warsaw Treaty Organization (Warsaw Pact) An alliance that was formed in 1955 as the Eastern European counterpart to NATO. Its current membership consists of Bulgaria, Czechoslovakia, the German Democratic Republic, Hungary, Poland, Rumania, and the Soviet Union.

SELECTED BIBLIOGRAPHY

2. Accidental Nuclear War

Ball, Desmond. "Can Nuclear War Be Controlled?" *Adelphi Paper* 169. London: International Institute for Strategic Studies, October 1981. A relatively non-technical argument for remaining skeptical regarding the claim that nuclear wars can be kept limited.

Bracken, Paul. *The Command and Control of Nuclear Forces.* New Haven: Yale University Press, 1983. A detailed but accessible argument that command and control structures are extremely fragile and that during a conventional war or in a deep political crisis, the probability of inadvertent or accidental nuclear war will probably be much greater than is commonly supposed.

Cox, Arthur Macy. *Russian Roulette: The Superpower Game.* New York: Times Books, 1982. A breezily written, highly readable survey of potential causes for inadvertent and accidental nuclear war.

Dumas, Lloyd J. "Human Fallibility and Weapons." *Bulletin of the Atomic Scientists* 36, no. 9 (November 1980): 15–20. An examination of the effects of drug abuse, boredom, and isolation on troops responsible for the protection and launch of nuclear weapons.

Garwin, Richard. "Launch Under Attack to Redress Minuteman Vulnerability." *International Security* 4, no. 3 (Winter 1979–1980):117–39. An argument for instituting a policy of launch under attack, to be implemented by a system of space-based infrared detectors, used to spot attacking missiles in their boost phase.

Perrow, Charles. *Normal Accidents: Living With High Risk Technologies.* New York: Basic Books, 1984. Although focused primarily on problems related to nuclear power reactors, this book also provides a useful theoretical framework within which to think about accidental nuclear war.

Perry, William J. "Measures to Reduce the Risk of Nuclear War." *Orbis* 27, no. 4 (Winter 1984): 1027–36. A concise survey of unilateral and bilateral actions to reduce the risk that human and technological errors will lead to nuclear war.

Posen, Barry R. "Inadvertent Nuclear War? Escalation and NATO's Northern Flank." *International Security* 7, no. 2 (Fall 1982): 28–54. Emphasizes the potential risks of inadvertent escalation to nuclear war incurred by NATO through its present strategies and deployments in Northern Europe.

Roderick, Hilliard and Ulla Magnusson, eds. *Avoiding Inadvertent War: Crisis Management.* Austin: University of Texas Press, 1983. A well-edited, highly informative transcript of a conference on crisis management that brought together many of the leading figures in this field.

Schelling, Thomas C. and Morton H. Halperin. "Preemptive, Premeditated and Accidental War." In *Theory and Research on the Causes of War,* edited by Dean G. Pruitt and Richard C. Snyder, 43–48. Englewood Cliffs, N.J.: Prentice-Hall, 1969. The outstanding single source for gaining a general understanding of the dangers caused by risk of nuclear weapons accidents.

Steinbruner, John. "Nuclear Decapitation." *Foreign Policy* 45 (Winter 1981–1982): 16–28. An argument for the central necessity of making U.S. command and control facilities less vulnerable and for avoiding strategies that emphasize "knockout" blows to the command and control facilities of the Soviet Union.

———. "Launch Under Attack." *Scientific American* 250, no. 1 (January 1984): 37–47. An essay that neither rejects nor espouses the strategy of launch under attack but sees it as a symptom of a deeper, unsolved problem: avoiding the tendency toward preemption in a crisis.

3. Surprise Attack and Preemption

Betts, Richard K. *Surprise Attack: Lessons for Defense Planning.* Washington, D.C.: Brookings Institution, 1982. A comparative case study analysis of why surprise attacks have succeeded. This analysis is then applied to current U.S. and NATO nuclear and conventional defense planning.

Betts, Richard K. "Analysis, War and Decision: Why Intelligence Failures Are Inevitable." *World Politics* 31, no. 1 (October 1978).

Chan, Steve. "The Intelligence of Stupidity: Understanding Failures in Strategic Warning." *American Political Science Review* 73, no. 1 (March 1979). The articles by Betts and Chan explore the effects of ambiguity on intelligence analysis, the effect of political considerations on the intelligence estimation process, and the interaction between intelligence producers and consumers.

Gross Stein, Janice. " 'Intelligence' and 'Stupidity' Reconsidered: Estimation and Decision in Israel, 1973." *Journal of Strategic Studies* 3, no. 2 (September 1980).

Handel, Michael I. *Perception, Deception and Surprise: The Case of the Yom Kippur War.* Jerusalem Paper 19. Jerusalem: Hebrew University of Jerusalem, Leonard Davis Institute of International Relations, 1976. The case studies by Gross Stein and Handel of the October 1973 war focus on the problem of estimating intentions and on the relationship among miscalculation, deterrence, and escalation in crises.

Knorr, Klaus. "Failures in National Intelligence Estimates: The Case of the Cuban Missile Crisis." *World Politics* 16, no. 3 (April 1964). Examines the effects of underestimating the adversary's propensity to take risks and of the adversary's underestimating one's own resolve.

Schelling, Thomas C. *The Strategy of Conflict.* Cambridge: Harvard University Press, 1960: 205–54.

Schelling, Thomas C. *Arms and Influence.* New Haven: Yale University Press, 1966: 221–59. These works by Schelling are the classic discussions of the reciprocal fear of surprise attack and the nature of strategic nuclear stability. They examine the importance of warning time, force size, and force survivability, and the requirements of stability in a disarmed world.

Snyder, Glenn H. *Deterrence and Defense: Toward a Theory of National Security.* Princeton: Princeton University Press, 1961: 52–119. Discusses the types of attacks to be deterred, the forces that are required to deter each type of attack, and the requirements of structural and preemptive stability.

Van Evera, Stephen. "The Cult of the Offensive and the Origins of the First World War." *International Security* 9, no. 1 (Summer 1984). Discusses the preemptive and preventive incentives that influenced the decisions leading to the First World War.

Whaley, Barton. *Codeword Barbarossa.* Cambridge, Mass.: M.I.T. Press, 1973. This case study of Germany's surprise attack on the Soviet Union during the Second World War focuses on the use of deception to hide preparations for attack.

Wohlstetter, Albert. "The Delicate Balance of Terror." *Foreign Affairs* 37, no. 2 (January 1959). This article drew public attention to the fact that retaliatory capabilities are more important than total nuclear capabilities and to the vulnerability of Western forces to surprise attack.

Wohlstetter, Roberta. *Pearl Harbor: Warning and Decision.* Stanford: Stanford University Press, 1962. This classic case study of surprise attack explores the difference between signal and noise in intelligence information.

4. Escalation in Europe

Beres, Louis René. *Apocalypse: Nuclear Catastrophe in World Politics.* Chicago: University of Chicago Press, 1980: 17–73. A discussion of different scenarios leading to a major nuclear war.

Collins, A.S. "Current NATO Strategy: A Recipe for Disaster." In *The Nuclear Crisis Reader,* edited by Gwyn Prins. New York: Random House, Vintage Books, 1984: 29–41. A good discussion of the consequences of theater nuclear warfare.

De Porte, A. W. *Europe Between the Superpowers: The Enduring Balance.* New Haven: Yale University Press, 1979: 166–96. An excellent overview of alliance relations in the postwar era.

Hampson, Fen Osler. "Groping for Technical Panaceas: The European Conventional Balance and Nuclear Stability." *International Security* 7, no. 4 (Spring 1984): 116–39. A critical discussion of the role that emerging technologies can play in improving the military balance and raising the nuclear threshold in Europe.

Holloway, David and Jane M. O. Sharp, eds. *The Warsaw Pact: Alliance in Transition?* Ithaca: Cornell University Press, 1984. An excellent analysis of the political, military, and economic problems facing the Warsaw Pact.

Kaldor, Mary and Dan Smith, eds. *Disarming Europe.* London: Merlin Press, 1982. A discussion of alternative strategies for eliminating the risks of nuclear war in Europe.

Lautenschläger, Karl. "Technology and the Evolution of Naval Warfare." *International Security* 8, no. 2 (Fall 1983): 3–51. An excellent overview of evolving technologies for antisubmarine warfare.

Mearsheimer, John J. *Conventional Deterrence*. Ithaca: Cornell University Press, 1983. A first-class analysis of the military reasons why conventional deterrence can fail and the role of the military balance in Central Europe.

Record, Jeffrey. *U.S. Nuclear Weapons in Europe: Issues and Alternatives*. Washington, D.C.: Brookings Institution, 1974. A definitive treatment of the evolution and development of tactical and theater forces in Europe.

Report of the European Security Study. *Strengthening Conventional Deterrence in Europe: Proposals for the 1980s*. New York: St. Martin's Press, 1983. A provocative and stimulating analysis of the potential role that emerging technologies can play in raising the nuclear threshold in Europe.

Sigal, Leon V. *Nuclear Forces In Europe: Enduring Dilemmas, Present Prospects*. Washington, D.C.: Brookings Institution, 1984. A short but highly informed discussion of the history of NATO's tactical and theater nuclear forces.

Smoke, Richard. *War: Controlling Escalation*. Cambridge, Mass.: Harvard University Press, 1977. A classic historical discussion of the problems of controlling escalation in war.

Steinbruner, John D. and Leon V. Segal, eds. *Alliance Security: NATO and No-First-Use*. Washington, D.C.: Brookings Institution, 1983. The best discussion of the whole controversy of no-first-use and alliance security issues in the eighties.

Wallin, Lars B., ed. *The Northern Flank in a Central European War*. Stockholm: Swedish National Defence Research Institute, 1982. An informed discussion of different scenarios for war in Northern Europe.

————, ed. *War in Europe*. Stockholm: Swedish National Defence Research Institute, 1982. An informed discussion of different scenarios for war in Central Europe.

5. Escalation in the Middle East and Persian Gulf

Chubin, Shahram. *Security in the Persian Gulf: The Role of Outside Powers*. London: International Institute for Strategic Studies, 1982. A good general discussion of current strategic issues related to the Persian Gulf.

Dismukes, Bradford and James McConnell. *Soviet Naval Diplomacy*. New York: Pergamon Press, 1979. Provides a detailed overview of Soviet naval deployments, with case studies of specific Middle Eastern crises.

Epstein, Joshua. "Soviet Vulnerabilities in Iran and the RDF Deterrent." *International Security* 6, no. 3 (Fall 1981): 159–80. Provides a detailed discussion of conflict scenarios in Iran.

Fukuyama, Francis. "Nuclear Shadowboxing: Soviet Intervention in the Middle East." *Orbis* 25, no. 3 (Fall 1981): 597–606. Includes a discussion of Soviet intervention threats in major Middle Eastern crises.

Glassman, Jon. *Arms for the Arabs: The Soviet Union and War in the Middle East*. Baltimore: Johns Hopkins University Press, 1975. Discusses the Soviet role in the Middle East between 1955 and 1973.

Guensberg, Gerold, tr. *Soviet Command Study of Iran (Moscow 41): Draft Translation and Analysis*. Arlington, Va.: SRI International, 1980. Translation of a Soviet General Staff study outlining plans for a Soviet invasion of Iran.

Heikal, Mohammed. *The Sphinx and the Commissar: The Rise and Fall of Soviet*

Influence in the Middle East. New York: Harper and Row, 1978. The last and most comprehensive of his three books on the Middle East, by a close confidant of Nasser.

Laqueur, Walter. *Confrontation: The Middle East and World Politics.* New York: Times Books, 1974. A study of the U.S.-Soviet nuclear confrontation during the October 1973 crisis.

Quandt, William B. *Decade of Decisions: American Policy toward the Arab-Israeli Conflict.* Berkeley: University of California Press, 1977. Analyzes American policies toward and interests in the Middle East, with special reference to the 1967 and 1973 wars.

Safran, Nadav. *Israel: The Embattled Ally.* Cambridge: Harvard University Press, 1978. Provides *inter alia* a detailed description of U.S.-Soviet interaction during all of the major postwar Middle Eastern crises.

6. Catalytic Nuclear War

Beres, Louis René. *Apocalypse: Nuclear Catastrophe in World Politics.* Chicago: University of Chicago Press, 1980: 99–118. Chapter 3 provides a general overview of nuclear terrorism as a path to nuclear war and addresses problems in combating this international threat.

Burns, Arthur Lee. *The Rationale of Catalytic War.* Princeton: Princeton University, Center for International Studies, 1959. In this game theory analysis following Thomas Schelling's work on surprise attack, Burns seeks to describe the case of a war between the superpowers deliberately caused by a third party.

Evron, Yair. "A Nuclear Balance of Deterrence in the Mideast." *New Outlook* 18 (July-August 1975): 15–19. Yair argues that the problem of catalytic war between the superpowers exists in theory only, although he believes that catalytic war could arise between lesser-powers states such as in the Middle East.

Gelber, Harry G. "The Impact of Chinese ICBMs on Strategic Deterrence." *Orbis* 13 (Summer 1969): 407–34. Gelber addresses the concern that if a war between two nuclear weapon states left each weaker and more vulnerable to the other nuclear weapon states, then each would have a great interest in a nuclear war between the others.

Goulding, Phil G. *Confirm or Deny: Informing the People on National Security.* New York: Harper and Row, 1970: 93–138. Chapter 4 presents a detailed discussion of the *Liberty* incident and offers an interesting perspective on attempting to identify an ambiguous conventional attack.

Kahn, Herman. "The Arms Race and Some of Its Hazards." *Daedalus* 89 (Fall 1960): 744–80. Kahn discusses the five major paths to war and concludes that catalytic war is the least likely.

Smith, Gerard C. *Doubletalk: The Story of the First Strategic Arms Limitation Talks.* Garden City, N.Y.: Doubleday, 1980: 281–97. Smith offers the best discussion of the Soviet preoccupation with "provocative attacks" during the SALT I negotiations. See chapter 9.

Szilard, Leo. *The Voice of the Dolphins and Other Stories.* New York: Simon and Schuster, 1961. Szilard relates the story of how during World War II, the Luftwaffe used Russian-manufactured bombs against Hungary, thus tricking Hungary into believing it was a Soviet attack and inducing her to declare war on the Soviet Union.

Tucker, Robert W. *Stability and the Nth Country Problem*. Washington: Institute for Defense Analysis, 1961: 21–24. Chapter 4 discusses the problem of catalytic war, with Tucker concluding that catalytic war arising by anonymous attack is doubtful.

7. Soviet Perspective on the Paths to Nuclear War

Berman, Robert B. and John C. Baker. *Soviet Strategic Forces*. Washington, D.C.: Brookings Institution, 1982. A good examination of Soviet strategic force posture in the seventies.

Douglass, Joseph D., Jr. *Soviet Military Strategy in Europe*. New York: Pergamon Press, 1980. A good analysis of contemporary Soviet thinking about war in Europe.

Holloway, David. *The Soviet Union and the Arms Race*. New Haven: Yale University Press, 1983. A general overview of postwar Soviet thinking about the nuclear arms race.

Garthoff, Raymond. *Soviet Military Policy: A Historical Analysis*. New York: Praeger, 1966. A good analysis of Soviet military thinking in the fifties.

Meyer, Stephen M. *Soviet Theater Nuclear Forces* (Parts I and II). Adelphi Papers 187 and 188. London: International Institute for Strategic Studies, 1983/84. An examination of Soviet theater nuclear warfare and linkages to conventional and strategic forces.

Valenta, Jiri and William C. Potter, eds. *Soviet Decisionmaking for National Security*. London: George Allen and Unwin, 1984. A useful collection of essays which examine Soviet decisions for national security from Stalinist antecedents on and decision making concerning weapons development, defense research and development, and SALT.

Wolfe, Thomas. *Soviet Power and Europe*. Baltimore: Johns Hopkins University Press, 1970. An excellent examination of Soviet postwar military policy.

INDEX